WOMAN IN THE MODERN WORLD

WOMAN IN THE MODERN WORLD

by

EVA FIRKEL

LONDON
BURNS & OATES

This translation from the original German,
Schicksalsfragen der Frau (*Verlag Herder, Vienna*) *was made by*
HILDA C. GRAEF

NIHIL OBSTAT: JOANNES M. T. BARTON, S.T.D., L.S.S.
CENSOR DEPVTATVS
IMPRIMATVR: E. MORROGH BERNARD
VICARIVS GENERALIS
WESTMONASTERII: DIE XVII SEPTEMBRIS MCMLV

MADE AND PRINTED IN GREAT BRITAIN BY
HAZELL WATSON AND VINEY LTD.,
FOR BURNS OATES AND WASHBOURNE LTD.,
28 ASHLEY PLACE, LONDON, S.W.1
First published 1956

CONTENTS

II. The Development of Woman

III. Perfected Woman

PREFACE

THIS book is addressed primarily to women and meant to appeal to their feminine human nature. It would encourage married as well as unmarried women to appreciate their own human values; hence the various questions are being discussed within the context of the individual feminine personality. This aim gives the book its special character. It is neither a manual of women's problems nor does it deal with 'concrete realities' only, but the actual situation is traced back to its spiritual foundations. Consequently theoretical preliminaries are cut out. On the other hand, we shall make a point of penetrating to the moral and religious roots of behaviour; hence one and the same question will sometimes be treated from different angles.

Since such is the leading idea of the book, there are no separate treatises on marriage, motherhood, education and professions, on which much excellent literature already exists. Here we would emphasize just those feminine characteristics that are less prominent elsewhere. We shall speak of the mature woman, who constitutes the other half of mankind; of her interior independence, her companionship with man and her cultural capacities, and we shall deal especially with factors both external and, even more, internal that tend to hinder this development. These inner relationships will always be given prominence; on the other hand, many of the ordinary features of books about women will be found to be absent. These have been eliminated deliberately, in order the better to bring out the principal aim of the book, which is the ripening of the feminine personality.

We have consciously avoided piling up masses of material, which is one of the main features of current education, since it prevents concentration on the spiritual aspects, with which we are concerned. Moreover, we intend from various points of view to attain to the Christian existence of woman. Nevertheless, the preliminaries to this will also be treated as valid human existence.

Since woman is in the centre of the book, man is relegated rather to the background. But this accidental consequence of its structure should on no account be interpreted as hostility. On the contrary, this book would serve to educate woman to be the true helpmate of man.

It is no accident that it should first appear in Mary's Year, which is meant to introduce a period of deeper motherliness and warmer love into the world.

EVA FIRKEL.

1954

PROBLEMS OF DESTINY

A MAN has reached the zero of his existence when he has become indifferent to everything: to the world, to his life in it, to his work. If he allows himself to fall still deeper, his feelings will be numbed. If he makes a new start, his interests will revive. Yet we may easily deceive ourselves if we think we are hardened to the vicissitudes of life. Man is normally more vulnerable and sensitive than he would care to admit; he is extremely interested in what he calls 'his destiny'. The psycho-analysts' investigations of the subconscious have shown that most people are far more affected in this respect than they know themselves.

Destiny means more than mere life; it implies origin, way and goal. It means that something is given to be used, to be enjoyed and formed. For man is the master of a number of correlated possibilities. He and his destiny are a mysterious power, and the more mysterious the more he is aware of the unseen reality. If a man realizes this power, he must determine his attitude towards it, and this demands a decision for or against it. He may blindly submit to his destiny, or he may obstinately refuse to accept it. If he freely comes to grips with it, he will have risen above zero.

If we blindly submit, we obey not our will guided by the light of reason, but a dark urge welling up from mythical depths. This would amount to falling a prey to horoscopes or some other magic arts; it would mean believing in empty invocations, in spurious 'facts' void both of cause and effect. Restless and highly strung people will go in for the latest prophecies and rumours without ever examining their origin and credentials. This sort of fatalism indeed titillates the surface of the soul; but while destroying its peace and troubling its clarity, it leaves its deepest thirst unquenched.

By obstinately refusing to submit, on the other hand, we deny that there is such a thing as destiny, that man is not his own cause and origin, and that he will one day be summoned to give an account of what he has become, of both achievement and failure. By such a refusal man rejects his human dignity that places him above mere physical existence; he mocks at a philosophy that, difficult though it may be to prove, will not accept tangible facts as final realities. Something is bound to be wrong if a man 'is finished with destiny'. He has, as it were, disconnected the flex and, through his own fault, is now sitting in darkness. For if we are 'finished with destiny', we have broken away from the meaning and purpose of life. We might as well try to make a plant grow without soil—the seedling would simply die. In the case of man, all faculties other than those needed for mere self-preservation would wither away. It is true, life can be sustained with a minimum of demands. Nevertheless, food, drink, sexual satisfaction and all manner of thrills and excitements affect only certain zones of the human being, while leaving its essence untouched. If this becomes a permanent state, it will have disastrous consequences—man's humanity will die. For being a man means to be in touch with one's fellows and with the spiritual forces above us. If we neglect these vital relationships, the result will inevitably be nervous disorders and a certain malaise. It may take a long time to discover the causes of melancholy, depression and disgust with life; it yet remains true that a man who is not conscious of a personal destiny will gradually languish and wither away.

"The stars of your destiny are within you", says the poet Friedrich Schiller, thus expressing the peculiar efficacy of the centre of the human being. This centre has a voice capable of saying Yes or No to the experiences presented to it, of showing pleasure and enthusiasm, disapproval and disgust. This centre is capable especially of contact. Like a tuning-fork, it is attuned to a tone that comes from far-away, from the supernatural world. Perhaps this is its deepest vocation, to be attuned to a beyond by which it has been decisively touched. Therefore it must always sound in response to such tones. The centre of man responds, attuned and responsible, to the coded messages of life. It is precisely in this that its mastery of life reveals itself.

It is surely no accident that life, its mastery and the powers of fate are so widely discussed today. For everything has indeed become questionable. We take this word in its most literal meaning : questionable, that is worthy of renewed questioning. Within the last sixty years scientists have made so many discoveries that allow us to see the foundations and relationships of life more comprehensively than before, and partly also differently, that it seems justified to pay special attention to this, and to interpret the many symptoms of unrest as signalling something new. Technical progress has outstripped our boldest expectations. Within a few decades our planet has changed into something small and easy to overlook; periods and places have been connected, the secrets of microcosm and macrocosm have been revealed through grandiose calculations. The mutation of energy which had hitherto been regarded merely from the point of view of physics points to the spiritual order of life; the atoms begin to dissolve into power fields. Here everything is very much in a state of flux, and will yet produce immeasurable changes in our view of the world.

Nevertheless, we have already fallen victim to one dark secret of this riot of discoveries : the consequences of their practical application have led to a technical civilization all but divorced from the world of creation. It has developed into an artificial world within the world, that carries with it the danger of man claiming an unlimited autonomy. Constructions are the basic elements of this world, far surpassing the creative and even the imaginative powers of the single human individual. The speed and mass production of technical progress create objects which both simplify and threaten man's life. Today life is unthinkable without machines, the use of which has considerably altered and flattened its rhythm. By this we mean that work and rest, tension and relaxation, the reception of a stimulus and its assimilation, follow each other more rapidly ; indeed, collective work in uninterrupted shifts almost destroys the natural rhythm of life.

Besides the growing speed, the technical world brings in its wake an immense increase in noise. A person constantly exposed to this will hardly be able still to bear complete silence, hence any occupation demanding it. Thus whole classes of working men and women have become incapable of certain wholly spiritual enjoyments.

In the modern world all our senses are being more intensely stimulated, whereas the human body is exercised less harmoniously than formerly. Moreover, such complicated, interrelated technical processes as land clearance, the construction of power-stations, canalization, etc., tend to spoil untouched nature, which would immediately impress every normal person as 'creation'. Everywhere man is faced with his own handiwork. Since this is fascinating, lovely and full of marvels, he is easily induced to worship this technical world which is so very much his own.

This world frequently operates with graphs; figures and diagrams express its mentality. There is no technical process that is not capable of 'graphic' representation; besides, statistics produce a peculiarly strong pictorial effect. We need only think of modern propaganda and advertising methods to realize how dependent our contemporaries are on visible presentation, which, on the other hand, is lacking in the sphere of the invisible spiritual realities.

The creative power of contemporary language rejects the images of bygone ages. It is true, even in those days men had perfectly sound views on the relationship between nature and spirit, between matter and form. But between that time and our own there intervened the 'modern period', distinguished for its misunderstanding of this interplay. And even if the modern errors were cleared up, it is impossible simply to go back to 'old times'. For though the eternal order was well known then, scientific knowledge, if compared with our own, was very scanty and partially faulty. It is our task to express what is true through the media of our own time. Admittedly these have greatly changed, hence the groping for adequate expression in all departments of life.

It is often assumed that this groping betrays an impoverishment in values, above all in the one that points beyond man, linking him to a higher destiny. The technical world is controlled by the constructive number, by the incessant growth of production and the myriad-armed apparatus; the relation to a personal destiny is absent from it. In the natural world as it used to be, this could easily be established. In the forest, on the summit of a mountain, man feels even now the call from something beyond and above himself. But on the tarred motor road or in the lift he hears only the noise of the machines. The world of today is breathtaking, it is amusing, but it remains essentially threatening.

It does not call man personally to an intimate talk, it only calls him to become a member of such and such a society. Man is nowhere any more *one,* he is always somehow organized and in the mass, pressed into some association, needed as a member of something. The ubiquitous craze for organized planning would let no one be just 'man among men'. Everything is too much split up. This is the reason why the call to the depths is lacking, or rather remaining unheard. For actually everyone is called, and the consciousness of this cannot be altogether destroyed. However, the 'concrete' everyday world gives no answer; the questions of value that spring from the living centre are buried in an underworld of roots, being subject, it seems, to conditions different from those of the 'concrete world' whose air we breathe. This brings about a cleavage.

Even in the most comfortable circumstances a man can be essentially dissatisfied, because his spirit remains empty. He cannot be satisfied by the spiritual treasures of the past, because they fail to appeal to his contemporary mentality. Today we no longer appreciate detailed descriptions and circumstantial approaches; long-winded titles make no impression, and methods manœuvring so to speak in a vacuum of pure reason find little sympathy. This is not due only to superficiality and haste. The immense destruction of material values has led to the discovery of indestructible value; incalculable events have shown up an arithmetic that is beyond steel constructions.

Modern man is aware of danger and 'accidents' that carry destruction. He is prepared for the essential, even though he is not yet quite sure where to find it. He has not yet an 'ersatz' for the rationalism of the Enlightenment. Up to the two world wars matter had supplied an unshakable support for man's need of self-reliance. Man had transferred to the outside world all that really belongs to the interior, to the soul; he had received the laws of his existence from the rationalized, and finally totally mechanized, structure of his surroundings. This has resulted in a way of life divorced from the human organism; it caters, it is true, for many of its needs, but disregards man's spiritual nature.

It remains true that spirit is not a blind natural urge which somehow split off or developed from *Bios*, but that its origin is the absolute Spirit—though again not a mere offshoot. The absolute Spirit is not 'something', but 'Someone', it is God. Or, to express it differently : God is Someone, He is a Person, and by His free creative will has made man, too, a person, a 'someone'. He has given him spirit, making him a spiritual person. Thus man is one, and every man is unique. The Creator Spirit has adapted him to an end, so that he should fulfil himself rather than achieve mere aims. Man may, indeed, legitimately aim at dominating nature, but not in order to rule it autonomously, but by subjecting it to fulfil the meaning of human life through offering creation to its Creator. The 'system' into which modern man is fitted to such an extent no longer affords this ultimate relation of all activity. Hence there is so much 'wrong with it', and the world is full of unrest, searching and futility. Yet the ultimate questions are bound up with man's true spiritual nature; therefore men ask these questions, and they will do so the more urgently the less satisfying the answers they receive.

Our present age is full of questions; it cries out for discussion, as is shown by the large number of discussion groups and by the questionnaires of our periodicals. Finally it all boils down to the main problems of the essence and meaning of human life.

The time is favourable to such questioning, which is urgent, straightforward and sober, animated by the desire to penetrate to the roots; the longing for truth is authentic. Men have become serious after the many searching trials of the last years, and they distrust exciting slogans. They are seeking genuine discussion as the best means to clarify the meaning of life. However, only the few are capable of true conversation; and only they will be susceptible to words carrying a deeper meaning. We ought not to be disheartened because the masses will not listen.

I

WOMAN'S NATURE

GENERAL HUMAN CHARACTERISTICS

W HEN man becomes conscious of himself he experiences himself as an individual, and now is just the right time to address the individual. For the question of 'destiny' is becoming urgent precisely because man is so poignantly aware of himself as an individual, and this question is linked to that of the value man represents in himself, as a human being. Hence we must begin by investigating this value more closely. This we have to do even though the following pages are devoted exclusively to woman and her nature. For being a woman does not mean being devoid of general human features and of the basic data shared by the other sex. We should always stress the essential sameness of man and woman despite their natural differences, though we ought certainly not to blur the psychosomatic difference of the sexes until nothing is left but a few unimportant biological dissimilarities that would not affect the shaping of one's life. It is, however, possible also to fall into the opposite error and to over-emphasize the natural difference. Then nothing would be left in the end which woman would understand and do in the same way as man, and thus artificial barriers would be erected that do not exist in actual life.

HUMAN DIGNITY

What makes woman—like everyone else—a human being is a special dignity and a spiritual centre. Human dignity is of great importance; it penetrates into the spiritual realm and is the ultimate source of all specifically feminine dignity.

What does the term human dignity really mean? It would give us pause if anyone were to speak in comparable terms of animal dignity. On the other hand, we can quite well distinguish the body of an animal from that of a man; for both have a body. In fact, they are both made of the same stuff, and yet they are worlds apart. The world of the animal consists in the surroundings that are within its reach, which it may use for its own preservation or for that of its species. But do animals create a civilization?

In the case of man there is no question of his being somewhat less like an animal, though still an animal, despite the fact that he is related to the higher animals through the structure and functions of his body. He is simply different. He lives not only by instinct, depending on reflexes and vegetative centres, but he is specifically human as a spiritual being. He is, as it were, a unity built up from layers, the whole consisting of body, soul and spirit in such a way that the lower serves the higher and is directed from the centre. Through this centre man realizes that he is one beside a second or third one, but also that he can say 'I' as opposed to the other's 'thou'. Besides saying 'I' and 'thou' and separating himself from the world outside, he also uses his judgement, another faculty of his centre, in order to attract what he thinks desirable and keep away what seems harmful to him. In other words : man is able to judge and discriminate ; he is born with a scale of values enabling him to assess the importance of various factors in a changing situation. By this we mean that conscience is able to respond and react, as we shall see later. This responsiveness depends on the sense of human dignity, which may be either keen or dull. In any case, it consists in freely using the faculties of reason and will, and in realizing one's share in the responsibility for fashioning the world. By this we mean cultural formation, not an uninhibited craze for power. Man's highest dignity will be realized, however, when he recognizes himself as the image and child of God and consciously tends towards Him.

SPIRITUAL CENTRE: CONSCIOUSNESS OF SELF AND CONSCIENCE

To be conscious of the spiritual power of one's centre is important, and indeed vitalizing. On the one hand it elevates our own self above the mass, putting a stop to the devaluation of what is human, and indicating that man is resting securely in himself. Even though this may not become an 'experience'—for woman even less than for man—the very awareness of authentic, invisible values that cannot be 'felt' is in itself highly significant. On the other hand, Rilke's words hold good precisely for the dignity of the human person : "More is given to many solitaries of the same nature than to the narrow one." There exists a communion of those retiring and silent ones who are drawn to what is beautiful, true and good ; for there exists a faith in the power of the spirit that cannot be taught—it is there or it is lacking. Life will not give us all we desire, nor can we expect all our longings to be fulfilled and all our enterprises to be successful. One can, however, react in a human way to the delay of good fortune. This depends on how highly one values one's humanity. It is no mean thing to be a creature made up of body, soul and spirit; it occupies the centre of the world, all things are made for it, and it governs from its own centre, first of all itself. We should well understand this art of governing. For the ordered possession of oneself will result in well-being; and through this well-being we shall be successful in our tasks, above all in our relation to our surroundings. This satisfactory relationship will give security, which in its turn will be perceived as an interior poise assuring us that life has a meaning. If we no longer think life meaningless, we shall have passed above zero. We shall then no longer grow giddy at the thought of moving towards a vacuum; death will lose its terror, for it will not be seen merely as the murderer of life. The devaluation of what is human starts from within; it begins with a spiritual flight from spirit, with being helpless if faced with silence and solitude, with interior images that are beyond reason. Being a man does indeed imply having at one's disposal an organism consisting of highly differentiated albumen molecules and being subject to an interplay of fluids and psychosomatic energies—but above all it means experiencing that many-tiered compound as one's own ego, and to express it in the irrefutable statement: I am.

If a man has never recognized the importance of this short sentence, he will miss the essence of life and easily fall a prey to fear and spiritual malaise. Today we feel a magic attraction for the 'dynamic flow of events'. We stare greedily at their kaleidoscopic groupings, and in the maelstrom of our crowded days all signposts and stopping points are effaced. Yet in his depths man is haunted by the image of a final repose. This is the cause of the many restless desires that seek their fulfilment 'in the stream of life'. Yet the restlessness remains. For man's life with its beginning, zenith and end is not identical with man himself. Before man 'does' things, he must be 'somebody'. If he makes his 'I am' the conscious basis of his spiritual existence, his life will rest on an unshakable foundation. To most men this will appear too vague; to be concerned with laying spiritual foundations seems to them to betray dreaminess and incompetence to tackle life. But they forget that this foundation may be capable of carrying the whole edifice of human destiny; it enables man to see life, not only as a unity, but as fitted together by the Creator. For the 'I am', if thought out to its logical conclusion, means being made by God for God Himself. In order to attain to this end man needs to be formed and prepared. If seen from this angle, life's catastrophes will reveal their meaning; for they will change a man's outlook by removing prejudice and false security. If a man is convinced of his spiritual dignity, he will not ask at every setback: 'Why should this happen to *me*?'; but 'For what purpose did it happen?' Just that retrospective question 'Why?' causes us to remain entangled in cares and worries, and prevents us from looking forward and discovering the silver lining on the horizon. For most of men's energies are spent not on coming to grips with reality but on manœuvring within a framework of possibilities. This is largely due to a lack of balance and self-confidence. We cannot develop these if we disregard our personal centre, and thus deprive ourselves of the faculty of making valid decisions. For if we have seriously faced this responsibility, we shall be given the perfect tranquillity that cannot be ruffled by external events which are outside our control.

The following considerations will prove that these are no empty words. We are keenly aware of moral value or unworthiness in society, economics or politics. If we knew the depth of our own personal being for what it is, its convictions ought to be sacred to us, and nothing ought to prevent us from putting them into practice. This will be more often a question of being than of doing; and in this case public opinion would not mean that of the masses but of responsible human beings. But if this intimate consciousness lies dormant, everyone will simply be parroting what 'everybody' says, and this sort of opinion will not be formed by true human values. For these derive from man's interior liberty, from his spiritual faculties of knowing and judging, from his powers of choice, decision and responsibility. If men used these faculties more consciously, they would lead lives of far deeper culture and avoid the emptiness of a mechanized existence. We resign our human dignity if we deliver ourselves without resistance to propaganda and profiteering. It is true, life becomes considerably easier if we simply follow the general trend; for then it will run by itself and be automatically deflected into the appropriate channels. Protected by the large front of yes-men in whose midst we march, we shall do quite well until the moment when everything will depend on the vitality of our personal centre. Such moments of destiny will come to all of us; we shall badly blunder in matters such as choosing a profession, setting up a family or discovering the meaning of the universe, if we think it possible to settle them with the help of ready-made solutions. At these turning-points of life it is essential to express one's own self, and this is possible only for a mature personality. Many let themselves be urged on and compelled in matters to which they should say yes or no from the depth of their own being and fully conscious of their responsibility.

We can experience responsibility only if we are aware that our conscience is functioning, which should be formed on the immutable principles of good and evil inscribed in the Decalogue. This standard is intelligible to everybody, and has remained unsurpassed by any other code of conduct to this day. To recognize oneself as a creature is a principle that separates order from chaos. Moreover, to recognize that other creatures are united to us in a common destiny is no more than a statement of fact. In the last resort our whole life consists in caring for ourselves as creatures. The Ten Commandments contain orders that can be carried out. Some readers may remark disappointedly: "I do all this, anyway." We would reply to them that it makes a difference whether our conduct be correct when there are no difficulties and when our personal advantage is not diminished by being faithful to moral laws, or whether we obey these from the conviction that we ought not to do otherwise even though this faithful observance might cost us dear. Besides, in most cases it will not be a matter of great things, but of containing or even fighting such everyday faults as envy and jealousy, suspicion, rude self-assertion to the detriment of others and a general, though not easily definable tendency to avarice in whatever direction; and to do this in the interest of a higher way of life founded on moral ideals. Happy the man whose decisions are made spontaneously in accordance with such principles. In the majority of cases, such an attitude of mind will have to be specially developed. This, however, is the way to form strong personalities, who make a success of life, face its difficulties and achieve purposes that are above mere financial profit.

The basic necessity is to recognize that man possesses a spiritual centre that freely makes its decisions and tends towards worthy ends. This means we deny emphatically that man is hopelessly given over to compelling instincts and demonic powers. It is true, there are spells of 'bad luck' and lives that are full of sorrow; but this does not destroy interior liberty. A person will prove that he is able to fashion his life satisfactorily, not by external success and a smoothly running existence, but by an inner harmony and spiritual balance that have gradually been achieved.

These conditions are as valid for women as they are for men. Woman, too, is conscious of her own self, and must needs realize herself if she is to develop in a healthy way. This remains true even if she fulfils herself largely, by turning towards others and to the world around her. It is possible for a person to find himself only through the response of another, and this is perhaps even truer for woman than for man. Nevertheless, these tendencies are inherent in primeval spiritual forces shared by man and woman alike. Besides, woman has her part to play in the task of fashioning the cultural world as much as man. Even the Biblical account of creation testifies that woman is accorded not only the hearth and the cradle, but also tasks outside the home.

THE CHRISTIAN POINT OF VIEW

W E have already said that in the reality of time and space
there are only men and women; but the fundamental value,
for the sake of which the sexual differentiation exists, is man as
made in the image of God. The Scriptural account of creation
says: "And God created man to his own image; to the image of
God he created him. Male and female he created them" (Gen. 1 :
27). Being in the image of God belongs equally to both man and
woman. It consists in the spiritual endowment of man, through
which he is able to do creative work, to investigate and make use
of nature, and, above all, in interior freedom. This as well as the
Creator's command, "Increase and multiply and fill the earth and
subdue it", applies to both man and woman. Both sexes are meant
to co-operate in the preservation of the race and in its cultural
tasks.

Hence the Creator has given man and woman an equal dignity—they are to rule the world together. This must not be understood as implying that woman's rôle is merely passive, that she
should be 'used' by man according to his ideas. Complementing
each other, they are both to serve God, though they will sometimes do this in different ways, according to their different natural
characteristics. Man and woman are correlated to each other. In
some respects this relationship implies a polarity, as may also be
seen from the Genesis account of the creation of Eve: "It is not
good for man to be alone; let us make him a help like unto himself" (Gen. 2 : 18). This is followed by the creation of Eve, whom
Adam recognizes as his true companion: "This now is bone of
my bones, and flesh of my flesh; she shall be called woman, because she was taken out of man." It is clear from this passage
that woman shares man's dignity; for as she was taken from him,
she can hardly be of less value than he.

Thus there can be no doubt that in Scripture, too, woman is
considered as an individual, divinely created as truly as man.
Hence wherever she must exercise her human responsibility, she
has to do the same as man : she must make decisions, act freely
and rationally and shoulder the consequences of her actions. But

beyond this woman has a special function in human society, where the division into male and female is of great importance. On this point, too, Holy Scripture instructs us, first of all in the above-mentioned passage from the creation account : the very creation of Eve implies differences of 'rank' between the sexes. For the narratives of Adam and Eve should not only be taken as referring to two particular individuals. Besides, Adam represents 'the male' and Eve 'the female' in the whole order of salvation. In this order Christ, as it were, preceded Himself in Adam as 'created', to appear in the fullness of time as 'truly born'. Eve as the female is the symbol of *ecclesia*, the Church. The Church is the community of all those who are 'called out' of the sinful world. Now Christ is the Head, the Creator and Lover of the Church. The Church is the Bride who through Him participates in the glory of the trans-figured Lord. In this relationship that governs the order of salva-tion woman is the image and 'the glory of the man', a theme de-veloped in the 11th chapter of the First Epistle to the Corinthians. For as the Church is introduced to the glory of God through Christ, the Redeemer, so woman through man. He is the first-created, as Christ is the firstborn. In the Church, Christ causes mankind to participate in the divine inheritance. The Church is the reflexion of His glory, and through Him the reflexion and the 'Thou' of the Father. She has received His love ; indeed, she is herself love that gives back what it has received.

This love is not a form of sexual attraction ; it is the giving love of God Himself flowing back to Him. Therefore God created man not as one but as two, as man and woman, so that together they should reproduce the self-giving love of God. In actual life this love presents itself as readiness to receive and accept, having its counterpart, of course, also in the narrower domain of sex. Yet this characteristic of woman's nature is nothing inferior. It is the specific task of woman to give back the life that has been formed in her and so to enrich the world.

In these questions, therefore, two points must always be borne in mind : Taken in herself, in her personal being, woman is a unique thought of God. As regards her primeval social function she is the image of man, himself the 'Thou' of God. He has the dignity of the ordained priest; woman, on the other hand, is co-redemptrix within the universal priesthood. The most perfect co-redemptrix is Mary, the mediatrix of all graces. The concept of woman being an 'image' as here described, confers an exalted religious dignity, and it is not permissible to hold it against her as implying inferiority in other departments of life. It is, indeed, important to pursue her capacity for receiving and loving to its spiritual origins. It is true, woman's receptive and protective powers are part of her organism; but in the matter of the universal vocation of the sexes it is not only, or not even primarily, a case of physical motherhood. Just as a woman gives a child to the world only after she has formed and borne it in her womb, and thus enriched it with her own substance, so it is the general characteristic of woman to add something from her own centre to every cultural activity.

THE PHYSICAL CHARACTER OF WOMAN

PHYSICAL motherhood receives its perfection from what a woman brings to it out of the depth of her own being. It is in the deepest sense a parable, hence its absence does not imply a diminution. A woman can realize this parable in a different way, though generally motherhood is believed to be *the* fulfilment. Besides, conception and birth are events in which a woman is supremely active, and in which she herself plays a formative part. It is true, femininity penetrates every layer of the personality, yet it is a complete whole in itself, with its own dynamism; this is evident even in the biological differentiation. The life principles of male and female ought not to be envisaged as reacting upon one another quite mechanically, especially not as if the male represented the 'life giver'. Male and female are equally alive. Being alive means being endowed with soul, subject to changes of matter, energy and form.

CHROMOSOMES

The biological constituents that build up the female body are situated in the sex chromosome, in the interplay of the hormones and in the diencephalon. The sex is determined from the moment of conception. The human being destined to be a woman has in each cell a pair of sex chromosomes. These chromosomes are tiny particles of the cell, carriers of hereditary matter; hence they have a decisive share in the development and influence the fate of the organism. In the sex cells (spermatozoa or ovules respectively) there are twenty-four chromosomes, but only one of them is a sex chromosome. There are two types of the latter, X and Y. One half of the sperm cells carry X, the other half Y chromosomes. The ovules carry only X chromosomes. If therefore a sperm cell with X chromosomes fertilizes an ovum, the resulting being will be female. But if an ovum is fertilized by a sperm cell with Y chromosome, a male being will result. Here is the root of the difference of sex. The ovule is the largest cell of an organism, the sperm cell the smallest. But it would be a rather cheap argument if we were to conclude from this that the female principle was material, the masculine spiritual. Should it not rather be taken as a symbol of help and protection, of the generosity of self-sacrificing love? It might point to the wealth of energy hidden in woman, which will help to shape not only herself but the world.

Woman, too, is creative, as well as man. Modern biology teaches that the old active-passive concept does not hold good for the respective shares of man and woman in the procreation of children. The female cell, too, is supremely active, and the chromosomes move apart by their own power. This mysterious fact makes it clear that man and woman are fundamentally co-ordinated; both together form an ordered whole, a single source of power, and it is difficult to ascertain whose is the more and whose the less important part in it. Conceiving, the woman will also give; begetting, the man will also receive. It is true, there is a polarity of the sexes, but this expression ought not to be pressed. Man and woman are attracted to each other, not by a mechanical opposition, but by the human desire for perfection and eternal life, for the good of which oneself is not capable; for the whole truth, the divine plenitude which the single individual can scarcely indicate. Both transcend themselves through each other; loving each other, man and woman give themselves to one another.

SEX HORMONES

Yet, as long as there are men and women, one will always mean to the other the opposite side of the world. Marvellously enough, the little girl already has within her body all organic potentialities of the future development of her womanhood. At the time of puberty this general sexual predetermination is enforced by the decisive hormonal sexual development which in its turn is directed by the co-operation of the internal secretory glands. In this the pituitary gland and the suprarenal cortex play a decisive part. The former produces a hormone that induces the germ glands to produce a sexual hormone. The interactions of the hormones are extremely complicated and very delicately regulated; research on this is still in progress. As in the case of the chromosomes, it should be noted that the ovary, too, does not produce a purely female secretion; what happens is that, of the male and female hormones that issue from the ovary the latter are more numerous. So we find here, too, as in the bisexual structure of the cells, that one sex predominates. The female body is

determined also by male elements even down to its individual cells
in the same way as the male body is determined by female ones.
This explains why there is neither a hundred per cent man nor
a hundred per cent woman, and why pathological changes of sex
may occur. The sex hormone is used, for example, to cure dilation
of the vessels; and the fact that these hormones are important for
the organism beyond their sexual function proves once more that
in the case of man the spheres of being are intertwined, and that
harmony is achieved only when the whole is governed from its
centre. On the other hand, the complicated physical structure and
the astonishing regulative capacity of the hormones and the vegetative centres suggest the thought that we must take sufficient
account of our bodily nature. We deceive ourselves if we behave
as if we were disembodied spirits; and we shall have to pay dearly
for such pretence in the course of our lives. Nevertheless, this does
not detract from the predominance of the spiritual element.

The rhythmic cycle of a woman's changing capacity for conception depends largely on the female sexual hormone. This factor
gives woman's life its special character by using her body in the
service of the preservation of the species. Physical motherhood is
the fulfilment of this capacity, and at the same time woman's
highest biological achievement. The so-called climacteric causes
the germ glands to atrophy, and this has a disturbing influence on
the harmony of the whole glandular system, and deeply affects
woman's psychosomatic life. In any case, the 'cycle' continues to
produce a periodic incision, the effects of which are felt even in
the spiritual sphere. Woman's delicacy of feeling, her capacity for
'empathy', her adaptability and vitality have a good deal to do
with the fact that she has to endure time and again the mysterious upheavals caused by the hormones, by which she is sometimes practically thrown down and built up again. Woman's life
is so truly a miniature of collapse, death and resurrection that she
is particularly familiar with the regenerating power of death and
rebirth. From the biological point of view we would also indicate
the importance of vitamin E. Despite their basic differences, vitamins and hormones are closely connected. Vitamin E, whose
effectual substance has been called tokopherol, is contained in
many vegetables. Germs of corn are particularly rich in it; but it
exists also in lettuce and fruit, and in very small quantities in milk
and butter. The influence of this vitamin on the female sexual
function is so great that it has also been called the hormone of

fertility. It seems to be essential for the development of the embryo, and must be present in the uterine mucus. Habitual miscarriages may perhaps be due to its absence, and can be prevented, among other measures, by feeding with vitamin E.

It is clear from all this, that woman is affected incomparably more deeply than man by the natural conditions of her sexual function. She is nearer than he to the creaturely order and its influences. In all civilizations man has been called the image of the deity; woman, on the other hand, is the image of the Great Mother, that is of the earth or, even more significantly, of the primeval womb. This is the deepest reason for her capacity for suffering, which is certainly a positive quality, unless it be understood in a wholly negative way, as opposed to untrammelled activity. For being able to bear and endure, to wait in patience, is not the same as being indolent and apathetic. Perhaps woman's capacity of letting it 'be unto her', exercised in the service of the race and also apart from it, may be sorely needed to save humanity from the consequences of our frantically active technical civilization. The words in which our Lady consented to her part in the plan of salvation, "Be it unto me", may be taken in a twofold sense as the perfect expression of woman's nature : they signify on the one hand readiness for responsible decision, on the other willingness to offer her life in the service of mankind.

BODILY SHAPE

The female body shows in its physical details how intimately related are body and soul in human beings. Apart from the primary sexual characteristics which exist for the sake of conceiving, bearing and bringing forth the child, the feminine appearance as a whole is, as it were, drawn to its centre. Her movements are not abrupt but swinging, as if embracing the outside world ; her walk, too, is in harmony with her figure. The round shape of the skeleton, together with the soft muscular structure and the delicate skin, all express the intimate union of body and soul. Woman 'experiences' her body far more than man, since she is strongly drawn into its life ; and by 'experiencing' we here mean being psychologically conscious of it.

4

HEALTHY PSYCHOSOMATIC CHARACTERISTICS

Wholeness

W OMAN lives as a whole; this is one of her decisive characistics. Her powers of soul and intellect are strongly bound together, hence they appear less spread out. This may be the reason why women are less apt to produce outstanding achievements which depend on the development of special abilities. Women are inferior to men perhaps, not in intelligence but as a rule in intellectual independence and productivity; as scholars they rarely blaze new trails. It is true there are many good writers and artists among them, but really outstanding women poets and creative painters and sculptresses are rare indeed. They are not sufficiently interested in the abstract and the universal, and without this no independent research can be carried out. This general lack of theoretical ability seems to be a structural feminine peculiarity. On the other hand, the gifts of reproduction and of entering into the thoughts of others are often remarkably well developed. Collaborating with man, woman will act as his supplement, putting his speculative trends in touch with concrete reality. Complicated systems of syntheses and abstractions will be concentrated in the lens of her heart, and reflected as ready understanding and warm sympathy, the stimulating preludes and interludes without which a man's creative imagination would lose its vigour. Perhaps women may not always understand men's work in detail; but they grasp their personality with unerring certainty, thus rendering them inestimable service.

Completeness

This certainty springs from the completeness of the feminine nature. A woman is there, she listens and takes in; she gathers, preserves and gives back. All feminine activity is shot through with protective motherly qualities. These emanate from every healthy woman, no matter whether she be married or single, whether she has children or not. This is the pivot of all feminine existence. Motherliness, however, ought not to be considered as a kind of metaphorical jumble-room, into which we throw pell-mell everything that we may find useful or even indispensable in times of distress, but which is otherwise entitled only to benevolent toleration. Feminine protectiveness and selfless generosity are not just pleasant ornaments of human society; they regulate the heartbeat of the world. Therefore, if woman is unfaithful to her own nature, she not only loses herself but at the same time human society will be deprived of its harmony. Where the gentle motherly qualities are missing, men's dealings with each other will be devoid of charity, and implacable fanaticism may well become the order of the day.

We read time and again that woman is more sentimental than man. Now women are, on the whole, more widely subject to feeling, because it is bound up with the psychosomatic events in their existence. Feeling hits them, as it were, more strongly than men, in whom it is less conspicuous, owing to the wider expansion of their interior powers.

Capacity for suffering

It is generally asserted that woman is more passive; but after what has been said, we would rather interpret this as a greater capacity for letting herself be formed. Her passivity is only apparent, as is shown by her share in the events of conception and in the final phase of giving birth.

Thou-relationship

Women are frequently accused of having a very limited horizon; and this may often be true. But this general idea is probably due to the fact that woman's perception is not as a rule focused on an object but on a person, on the 'thou'. By this we do not now mean her husband. For a woman's whole personality is directed towards other persons. She plans and thinks with the reason of her heart; therefore she sometimes staggers others by her bold conclusions, which are right, though it is impossible to see how she has arrived at them. This explains why abstract syllogistic thinking (the only one that is recognized as 'objective') is normally foreign to her. Man leaves the personal sphere in order to go forth into the sphere of objects, to investigate and form them. Woman takes what is personal to her with her into the sphere of objects—not necessarily to their detriment. Woman's thoughts and desires circle more round her own centre than man's. This means that she takes the outside world into her heart, and sees the objects through the medium of her personality. Her tendency towards the personal is concerned with the living 'Thou' rather than with the needs of her own person. She turns towards this other from the fullness of her own peaceable being; since this capacity for companionship has been given her at her very creation, in the words of the Genesis account cited above. Thus her cultural task is personal in a twofold sense : she takes her share in preserving life with her whole person, body and soul. In other words, she protects, nurtures and conserves not only physical but especially also spiritual and intellectual life.

Such a vocation presupposes understanding and sympathy for others, else it will degenerate into a mere technique that leaves us cold. On the other hand, it requires that the demanding ego should be silenced; it needs the strength that is able to sustain the helpless and needy and to shoulder the daily burden; in a word, the essence of motherliness, which may also be defined as capacity for suffering. As has already been said, this quality is a feminine characteristic, which we would not, however, wish to be mistaken for weakness or inferiority. It endows the impatient, energetic will with the elements of humility and trust, and symbolizes the genuine religious faith in Providence. True womanhood needs self-confidence and activity as well as patient expectation of the appointed hour, and courage to bear the manifold pains and sorrows inescapably bound up with our daily humdrum existence.

CAPACITY FOR LOVE

Thus woman's nature reveals itself in 'meeting', or rather in the meeting of love. Man is called to love, which is, indeed, the fundamental law of the redeemed world; and woman in particular, being so close to life, and so ready to turn towards others, cannot disregard it. She should certainly have the courage to be herself, to keep her heart prepared for love as a woman should. It is true, she may sometimes show kindness to someone unworthy of it; worse, her friendliness may occasionally even be misinterpreted and lead to unpleasant situations. Sincere goodness of heart is not always accepted in the way it is offered, and may even suddenly change into something less sincere. But possible dangers ought not to cause timid withdrawal. We can indeed learn certain principles of behaviour; yet it is impossible to foresee all possible complications of a situation. Love, on the other hand, cannot be learned, it is always a new creation, a new grace —a new risk, too, hence a new source of suffering. Since woman is the 'advocate' of love, she will sometimes have to prove her capacity for suffering in this sphere. But we should remain poor, indeed, if we would always be afraid and hold back. With the poet Rilke we would say to those who are shy and yet hunger for life: "Let everything happen to you: beauty and terror", for only thus will you reach full human maturity.

The specially religious form of love shows the same psychological characteristics as love for a human being. For the lover says Yes to another, whose individuality attracts him particularly and whose worth he recognizes intuitively. Love radiates between persons, and God is a Person of inexhaustible individuality and infinite worth.

To be religiously alive needs precisely those qualities with which woman is so richly endowed, the gift of personal relationship, instinct for vital values and the capacity for giving oneself completely to another, to The Other. Nevertheless, just the intimate interrelation between body, soul and spirit which belongs to her nature may sometimes make it difficult for her to worship "in spirit and in truth". The personal bond may become an obstacle; for not all love of Jesus is true love of God. However, religious development admits of stages, and a faulty ideal may be transformed into the true one. It should not be too difficult for a woman captivated by the artistic beauty of music and ceremonies, or by stirring sermons and attractive religious personalities, to be gradually guided to a purer faith, since the concrete and visible things may be turned into points of departure for this.

SYMPATHY AND COMPASSION

The question of a person's capacity for love is a decisive question for everyone—for a woman it is *the* question, because her whole nature is meant to care for all that is alive. However, her biological capacity for love is only part of this function, not the other way round. Love should approach its object immediately; 'higher love' is not an *ersatz* for something else, it is essentially spontaneous. Nevertheless, it cannot be forced. An authentic love of God will not exclude love of men, and all truly human earthly love will yet leave room for union with God. If we have not been

given a definite human partner to love, and if we have not yet
found God, we may well find an outlet in love for our neighbour.
But perhaps we had better not call it that, since 'love of our
neighbour' implies for most people something that is forced and
'in the air'. Hence we would rather call this immediate form
human 'sympathy'. It springs from woman's intimate communion
with life. Woman loves other human beings, whereas man views
them with detachment. Even personal matters he will mostly
judge and value from an objective point of view. From the moral
standpoint this may, indeed, be just; but it tends to create a cool
atmosphere, productive only of an 'official act', whereas a woman
would quickly turn it into a personal meeting. Whenever she dares
to follow her feminine nature, she will infuse human warmth into
the notorious proceedings of officialdom and red tape, so that
even abortive negotiations and negative answers will have a con-
ciliatory spirit about them. This feminine sympathy that bridges
gaps and reconciles opposites has surely a 'productive' quality of
its own.

Unless we practise this spirit of reconciliation and loving acceptance of foreign ways of life and thought, the world will surely be
scattered with new ruins. Such considerations should open
women's eyes to their own power. This does not consist in taking
up prominent positions, it uses no external means to express itself;
yet it is a legitimate power, for it is power over human hearts.
Unless the masculine thirst for material power be restrained by
moral considerations, the technical mastery of the world will end
in failure. Women ought to be able to induce men to fashion the
world in such a way as to make it a place where people can live
together peacefully. It would be a big step in the right direction
if women would only become conscious of this task. For then
they would also teach their children to be charitable and peaceable. It goes without saying that women must first teach themselves these things; and in order to do this they need to realize
clearly that a perfect home requires more than a number of efficient household gadgets. We would certainly not deprecate technical progress, but it ought to be used as befits human beings.
With the proper training women should surely be particularly
suited to develop the sense of its right use. In sympathy and com-
passion they are hardly inferior to men, for these are their special
gifts. It is certainly true that achievements in this sphere—if we
except some recent publications—have never been valued nearly

as highly as achievements in art, scholarship and economics. Perhaps hitherto we have been too one-sided in our judgement on values; it is time to become conscious of what has been relegated to the subconscious, and to acknowledge the great value of active love and of those who can teach this better than anything else.

In the rationalistically inclined period which is now past, mere reason had probably been overrated at the expense of the qualities of human sympathy that are especially the domain of woman. This, however, is not meant as a defence of unthinking sentimentality. On the contrary, we envisage feminine characters fully formed under the inspiration and guidance of reason. Besides, mankind has never suffered from an excess of reason; even in our present civilization we would not like to see less of it; else the result would be only useless irrational extravagance. On the other hand, we could well do with a little more spiritualized sympathy and humanity.

Mankind needs more motherliness and less merely masculine thought for its happiness. We need people capable of regarding foreign ways not only without prejudice but with love. It is quite possible to foster such an attitude, if its importance be recognized. It can hardly be said that women have so far failed men in this respect. Quite honestly, the fact of the matter is that for a long time men have not given women the chance to help them. Even now many men feel uncomfortable if women take part in a discussion. Women will best help to govern the world more humanely if they teach the meaning of sympathy and humanity by their own example. They will scarcely gain the positions due to them by storming barricades; they will do so far more surely if they set an example by what they are and do, if their professional achievements are unexceptionable, and their personalities so pleasant that no one would like to miss them from the economic machine. Then men will be convinced that their growing capacity for good is their own achievement; they will not suspect that the feminine influence has no mean share in this development. But this slow 'advance' requires a very great deal of discipline and self-sacrifice on the part of women. Much is yet to be done on both sides. Women must become conscious of their own true worth, and men must get ready to appreciate it. The motherly woman can contribute to the moral goodness of men the more, the more securely she rests in herself and the more satisfied she is with her own being and her sphere of activity. On the other hand, it is indispensable that man should accept what woman has to give him, and submit to the elevation of his own nature. These frequently discussed problems make demands on the adaptability of both sexes. If the 'masculine' woman—which is an exceptional human formation—should rise to a leading position, this would be largely due to the fact that effeminate men would have it so.

WOMAN ACCORDING TO PSYCHOLOGICAL TYPES

This book has been written so that women may know themselves better. We have therefore first made some statements on woman's nature, and will then describe the various phases of her life. But before doing the latter, we would deal with psychologically recognizable differences. This will make it easier to understand more clearly the individual destiny, including—and especially!—one's own.

Definition

If we here use the word 'type' we do so with some reserves. In their efforts to establish a scientifically acceptable characterology, scientists have tended to abandon the 'type' and to devote themselves to examining and describing the individual. We assign a person to a type simply as an aid to sketching an outline. Nevertheless, the science of typology has retained its importance for theoretical characterology. Yet it is necessary also from the practical point of view to realize that the many special characteristics derive from a few basic features, and that there are biological relations between physical and psychological characteristics, though not in the sense that every human being could be fitted into a pattern. The relations between physical form and character are the basis of the brilliant characterology of Ernst Kretschmer, who made his psychiatric findings the point of departure for his work. He was able to establish that certain forms of mental diseases occur mainly where a certain bodily structure is present, so that he finally succeeded in proving a definite relationship between physical features (*Koerperbauformen*) and mental diseases.

The classification of men according to their physical features goes back to antiquity. Even Hippocrates distinguished between the *habitus phthisicus*, which is long and narrow, and the *habitus apoplecticus*, which is broad, short and stout. If scientists speak of the structure of the body, they mean the constitution; that is, the *ensemble* of all physical hereditary traits. This is a very controversial notion. If the well-known Viennese scholar Julius Bauer classifies physical constitutions as asthenic and arthritic, this differs scarcely from the Hippocratic types.

Now Kretschmer describes on the one hand the slim figures of the *leptosomi* and the muscular ones of the athletic types; to these he opposes the *pycnici*, who tend to be large and fat but have weak bones. The first group exhibits chiefly the cycle of schizophrenic symptoms, the second that of melancholia. From the observation of sick patients Kretschmer extended his typology to normal persons, assigning the schizothymic character to the *leptosomi* and the cyclothymic to the *pycnici*.

The schizothymic character is complicated and difficult to understand. It shows only its surface, which may express itself in many different forms, varying from the artificially gay, joking and talkative person who may even be invariably friendly and apparently tranquil, to those that are shy, sensitive and always inhibited. None of these show their depth, which may even be diametrically opposed to the visible surface; for the schizothymic person is an introvert.

The principal characteristic of the cyclothymics is their excitability, to which is joined their need for expressing their feelings. The average cyclothymics may be grouped according to their prevailing moods. There may be those who tend to depression, but also others who are serenely balanced. These will be active business-men, charming companions and energetic politicians. The cyclothymics present few problems, and it is easy to make contact with them. There may occur sudden changes of temper, but no completely unforeseeable eruptions from an unknown depth, as in the case of the schizothymics.

Kretschmer's typological classification has one disadvantage for the medical layman : it rests on biological investigations which the latter cannot carry out. And these matters especially cannot be judged according to one's 'feelings', else the classifications are worthless. Besides, for purposes of self-instruction it is best if such scientific terms of reference are as general and elastic as possible. We would repeat that theoretically the term 'type' signifies an artificially constructed human specimen possessing all the characteristics of a group and only these ; whereas in practice 'type' signifies an actual individual who exhibits a particularly large number of the characteristics of his group in a striking manner. This, however, ought on no account to give the impression that the knowledge of one's own type is a magic formula dispensing people from all character training, as if it were enough to fill in a questionnaire in order to hold the key to one's life. The reason why we make these scientific findings available to a larger public is to encourage people to take their own character training seriously.

We will now, however, leave aside the biological data and confine ourselves to an easily recognizable psychological characteristic common to either group; we shall find that all schizothymic types are in some way or other introvert, whereas on the contrary the cyclothymic types are extrovert.

The types according to C. G. Jung

So we come to the purely psychological classification of types according to the Zürich psychologist C. G. Jung, who has described these two types of introverts and extroverts. This differentiation indicates whether a person's attitude to reality is mainly subjective or objective.

The first question to be asked is how 'experience' comes about. It presupposes someone who experiences and something that is to be experienced. Differently expressed : an ego is the experiencing subject, and something else, generally outside the self, is the object that is being experienced. Perhaps it may seem strange that we should first speak of the 'ego' and then of the 'self' in the same sentence. This has its reason. For this differentiation serves to express that the two, 'ego' and 'self', form the whole human person, composed as it were of shell and kernel. The mere individual, distinguished solely numerically from another individual of the species man, will be transcended in the ego only if it is capable of giving meaning to its life by directing it from its depths and harmonizing its spiritual and instinctive powers. This direction derives from the self, or the personal centre. We might also say that the ego can become the contents of consciousness, whereas the self in its fullness can never be apprehended in a conscious act.

The oldest of the modern typologies that are based on 'psychic energy' is probably that of Jung. It is very useful for practical purposes; for it is arranged according to general principles, corresponds to easily verifiable rules, and, as has already been said, does not go beyond the statement of psychological data. Jung himself gives the following rough outline of these types :

The introvert "if normal, is characterized by a hesitating, reflective and retiring temperament; he will not easily yield himself, shies at objects, is always somewhat on the defensive and prefers to observe others suspiciously while himself remaining hidden".

The extrovert, on the other hand, is characterized "by an obliging, apparently open and eager temperament; he will easily adapt himself to any situation, make contact quickly and often confidently venture upon the unknown, taking no account of possible objections" (*The Unconscious in Normal and Diseased Psychology*, Zürich, 1926, pp. 63 f.).

Hence the actions and decisions of the introvert will be chiefly motivated by subjective, those of the extrovert by objective, factors. Consequently the extrovert will live in accordance with external circumstances, whereas the introvert is guided by personal motives.

This comprehensive classification corresponds to natural data. There are creatures which multiply very quickly and abundantly but enjoy only a short span of life. They are characterized by the extroverted tendency. In contrast with these there are others whose individual lives are carefully protected, so that the preservation of their species is assured despite their comparatively poor fertility. They follow the introverted tendency.

The mainly extroverted person quickly grasps the impressions that offer themselves, adapts himself and his behaviour to them and is influenced by them. The introvert, who lives inwardly, withdrawn into himself, will react quite differently to the same external stimuli. His own inner world forms, as it were, a wall of partition between him and the world outside. Or, to use another metaphor: he receives no impression that has not first passed through the filter of his own individual mentality. Examples from different schools of art may illustrate our meaning. The 'Impressionists' paint their object as it appears to the eye; they reproduce their 'impression' without transforming it. The Expressionists and others, including the Surrealists, aim at representing the idea of the object as the artist sees it. For them their own inner world is the decisive factor.

Jung's classification, which stresses the basic tendency of the 'psychic energy', also states the psychic functions by which this fundamental tendency is perceived. Two pairs emerge: thinking and feeling on the one side, sensation and intuition on the other.

The two former are rational, the latter irrational. It is not immediately clear why feeling should be rational, as Jung states emphatically. By this he means judgements which, though springing
from a particular emotional situation, are based on the intellect;
whereas he wants sensation and intuition to be understood only
as conscious or unconscious perception. Sensation and intuition
merely perceive, they neither judge nor value. These four functions suffice to explore the world of the psyche. However, useful
though these types indeed are, they do not exclude quite different
possibilities of classification. This is sufficiently attested by the
innumerable psychological types put forward by other scholars.
We have, nevertheless, decided to use the types of Jung, which
we now propose to illustrate by various feminine temperaments.

The scale of female types from the extremely extroverted to
the extremely introverted might be headed : From the *exaltée* to
the inhibited. The other forms can be fitted in between these two
limits.

Women of the extroverted emotional type are very excitable,
quickly enthused; they make most appreciative concert- and
theatre-goers. Many girls belong to this type during the teenage
period, but do not carry it over into maturity. Such women are
influenced principally by people, much less by events or ideas,
though an idea may be readily accepted if it be attractively represented by a person. They feel magically attracted to the 'object'
of their affection, and as they are governed by their feelings, their
thought may sometimes be somewhat defective. They do not
form their own judgements, but repeat those of others and let
their emotions colour their views. Hence their conversation will
often be trite, sentimental and unconvincing. They have a wealth
of stock phrases at their disposal, by which they may give an
impression of intellectual independence that does not actually
exist.

We would once more repeat that all experience presupposes
an experienced object and an experiencing subject. A properly
balanced person will always be able to satisfy the legitimate needs
of her own nature, even though she may be powerfully attracted
by an object. For it is a psychological axiom that every human
being requires a certain measure of self-assertion. To be true to
oneself means to say Yes to, and to develop, oneself. It is impossible completely to give up one's own personality. We may,
indeed, devote ourselves entirely to some task or ideal, but never

by abandoning our own nature. There are women who, guided by their emotions, would give themselves utterly to someone or something, who would like to pour their whole interior energy into one object. Later they will often painfully realize that their own self has suffered grievous loss; it has fallen ill because it had been neglected. This, it is true, developed at first very slowly and almost unnoticed, for such an illness will not grow on the surface, it rankles in the unconscious.

What is this much discussed unconscious? The psycho-analyst (Freud) discovered that beside the conscious there must be an unconscious sphere in man, by which is meant the psychologically unconscious. About the turn of the century all European schools of thought restricted psychology to the psychology of consciousness, the latter was even identified with the soul. In this situation it was a step in the right direction when psychologists realized that all conscious experience rests on a deeper layer in the life of the soul. On the other hand, the idea of the metaphysical unconscious as the primeval centre and foundation of all being has long been familiar. Especially after Leibniz had developed his teaching on the structure of the psyche and of the universe, theories of the metaphysical unconscious played an important part in philosophy.

In contemporary medical psychology the assumption of an unconscious may be taken for assured, though it seems an exaggeration to consider, as Freud does, those impulse-energies that have been repressed and relegated to the unconscious as the real and only formative powers in human life. There are, indeed, psychic disturbances which require imperatively that, with the aids furnished by depth-psychology (such as spontaneous ideas, dream interpretation and psychological tests), the unconscious should be represented and made conscious to the patient. This, however, can only be a subsidiary means added to biographical data acquired in other ways; and, the cure of neuroses apart, we cannot possibly question the necessity and value of our whole conscious training in self-mastery. Once those unconscious factors that have produced neurosis have been discovered, even the patient who has received depth-psychological treatment will have to turn to the conscious direction of his life.

Without going more deeply into the definitions of the unconscious according to Freud or Jung, we would use the metaphor of the ocean, to which the whole psychical complex may be com-

pared and of which the conscious sphere constitutes only the surface. These psychological spheres or layers, however, should not
be pictured as neatly separated from each other. Thus one speaks
also of a subconscious, which comprises the not strictly defined
realm of the faintly conscious, or of the actually unconscious psychological events. Within these layers the current is incessantly moving up and down, now bringing one of them to the surface, now
submerging it. Images and ideas will vary in intensity and clarity.
Whatever has been suppressed or neglected sinks into this unconscious. If a person can bear the tension of life no longer, if the
exuberant woman has cast herself too vigorously into the 'object',
having spent her whole spiritual energy on the person she wor-
ships or the ideal she desires, the moment may come when the
tension snaps and the breakdown follows. The desired object
which has remained unattainable is, as it were, dropped and
broken; a flood of unobjective and unbalanced judgements will
be let loose from the mass of inferior thought that has been
stored up in the unconscious.

This is the reason why over-emotional people so often release
floods of spiteful remarks from an otherwise hidden depth, when
their dikes break because they have failed to achieve their purpose. Often just such sensitive girls and women who look most
unselfish and full of sympathy may in fact be deeply egocentric,
as can usually be guessed from some certain slight indications, and
will be clearly seen when they have a breakdown.

The subjective catastrophe will occur when the person is so
deeply affected by the conscious happenings that her ego can no
longer breathe, and the 'object' mercilessly absorbs all her powers.
At this moment the overburdened unconscious surges up violently.
The threatening danger shows itself in wanting too many things,
and no longer knowing what one really wants. For a time the
approaching breakdown may be delayed by the use of narcotics,
though it may also quite suddenly be consummated in suicide.
In general, the pathological perversion of the extroverted type
will be hysteria, by which we do not mean an emotional statement of the medical layman, but a scientifically diagnosed disease.

If the extroverted woman, guided by her feelings, is a strong,
balanced personality, she will be in some way creative. It matters
little in which sphere this will be expressed; she may as well be a
manageress in a fashion house as the mother of a family. Such
women will be popular with their colleagues; they know how to

adapt themselves and will bring a human element into the dry atmosphere of an office. Their home will be comfortable and their guests be made welcome.

A community deprived of such types would be lacking in harmony; for they are its indispensable connecting-links. The richer a person's interior life, the nobler will be the object that attracts her and occupies all her faculties.

If a woman is obviously guided by her reason rather than by her feelings, she will be of the energetic and active type; if sufficiently gifted, she will be a good organizer. Such are the typical leaders. The more exclusively their thoughts are in the object, the more they will spend all their energies on their task. If this should consist in realizing an idea, it will become *the* idea, the only one in the world which they will admit; and if there be neither compensating efforts of their own nor obstacles from outside, such women may become rigid dogmatists, devoted only to the one cause. The more they turn into a 'type', the more they will shut themselves off from all other interests. But if their thought be properly integrated with their other powers, it will be especially constructive, directive and purposeful.

Cerebral types of this kind are generally endowed also with a strong will, which to their entourage often appears as severity. As superiors they will be very exacting. Such are the hospital sisters who notice every slip of the student nurse; the headmistresses who may become a burden to their staffs. It is a common experience that even their most intimate collaborators will have a hard time and have it 'taken out of them', though their work will enjoy the highest reputation outside. It is quite true if congratulatory addresses and biographies praise their energy and creative genius; the achievements of these characters are, indeed, greatly to their credit.

On the other hand, extrovert cerebral types are frequently oversensitive, and we may meet with the curious phenomenon that they will be all the more easily hurt the more selfless they appear. The slightest criticism will often be enough to spoil their temper. Hence their underlings will quickly remove any unpleasantness, and so such weaknesses will grow quickly. The more these people throw themselves into their work, the more they will neglect themselves. Now experience shows time and again that nature cannot be disregarded. The fettered part of the ego will surge up from the unconscious in the form of excessive emotional reactions. For in predominantly rational types the emotions, which are essentially linked to the ego, are forced back into the unconscious. There they are unable to develop normally and to affirm their own legitimate value, which is necessary for one's mental health. This explains the fact that great men and women so often take umbrage at the slightest provocation and that 'strong souls' may be quite unreasonably touchy. The prejudices of such people against others who go their own way are not so much due to the fact that their thought is totally occupied with their own form of life, but that this form restricts their suppressed feelings to their own ego.

Here, too, the conscious and too rigorous elimination of the ego, the repression rather than the slow purification of its desires, will one day lead to the catastrophe of a breakdown. Then the wiring will be torn and a complete short circuit is the result.

There are hardly any purely cerebral types; for the function of thought is combined with the gift of intuition or with sensation, by which we mean external perception.

In order to remain healthy such persons should not neglect compensational occupations in their spare time. It should indeed be a general rule for everyone not to devote themselves one-sidedly only to professional work or any other single occupation. No one can live without relaxation. Now, in order to relax we must quieten all those faculties that are normally in action, and activate others that are not, to whatever sphere they may belong. For energetic leaders always applied to their task, devotion to a hobby or to some artistic pursuit should be real leisure. This personal inclination ought not again to serve another purpose, however noble that may be. For it is supremely important for all those who give themselves to outside activities that they should find time to take in and gather. If they fail to do this, they will in a few years' time work like machines; they will indeed still be active, but much less truly effective. If they love music, pictures or poems, this love should remain secret. For once it is advertised in order to adorn the portrait of the great woman, its healing power will be gone. This power consists in activating all sides of the personality and allowing none to wither away. For only thus can she mature into a harmonious personality.

Apart from the pronounced leader, there are women of smaller stature who yet embody no less valuable qualities. These are prudent, open to the world; they are turned outward, and, stimulated by their surroundings and controlled by reason, they will do useful work, especially in 'shaping the world', as has been mentioned before.

It is more difficult to pigeon-hole the erratic, impulsive woman, since she may belong to either type. Intuition is her leading quality. In practice she is a person on whom one cannot count permanently. The impulsive person who belongs to the extroverted type will be an inspiring and original companion for a time; but then she will disappear as suddenly as she turned up. The more developed her intuitive faculties, the more ideas her surroundings will suggest to her, though it will not always be possible to realize them. Whims will chase each other, but not all will shape themselves into definite plans. This erratic temperament must be balanced by getting accustomed to steady work and regularity, independent of such fancies. Desire for the sensational ought not to be encouraged too much, else psychological tension might produce feelings of anxiety and insecurity.

For completeness' sake we may also mention the extroverted emotional type to which belong pleasure-loving women, who easily give way to sensual debauchery. But it will hardly be necessary to deal with this type in detail.

We would now summarize once more the principal characteristics of the extroverted types. They live in close relation to their surroundings, taking their clues from external facts, and adapting themselves easily to circumstances. They may be totally absorbed by their milieu, but also by devotion to a cause, an idea or a person. They will be balanced and healthy unless they disregard their own subjective needs; they should not spend themselves utterly in their work or their organizing activities, and ought not to prevent themselves from occasionally doing things solely for their own pleasure. Hence it is inadvisable to turn to public use all the talents of those who work, anyway, mostly for others. If their spare time is not spent in real recreation, it will not yield the necessary relaxation. If things go wrong with them, the result will be not so much some strange twist in their nature, but they will become hardened, over-sensitive or suffer a sudden breakdown The extroverts will always form the majority of a community, because they are sociable and adaptable. The introverts, however, as we shall now show, are no less important.

Though they are mainly turned in on themselves, they have nevertheless also to gather their impressions from the outside world, since to them, too, knowledge comes through the senses.

Yet the true form of an object may become blurred for them by the interior images it will call forth in their minds. All external events are digested in a way peculiar to this particular person. The extrovert argues: It is cold, therefore I am going to take a coat. The introvert: I have the feeling I need a coat. The extrovert who is listening to a good singer will exclaim: What a marvellous voice! The introvert: I have rarely been so impressed. Of course the actual living person may strike us sometimes as more extroverted, at other times as somewhat introverted; for a human being is not a 'type'. Nevertheless, there can be no doubt that many people are developed very much in one direction.

In the case of the mainly introverted type the individuality is a very important factor; for it experiences the outer world only through the medium of its own inner world. The introverted attitude becomes pathological if the inner world is so cluttered up with images that the multitude of ideas prevents contact with the external world. In this case the object, which nevertheless called forth the experience, will be repressed into the unconscious with its store of imaginary possibilities, which it will consolidate into firmly fixed pictures. If people cannot get on with themselves, are tormented by scruples, suffer from painful, interminable introspection and fixed ideas, these symptoms may be caused by undigested experiences that have taken firm root in the unconscious, when a richly developed self has taken possession of this material, which itself remains quite unconscious.

We now turn to the cerebral type of the introverted group which, in a feminine form, we would call 'the rare woman' (*die Aparte*). By this we mean the pensive, silent woman who mostly goes her own way. She surprises by her original ideas if she expresses them, and her whole behaviour and appearance strike a peculiar note; her clothes could not be worn by anyone else, but they suit her perfectly. If she is of more than average intelligence, her thought will produce new opinions rather than new facts. Such people are considered clever, but their thought differs from that of the generality of men by its lack of purpose. Introverted thinkers may pose new questions, they will not create universally accepted bases of thought. If they are exceptionally gifted, they will produce theories and devote themselves to abstract scholarship. If a person of this type is engaged in reproductive work, she will be occupied with theoretical rather than with practical questions; if she has devoted herself to a cause, she will not easily be turned away from it, and even cling to it tenaciously.

The 'rare woman' who is of weak constitution and not remarkable for intellectual or indeed any other qualities will make, so to speak, a threadbare impression. Those are the delicate women who find it difficult to make contact or to arouse interest. They quickly collapse, whether in their work or in the emotional sphere. This insipid exterior may, nevertheless, be deceptive. Such natures will frequently have a rich interior life and especially a strong capacity for love; but they fail to find the way to the other person. In order to become healthy they should be loosened; but this we shall discuss more fully in the second part.

The emotional introvert may sometimes appear as passive; the saying that smooth waters run deep applies especially to her. These pale and silent women withdraw as soon as they are approached, they appear cool and uninterested, where the extroverts are enthusiastic. As their feelings are drawn inwards, they give those who meet them the impression of not being wanted. They seem not to notice others, and appear superior and critical without saying anything. Through this behaviour they separate themselves from their surroundings; nevertheless, just such women have a particular attraction, probably because they produce a sphinxlike effect.

While those around them suppose them to be cold and devoid of all feeling, the truth is, on the contrary, that they are actually overwhelmed by their emotions; they are only either incapable or afraid of expressing them. Their interior life is highly agitated, it has its innumerable battles, high lights, fits of despair and complications. Yet their feelings do not overflow, as those of the extroverts, but seep into the depth where they will not come to rest. Perhaps they are tormented by some affection, even by some passionate love, without the 'object' in question having the slightest notion of it. But if the emotion is too much dammed in, there may some time be a sudden outburst. It is also possible that such a person who usually keeps herself quietly in the background will on some occasion suddenly perform an heroic action. The unforeseen opportunity has produced such a strong emotional inrush that the restraining dike—that is to say, her peculiar temperament—has become flooded. Such occasions will reveal a powerful energy which, until then, had lain either dormant or been at work only interiorly. Such an eruption, however, will not remove the plug once and for all. Later these people will probably once more withdraw into themselves.

In any case, such pensive women may be expected to have a rich interior life, though it will be difficult for others to gain access to it, and unfortunately they rarely meet friends sufficiently patient to open up an entrance. They will not often expand on their own account; they expect the mountain to come to the prophet. But once they know that they are being understood and taken as they are, they will show their interior riches and depth as well as their longing to be understood and an astonishing capacity for love which may well put to shame those who make contact easily but superficially. Such people will be punctual, accurate in their work and correct in every way; they are tidy, tending to be pedantic, love regular habits and are easily guided by regimentation, but are equally susceptive to its dangers.

If the type of the pensive woman becomes more pronounced, it may lead to excessive reserve. If this continues to increase, she may become inhibited, a state bordering on the neurotic. A note of depression will be present with the languishing type. These women are permanently unhappy; there seems no remedy for their misfortune. Thus we have traced the way from the over-enthusiastic to the melancholy woman, going from the extreme right to the extreme left, so to speak. Those introverts who are strongly inhibited are often very tense; their conversation will be halting, going round and round the same subject or petering out; they do not take up hints, and their sentences will often remain unfinished. They are unable to get away from themselves and have no gift for social life, though they may desire it.

The modern woman artist often belongs to the introverted emotional type. The strength of her emotion is dependent not on the object but on her idea of the object. This way of perception is capable of uncovering the ideas beneath the surface of the world, and will express itself in symbols. Such artists represent the object under the sign of their own inner experience. Now symbols always emerge from the common treasure of mankind, no matter at what time they may come to the surface. The artist's introverted perception clothes the object that is to be reproduced with the images it receives from primeval sources and from future subjective experience. Thus the mere sensuous impression is deepened and enriched with suggestion, producing an art form which is of special significance in a period of technical proficiency. The obscure image language of the introvert also represents a side of life; it tries to express the fact that what we call nature emerges from depths that lie beyond the visible world.

We are too much inclined to forget that the world is not a surface, but space—space which, according to the philosophers, is finite, yet without limits. The interior space within men's souls is in the same way limitless, yet finite. An artist may give expression to this, but many others will be denied it; they carry within themselves their rich, not readily understandable interior world without being able to relieve its pressure. While things are going well, the manifold illusions of these people will hardly reach the surface. But if the inner burden increases, former external impressions may surge up from the unconscious, and then images and perceptions may turn into hallucinations that will oppress the sufferer and be incomprehensible to critical reason. To begin with, many people are, in any case, quite incapable of reading the souls of others; but then it also will often be impossible for many external or internal reasons. Nevertheless, regard for our neighbour demands that we should admit with Shakespeare that "There are more things in heaven and earth than are dreamt of in your philosophy". It will be a great step forward towards understanding each other if we admit that there are other valid forms of humanity beside our own.

Let us take for example the introverted intuitive type, exemplified in the reserved, 'clever' woman. Hers will be a silent, retiring femininity that is intellectually and spiritually receptive and activated by its own creative impulses. Such a woman will produce original work in any sphere; her experiences will call forth interior images which, if she be a strong and balanced personality, may be significant beyond her personal sphere, though this is not essential. We are only concerned to show that mankind as a whole would be poorer without this type. Here the external event will stimulate inner experiences; the mind will fertilize the object. It is true, in the extroverts the mind will also form the experience; but in their case the mind works outwards, whereas in the introverted type the external energy is less active than the interior creative power. This holds good regardless of whether it is a question of more than average creative gifts which, in the long run, will yet have external effects, or of ordinary people performing their everyday duties.

The balanced, mature person is both extroverted and introverted at the same time. The value of the introverted type may be seen in the case of a teacher, who educates not so much by what he teaches as by what he is. For true education is more than a mere accumulation of knowledge—it is fully developed life and, being that, forms both its inner world and its surroundings in the right way. It is no mere assimilation of facts like the material of a card index; it is the fruit of personal and spiritual influence.

A personality will be perfectly formed only by love. It is significant that the commandment that binds all men should run: "Love thy neighbour as thyself." This means: Go out and draw the world to yourself; or in the words we have been using above: Behave as an extrovert, but relate this outgoing to whatever has been revealed to you when you withdrew into yourself to commune with your own thoughts. Healthy introversion does not separate a person from the outside world, but it is needed both to make a start and to reach the goal.

We would repeat that pure 'types' do not exist in concrete reality; nevertheless, in some people one function may predominate either temporarily or permanently, though generally associated with another. Thus the practical intellect will be combined with sensibility, the artistic intuition united to feeling, philosophical intuition married to discursive reasoning; and there are innumerable other possible combinations. Reality will never exactly correspond to a given scheme, and this applies also to other psychological or biological types which we will describe, for many more have been discovered by characterologists. Nevertheless, it will be helpful to remember that a person's attitude to reality may be conditioned by his type. By dividing human behaviour into thought, feeling, sensation and intuition, we shall gain practical subdivisions which will be supplemented by the secondary functions mentioned above. It is important to recognize these latter, since they will balance the personality. For example, if we are trying to help someone to overcome a cramped attitude, we must make use of the secondary function and direct him in such a way that he is compelled to acknowledge it. He may be so deep in organizing activities that he becomes harsh and brutal, wasting his own and other people's energies. If he is at the same time sensitive, this tendency should be encouraged by procuring for him experiences from the sphere of art or nature, which would make him aware of the failings he should correct. An intuitive type who causes agitation by his impulses and ideas should be given work that commands the attention of his thought. If, on the other hand, someone is abnormally obedient and submissive, we should find out whether this may not be due to his 'type' rather than to virtue. In any case, access to the unconscious should never be sought immediately, but always over the secondary function. These considerations will make it clear why admonitions are so often futile, and why in many cases the appeal to the will must remain ineffective. The causes of many wrong attitudes are not to be sought in these attitudes themselves, which are but the results of quite different failings. The existing attitude cannot be changed unless the surface be penetrated until the motive of just this attitude becomes visible. Perhaps this will not always be possible; in advanced years not even with the help of a trained psychiatrist, but much will be gained if a person knows that an undigested past experience which has 'settled' in the unconscious may lead to a disturbance, and that he should aim at balancing the psychological faculties. But how is it possible to aim at this if a person has no idea of his psychological make-up?

It may also be apposite to say something about diseased psychology, which may painfully affect a woman's life, whether temporarily, repeatedly or even permanently.

Pathological types

In connexion with the division into types we would point out that there are permanently pathological types, though not immediately related to these groups. They are called psychopaths; that is, mentally abnormal persons. According to K. Schneider, it is a principal characteristic of the psychopathic personality that either the subject himself or society suffers from his abnormality. Without going more deeply into scientific questions, which are still very much in flux, we would note what is essential, from the practical point of view; namely that in these cases, as opposed to neuroses, hereditary disposition is a very important factor, so that lasting cures are difficult to effect.

The medical layman notices usually only those people of abnormal mental behaviour who are called schizoids—an unfortunate expression. These psychopaths have little connexion with the outside world; they find it very difficult to approach their fellow-men, whom they put off by their stiff, cold behaviour. Besides, they are odd, devoid of human warmth, yet extraordinarily sensitive. On the one hand they will often seem, or even be, violently hostile to some people; on the other they will attach themselves exaggeratedly to those who appeal to them or to whom they themselves appeal. These are the only people who cause them to thaw and from whom they will take advice; though even they will not be able to exercise a lasting influence on them. They find it hard to understand others, and it is equally difficult to understand them. These abnormal people, too, may have a rich inner life. Such women will often be almost fanatically attached to one-sided ideas; they will swear by a certain sect, a diet, a particular form—or reform—of life. Those that may justly be considered abnormal or psychopathic will always show a lack of balance. They will strike others as crazy; but this does not mean that they may not do good or even excellent work in their profession or in other spheres congenial to them. Very often they tend to be hypochondriacs.

This psychological make-up may become tragic if it is connected with features which torment their victim and which she herself realizes to be abnormal. Here we have in view a disease which is known also to the lay public as compulsion neurosis. Since we are not writing a manual of psychiatry, however, we can here do no more than just list these often very troublesome diseases.

5

PATHOLOGICAL ATTITUDES OF MIND AND SOUL

THE knowledge of permanent abnormal features in one's own character should on no account lead a person to think that efforts to improve will be of no avail. Every man possesses a certain measure of freedom as well as the capacity to use it, but it needs one's own constant co-operation. This will be especially important and successful in the case of acquired faulty attitudes, which make so many people's lives miserable. This brings us to the subject of neurosis.

NEUROSIS

Neuroses are psychologically conditioned disturbances of balance, which may express themselves either purely psychologically or purely physically, but also psychologically and physically together. It is essential to speak of neuroses only if a physical cause of these complaints can be excluded with certainty; though there are also patients who are physically ill but at the same time neurotically affected. Apart from this the doctor must exclude mental derangement (psychosis). Thus neurosis may almost be called 'the disease of the healthy'. It is brought about by some unmastered misfortune, some obstacle which has caused an interior fall, so to speak, and produced a wound that has long remained sensitive. It is, moreover, characteristic that this misfortune is by no means clear to the sufferer himself; on the contrary, the knowledge of it is generally buried in the lowest depth, and it requires long-drawn-out, patient and efficient work to discover it. The conflict and the behaviour resulting from it must be intelligible and accessible to closer investigation, else neurosis could not be called 'the disease of the healthy', for it excludes hallucinations.

A neurosis, then, may develop if somebody has not been able to master a situation no matter in which sphere of life. This may be especially an unhappy childhood, in the case of women frequently a lack of understanding on the part of the husband, or a disappointment in love. Every department of life, whether one's profession, politics, family or religion, may become the occasion of neurotic tensions. It may become this—it need not do so. Not every person would develop a neurosis in a given situation. There are enough robust natures able to bear many hard blows and complications. A certain degree of connatural instability may well be considered a subsidiary cause. Add to this unfortunate conditions of life and surroundings, for example discord between parents and defective or wrong education, and the prerequisites of a neurosis are there.

As neuroses have been more closely studied only within the last few decades, their multiple manifestations have not yet been brought into a uniform system. The different scholars proceed in different ways. Neuroses may be classified according to their 'seat' within the personality (thus J. H. Schultz), according to the sphere of life affected (so L. Binswanger, V. von Weizsaecker, V. E. von Gebsattel, Igor A. Caruso, V. E. Frankl), or, which the layman will understand most easily, according to the forms in which they appear. Thus there is neurotic insomnia, and physical symptoms affecting the function of an organ which is, nevertheless, neither physiologically nor anatomically diseased. Some of the obsessional or compulsion neuroses belong to this category. They are so called because the subject is constantly obsessed by certain ideas or compelled to behave in a certain manner. The exhibition neuroses of hysterical characters are important and not infrequent. They are also called conversion neuroses, because the conflict is 'converted' into a physical symptom. These will be discussed in the section dealing with the hysterical character. Finally we would mention the sexual neuroses, through which many a marriage has been destroyed.

Summing up, we can say of the neuroses that, however different they may appear to the different observers, they have one striking feature in common : to all of them belongs, not, indeed, a wounded organism, but a wounded texture of life. It is always possible to point out frictions between the ego and its surroundings and a misdirected striving for love. Besides, in the context of his neurosis a person will not behave in conformity with his adult age and find it difficult to accept reality as it is. Seen as a whole, every neurosis seems to be a kind of puberty crisis become chronic.

Today those complexes of symptoms that cause defective functioning of the autonomous or vegetative (spontaneous) nervous system are called pseudoneuroses. They differ in origin from the psychoneuroses that have been enumerated, but are partly treated in the same way as these.

FEAR

So far we have intentionally left aside a symptom that is present in every neurosis, because it must be given fuller treatment. This symptom, anxiety or fear, is in many cases the most important or even the only one; we speak indeed of special anxiety neuroses. We will now describe this particular state in greater detail.

Take as an example a young girl fresh from the domestic science school, who gets a job and is to cook her first dinner alone. Everyone will understand that she will be afraid of making this start. But now take another case. An hotel cook with many years' experience one day has to prepare a gala dinner. She suddenly feels no longer equal to it; she has palpitations, fits of giddiness and perspiration. She herself is quite astonished and admits to herself : I am terrified of it. So in both these cases we have a different situation. The young girl is simply afraid, the experienced cook is in the grip of anxiety. In the former case the reaction is proportionate to the risk, in the latter it is out of proportion; indeed, there is probably no risk at all. Now, the difficulty is that such reasoning does not help the person in the grip of fear; for her anxiety is not related to the situation as it actually is but as it appears to her. What is it that so many people are afraid of? Some have a vague, general fear; others suffer from veritable attacks of it, which may also be connected with regularly recurring situations or activities, such as staying at the top of buildings, walking in streets or moving in society. Fear may also have a specified content such as illness or professional failure.

Finally there are also women who are aware of depressions, feelings of inferiority and inhibitions, but who do not realize at all that they ever feel fear. Closer investigation will prove that they are very much mistaken. Only their fear is situated beneath the surface and does not become conscious. Yet the degree to which a feeling becomes conscious gives no indication of its strength and effectiveness. This is one of the most important results of depth psychology.

In fact, much fear is stalking the world today which is the source of great distress, though everything is being done to escape or avoid it altogether. For the most uncanny thing about it is that one feels completely helpless before it.

Moreover, the apparent unreasonableness of this kind of fear causes uneasiness. Now, the very fact that it cannot be explained proves that we are faced with interior forces of which we cannot dispose with mathematical certainty. Our soul is capable of unforeseeable reactions—which is no doubt uncomfortable, because such signs indicate that something is not as it should be. The symptom of fear is a signal urging us to find this something, to examine it and to put it right. All this is not consciously realized; yet the demand to approach this threatening something cannot be refused, though no one is pleased with the idea. For there is nothing a person resents so much as the knowledge that he will have to change his attitude. This is of course quite understandable, since human nature is in itself lazy and dislikes making an effort to rise above itself. Those people, however, who are used to examining themselves and their actions in the light of objective standards will be far less inclined to relegate unpleasant things to oblivion. They will admit a fault to themselves and try to avoid it in future. But those who never practise self-control will easily drag 'undigested' remains along with them. So it happens that gradually an inextricable tangle of fear and defence measures against it will come into existence. "But this is not fear", such people will say, "it is well-founded concern." The victim of fear will cling all the more to the illusion that he is always right and quite perfect; he will vigorously reject even the slightest suggestion that something may not be right and needs to be changed.

There are several principal methods of escape from fear. The first consists in giving circumstantial reasons for everything that is likely to put a barrier between oneself and one's fear. The over-anxious mother, for example, will state emphatically that her attitude to her children is dictated only by love and her sense of duty. In fact, however, it is the expression of personal fear.

Another possibility is to deny fear. All that becomes visible is physical symptoms such as shivering, perspiring, flushing, palpitations, frequent urination and diarrhœa. In such cases the person in question knows only that in certain situations he has frequently to pass water, that he feels sick in a railway train, that he sometimes perspires freely during the night, and similar things.

People also seek to rid themselves of fear by using alcohol and other intoxicants. But there are innumerable ways of camouflaging this desire so that the connexion with fear is not revealed. For fear of loneliness one may perhaps cast oneself into a whirl of social life, one may become an addict of the cinema, of novels or of sweets. Fear may also be dulled by a mad craze for work, supplemented by the well-known nervous dislike of Sunday. Inordinate need of sleep may be another symptom; but this enumeration is by no means exhaustive.

The most radical means by which to escape fear is no doubt the avoidance of any thoughts and feelings that might tend to produce it. This may be done quite consciously; on the other hand, somebody may be only vaguely or not at all conscious of his fear, and therefore not realize at all that he is avoiding it. Thus one may delay things connected with one's fear without knowing it, such as making a decision, writing a letter or concluding an agreement. The next stage will be that such an avoidance will come about automatically when the same action is imminent. Thus insuperable inhibitions will originate in some sphere of life or another.

One might think the easiest way to master fear would be either consciously to deny it or to try to conquer it. For example, the shy, stammering pupil teacher might volunteer to give difficult lectures. This rigorous method will succeed almost only in cases of an ordinary constitutional weakness which does not rest on an unconquered experience or an unacknowledged general situation that would foster fear. Experience teaches in all these cases that such a 'pulling oneself together' may well cause a certain manifestation of fear to disappear, but that the vital disturbance that causes it will remain unaffected.

These disturbances must be treated more fully in order to teach the right manner of self-examination. This is important especially for religious people, who are troubled about their own faults. Often character training will be unsuccessful not so much because nature is weak and easily tempted, but because human actions are viewed too superficially; we consult hastily composed lists of faults that are quite irrelevant to the true structure of these actions. Moreover, the 'deed' will itself be the result of faulty attitudes that go deeper. Their roots are contained in the seven deadly sins; only most people are not accustomed to ask themselves for what reason they have done or not done something. The action itself reveals only the external occasion; if we would avoid permanent faulty attitudes, we must penetrate to the deeper reasons. And, as we are now going to show, we often cannot arrive at these inner reasons (we deliberately avoid the term 'causes')—that is to say the motives—by simple reflexion.

Surely everybody will have found it difficult at one time or another to pronounce a certain name. It is odd, we have never been able to say Mrs. Hintermoser—it has always turned into something else—Hinterhuber or Hubermoser. Our friend could not help laughing. Every time she has to correct us : "Her name is Hintermoser." One may be quick in the uptake and possess an excellent memory—no matter, on certain occasions a reminiscence comes into play whether we want it or not. One would like best to wipe out the whole story, but as this is impossible, it is relegated to the farthest corner of our memory. Learned psychologists call this repression ; forgetting and mislaying things, as well as slips of the tongue, all belong to this same category.

The explanation of our example is this : Mrs. Hintermoser once made a slighting remark about us to Mrs. Pokorny, which the latter reported to us with suitable 'frills' twenty-four hours later. Of course this did not leave us entirely unmoved ; and, to be quite frank, Mrs. Hintermoser's remark did contain a grain of truth. "Stuck-up creature" she had called us, not without giving some details of our behaviour. These, it is true, had been sheer gossip—but, as a matter of fact, we are sometimes arrogant. Therefore the remark was a direct hit and is hurting us a good deal even now. Nonsense, this. "Not entirely," whispers an irritating little voice. "Be quiet," we hiss inaudibly. It is no use ; the undigested realization of our weakness is an obstacle holding up our thoughts until they have learned to take it in the school of sound self-knowledge. All we have to do is to admit privately to ourselves that Mrs. Hintermoser is not altogether wrong. It would be ridiculous if we could not behave more unassumingly, which, in fact, is much more natural to us. Our arrogance is really only put on to hide some uncertainty which is sometimes worrying us.

But to go back to unpleasant memories. The case we have just been describing is quite harmless ; we do not worry much if we only mix up a name, a mistake that can be put right in half a second. It is much more serious if the disturbance continues for some time. For example, an experienced book-keeper always stammers in the presence of her boss ; a teacher gives her lesson with a lump in her throat ; the housewife is terrified when she has to cook a dinner for her guests. We must here distinguish, however, whether this happens only rarely, in which case it would be irrelevant to our subject, or whether it is a regular occurrence.

Here we are thinking of chronic fear, when one's performance is actually out of harmony with one's personal reactions, when one is terrified of things in which one is perfectly competent. It may be that outwardly everything goes well. The book-keeper gives her account satisfactorily; the teacher presents her subject adequately, the housewife satisfies her guests. Nevertheless, all this will be done with a disproportionate expenditure of energy. This will frequently be due to an exaggerated sense of honour coupled with inordinate ambition. The sufferers themselves, however, will not have the faintest idea of this. In fact, they completely fail to realize that deep within themselves there exists a truly compelling desire to excel.

Consciously, they suffer quite on the contrary from inferiority feelings. They do not think they are able to do this, that and the other. Everybody else is more efficient. Please, please after you! . . . They want to pass quite unnoticed and pretend they are only happy when they are hidden away in a corner. Nevertheless, appearances are very deceptive indeed. We are here confronted with the second stage of unfulfilled ambition. The inferiority feelings serve to squash their own immoderate desires. This may seem complicated; however, human nature is like that. Psychological examination may bring to light that extravagant ideals and festering ambition are often due to a wrong education or a very painful humiliation in childhood, though frequently only to a weak constitution. The grown-up person, however, behaves not simply in an infantile way, but displays a chain reaction which the expert has to undo link by link.

But what about helping oneself? Every swimmer knows the exciting moment of starting off into the cold element. This is indeed unpleasant, but only for a second; then it is past and one only feels extremely comfortable. It is the same after one has mastered one's fear, for example of not daring to go to a party or to speak before others. Shy people should accustom themselves to taking part in things, and not give in to their impulse to stand aside and leave all activities to others. One should not intensify such inhibitions by trying to justify them. On the contrary, one should quickly find counter-arguments. For here we have to do with nothing worse than a very slight hesitation before a tiny threshold; it needs but a scarcely noticeable effort to pass it, which really should be made, for it is worth the trouble. The satisfaction after overcoming our weakness and the increase in strength it brings are quite evident, and these good results are so certain that it really pays to rouse ourselves time and again to make this small effort.

No doubt the situation is more complicated if we have to do not with some general anxiety but with a full-grown fear of a certain thing, which even the sufferer himself will consider unreasonable. Somebody may always avoid a certain crossing, another may never make a certain appointment. The question is whether one should avoid the object of one's fear, or whether it should be attacked as energetically as possible. In such cases it will be a help to encourage oneself gently, and not to attempt to use violence in order to remove something that defies violence. For fear is an intangible and formless feeling. It is no use trying to persuade ourselves that we are really not afraid, while every hair on our head is standing on end with fear—for it is simply not true. We should, however, keep on telling ourselves quietly that there is no reason to be afraid. We should conquer fear by quiet reflexion, convincing ourselves by looking at the evidence that no danger is threatening. Here many will sigh : "But how often have I done that! But without the slightest success. Even before the occasion in question actually arises, I keep worrying how things will go."

This brings us to an important point : the fear of having fear is worse than the actual fear, and poisons one's days. For example, we may be afraid of blushing or of having damp hands when we must shake hands with somebody. We need only think of it and we are already blushing and our hands are getting damp. This is really a vicious circle which has to be broken, else our fear will grow to infinite proportions.

To conquer it we must change our method. It would be quite wrong to try not to blush by hook or by crook. On the contrary, one should say to oneself : "Today I shall blush all over, in fact I shall get as red as a poppy. And all will be flabbergasted—just as before. There will be thunder and lightning, when I shall blush like that—just as before. Darkness will cover the earth—just as before." Who would not smile at this?

For what has so far happened when we did blush? Nothing, absolutely nothing. Life went on as before : the boss carried on dictating his letter, people went on talking, the earth still moved round the sun. Much will have been gained if we actually desire the thing we are afraid of. Then a person will no longer be in the grip of fear, but will have vigorously come to grips with it and broken the vicious circle by rising above it. If we have learned so to change our attitude to fear, much will have been done to master it, and a little sense of humour applied to ourselves will do the rest.

Many things must have happened before fear can become so ingrained that it will recur again and again. A person must have been afraid for the first time, probably under the impact of a great shock. It may be helpful if we succeed in tracing back the experiences to the first attack of vertigo or failure, though it need not be. For by doing so we only bring to light a past event, perhaps even a forgotten childhood experience. Fear, however, is effectively overcome only if the anxious anticipation has been removed, for it has attached itself to this rather than to the earlier experience, though the latter may be considered painful in retrospect.

As we have said before, it is advisable to attack ingrained fear from quite a different angle, with a sense of humour capable of laughing at the fear itself, which will solve the difficulty of transcending oneself.

People with an over-excitable spontaneous nervous system are a particularly easy prey to fear. Since they are therefore naturally inclined to it, they will be able to assist the fight against it with approved sedatives. On the other hand, it would be utterly wrong to attempt to dull it with various stimulants, which would only do harm.

Now, there are undoubtedly spiritual and mental spheres which do not respond to mere volitional energy and from which interior attitudes are fed. Timidity before the demands of life, a melancholy disposition, inordinate reserve, inclination to brooding and the whole complex of fear which is so difficult to describe—they all cannot simply be turned into their opposites by a dose of energy and will. For will itself is blind and needs to be guided by reason. In these difficulties the dark and hidden understanding supplied by one's whole attitude to life (*Lebensgefuehl*) has no doubt been led astray and needs being harmonized with the bright surface will; else all efforts will be in vain. It is a mistake leading to discouragement to think that all the imponderables necessary for interior balance can be produced simply by a 'good will'. A good will can be effective only if it be founded on a sound sense of life, else it will have to be acquired by a suitable training.

It must be admitted that a sound attitude to life can be achieved only through suffering. Those who are sufficiently discerning will not be able to escape the painful knowledge that the stream of life itself offers no ultimate securities. Here the only sensible thing to do is to realize that this is so and that neurotic fear springs from a root of genuine fear. This latter must first be admitted and confronted by placing ourselves and our fear within a sphere devoid of fear. But where is such a sphere to be found? Nowhere except in absolute truth, which is God Himself. It is indeed possible to remove much of the mammoth growth of neurotic fear; but this is no real remedy. On the contrary, fear can begin to be cured only when we affirm its cause, which is bound up with the insufficiency of all that is merely human. The complete cure of fear brings us face to face with salvation, which will unlock the centre of our being and unite us to God. Only if man is united to God will he know that there is no world without fear, but one who has "overcome the world" (John 16 : 33), in whom alone man can overcome his fear. Nevertheless, this does not rule out the existence of many emotions of fear, which are simply connected with an unstable constitution, with hormonal disturbances or nervous excitements. This form of fear, too, will not be totally destroyed; but it will be borne more easily if it be reckoned with.

Nevertheless, a well-ordered way of life with physical recreation and sports will do much to lay the ghost of fear, or to expel it where it has already become a tormenting reality. Besides, we must be gentle and patient as well as firm with ourselves. For in this sphere the psychosomatic relationship is very evident; though the spiritual superstructure, or rather the spiritual centre, of the human person is no less certain. For from there all faculties are united and guided. Now, to be a person in the sense in which the term is here used is an attribute of every human being; this can never be sufficiently emphasized. It is true, there are instincts in man which a wrong attitude may bring out, so that they will demand their rights by force and take the lead. Yet the impulses of self-assertion, which at first aim at forming and asserting themselves, are by no means fed only by blind instincts; for every human nature demands a fullness of life that survives the mortal body; more, it desires even to be united to a community of those like to itself. All this is very intricate; hence we have so far avoided to investigate the causes of this or that attitude. For this might give the impression that it was a question of mechanical connexions which could simply be unravelled like stitches of a knitting. Such a view would not do justice to man and miss the point from the start.

Every individual is a self-contained world, an incarnate idea of Him who has willed life to exist. Therefore we shall never receive a satisfying answer if we only strive to remove existing defects and whitewash dark spots in the hope of thus reaching something outside ourselves. The real question is : How can I find fulfilment as a human being, and, more especially, as a woman? We should hold on to this, for thus the vital question comes back to the inquirer, who will always be a complete human being, regardless of whether she be altogether or only partly ill, or on the contrary perfectly healthy. This question cannot be answered except from one's own centre, from one's heart and conscience. And, leaving aside all details, explanations and analogies, it will finally boil down to the question : Have I loved enough? In the case of a man this aspect may more easily be left out, provided his work stands, for this may be the fulfilment of his life. But a woman's life can be fulfilled only in herself, all depends on how much her heart can contain. This will certainly not always be her own family, which may often turn out to be a burden of sorrow and sacrifice, and this can be a fulfilment only if it be accepted. Of this we shall have more to say in the later chapters. The achievements of creative women do not contradict what has just been said ; for they will be valued precisely as women only if their personal powers show forth in their work.

HYSTERICAL REACTIONS

In this section on psychological diseases we must refrain from dealing with the great cycles of the so-called mental illnesses (psychoses). These are manic depressive states, as well as the complex of schizophrenic symptoms which shows itself in certain disturbances of the emotional, volitional and reasoning faculties. But it will be useful to conclude the discussion of the pathological side of feminine psychology with a description of the hysterical character, because it is fairly frequent. By this we mean a deformity of character manifesting itself in an exaggerated desire to shine and attract attention. The urge to be talked about and to be at the centre of things causes the hysterical woman time and again to make an exhibition of herself. Hysterical people are extremely susceptible psychologically, and they will react violently where others show no sign of emotion.

It follows from this that the question of hysteria is intimately connected with the character problem, which is complicated. It is certainly easy to describe an hysterical woman with all her exaggerated behaviour and grand theatricals. It is much more difficult to form a correct opinion of her real intentions. One ought not to pronounce moral judgements without an adequate knowledge of the difficult subject of scientific characterology. The onlooker dislikes the behaviour of these people and is disgusted by the purposive nature of their reactions. Nevertheless, their whole conduct is fundamentally due to their effort to achieve some interior balance. Their desire for harmony and fulfilment is working unconsciously and expressing itself as a varied play of many scenes. It is true, the hysterical woman does not appear to be genuine; yet her attitude is not 'put on', it is pathological, due to deep-seated disturbances. To the medical layman hysterics may seem to be in the same category as frauds and shammers; but this is not so. The shammer wants to *appear,* the hysteric to *be* ill; the psychological premises are different. A kind of desire for salvation is at the root of the hysterical character. Such people would like to be freed from their own egoism and their inner futility; therefore their purposefulness and their calculations serve a desirable end. Nevertheless, everything becomes entangled, because this desire may be far from the threshold of their consciousness.

Certainly all this is not due to a defect of the will, as one may often be inclined to think. Such characters are at the mercy of psychic intentions which have usually already become divorced from conscious volition and have gained independence; they may even appear against one's will. The ultimate, though hidden objectives can only be understood as the desire to be set free from one's own unhappy character.

The psychologist will be able to direct hysterical women in such a way that their desire to make an exhibition of themselves will serve a useful purpose. One should remember, however, that because of their unbalanced and unstable character one will hardly be able to count on constancy, reliability, discretion and faithfulness.

If it be admitted that deep down in the nature of hysterical subjects there is waiting a readiness for being changed, it will easily be understood why there are intimate relations between religious devotion and hysteria. Hence it is no accident that in the various religious groups many such women will be found who are in need of individual direction. It will certainly be possible to guide and find a place for them, as well as to help them personally, on condition, however, that one will not quickly decide that one has 'seen through' them, but will diagnose their state of mind correctly.

The hysterical woman is a sufferer whose suffering is caused more or less by her own fault; in so far as her illness is based on selfish deception, it can be regarded as a punishment. Just this 'religious basis' is often the reason for the goings-on of hysterical subjects that drive those around them to distraction. But this is realized neither by the victims of hysteria themselves nor by those whom they torment. Now, hysterical subjects need sympathy and suitable assistance. This does not mean that their attitude should be approved; they should not be weakly pitied, but pardoned and understood, else one may easily put oneself in the wrong. The emotional outbreaks of hysterics quickly rouse the angry emotions of others. Most people, no doubt, resemble the self-righteous Pharisees and readily condemn what offends their feelings. Now, hysterical behaviour immediately calls forth disgust. Hence hysterical women (we have only these in mind, though this character deviation is not confined to one sex) are more easily wronged than any other sufferers in need of help. Moreover, the very common attitude of scornful, pharisaical condescension will make all access to such people impossible. As hysterical subjects are particularly sensitive, they quickly discover the weak point of their opponents; and no weakness will be more mercilessly exploited than injustice, especially by people whose own injustice has time and again become a snare to them.

From the educational point of view we shall be most successful in our dealings with hysterical women if we take up the unassuming attitude of a person who knows herself to be imperfect and takes the world as it is. Emotions and counter-emotions are uncalled for; the hysterical game should not move the spectator to tears, whether of sympathy or of wrath. But genuine simplicity will have its effect, because the hysterical subject herself would like to be like that, though this desire to change her character may be largely unconscious. If she recognizes this quality in her *vis-à-vis*, she will be attracted by it.

In any case, it will be a good thing to know that hysterics are psychologically vulnerable. Everyday experiences may cause interior wounds which in their turn will call forth hysterical symptoms. Being hypersensitive, they also react with great violence and may become very aggressive. They tend to embellish or misinterpret facts quite fantastically, and immediately take advantage if one believes them. In communities it is not advisable to entrust leading positions to women subject to hysterical reactions; it would cause no end of excitements and quarrels. Nevertheless, many persons of this type will try to reform themselves, and there are instances of very satisfactory permanent changes. Psychotherapeutic treatment is advisable in such cases; it can be surprisingly successful, because cases of hysteria that resist all treatment are not very frequent. Generally it will be a case of hysterical behaviour, whereas the character is otherwise intact. An emergency has once been mastered by hysterical defence, and since that time one employs it as a means of escape. The hysterics hardly know it themselves—and there they are already taking this line despite themselves, finding no other way out. Here, too, our advice of changing the inner attitude to life holds good; those women who do not shirk an authentic change will find themselves richly rewarded.

II

THE DEVELOPMENT OF WOMAN

THE YOUNG GIRL

On the following pages we are going to describe the various stages in a woman's life. The transition from the child to the girl marks the beginning of a change from the preliminary form of childhood to the maturity of womanhood. This period of physical but also of psychological transformation is called puberty. It is especially important for the girl, who has now reached her decisive hormonal and sexual development. The first menstruation occurs between the twelfth and the thirteenth year, in our latitudes usually a little later; with this the 'teen-ager' comes into existence. Until her eleventh year a girl may have been very much like a boy; but then she begins definitely to develop into a woman. The sexual maturity is often preceded by a rather restive period, with difficulties at school and sometimes nervous symptoms such as bed-wetting, distracted behaviour and unreasonable nerviness. Girls who have hitherto been obedient may become refractory and neglect their normal interests. But once menstruation has become regular, all these disquieting symptoms will disappear by themselves. It is important for a girl's harmonious psychological and physical development that she should be properly instructed on the menstrual cycle in good time. It is a mother's duty to tell her daughter openly and adequately what to expect. The way in which the happenings in her body have been explained to her will determine to a large extent a girl's feminine self-respect and tact, and especially a healthy attitude to motherhood.

Gynæcologists and psychotherapists can tell a tale of the tragic consequences if such explanations have not been given. If these unintelligible happenings suddenly come upon the unsuspecting girl, they will appear to her unclean and terrifying. This may later produce anxiety neuroses or a permanent disgust with regard to sexual matters. Another consequence of ill-advised silence on this subject may be unwholesome curiosity, which will sometimes develop into a vague yearning for erotic experience. These forbidden things will attract, though they are consciously resisted.

It is easy to see how girls who were once imprudently left to themselves will later yield to sensual temptations without resistance.

Half-explained mysterious hints may also be harmful; nor will melodramatic enlightenment and unreasonable softness during these days provide the foundation for a sound feminine development. Though it is necessary to be more careful during the period, this should nevertheless not be exaggerated; the young girl should not be encouraged to regard herself as ill and to feed her imagination on such ideas. The fact that girls engaged in intellectual work often menstruate earlier than others is of course no reason to oppose such activities.

It is all-important that the child—for such a girl still is at the beginning of menstruation—should be imbued with reverence for the happenings in her own organism, and should know that such mysterious events are necessary so that she may later be able to bear a child in her own body.

MATURING PHYSICALLY

We will now give a detailed description of the events in menstruation, so that mothers may gain sufficient information and certainty to discuss these matters with their daughters. The female germ glands are formed by the double ovaries. In these the female germ cells or gametes originate and develop so that they can be fertilized, until they are ejected. From their place of origin they pass through the tubular canals of the oviduct. The unfertilized ovum passes the uterus without embedding itself; if fertilized, the uterus will build it up. Through the entrance to the inner sexual female organs the vagina leads outwards; it is a flat skin passage whose built-in muscles cannot be moved at will.

We will now describe the activity of the female germ glands in greater detail. The female gametes or ova are formed before sexual maturity has been reached, even before birth, as we have said in one of the first chapters. In the very earliest stages of the development of the human being in the womb, cells are separated, put aside, as it were, as building materials many years beforehand. For the ova must be capable of building up a whole organism with all its many separate organs. Hence they must not be so specialized as the various other cells become in the course of building up the body, when, for example, the nerve cells are capable only of forming nervous organs. In the anatomical preparation such primitive germs can be proved to exist already in the first stages of a human being; they multiply without special organs by dividing, and about the time of the birth of a girl the formation of all the original ova is finished. Thus they lie ready in the ovaries, in much greater number than can ever be ejected from a woman's germinal glands. For of all the primitive ova numbering several hundred thousand, only four hundred to five hundred reach their maturity and are expelled in the life of a woman during the time of her reproductive capacity; that is between the ages of fifteen and forty-eight. At certain intervals, corresponding to the periods of menstruation, only one of this multitude of ovules matures sufficiently to be detached from the ovary so as to move outward in order either to perish without being fertilized or, in the opposite case, to be embedded and developed.

The maturation of an ovum comprises two simultaneous processes. In the first place the ovum itself grows to approximate sand-grain size and undergoes certain divisions; the ultimate end of this is a halving of the hereditary matter as is found in all sexually reproduced beings; for the other half of it is destined to be supplemented by the male sperm with its hereditary matter, which has also been halved during maturation. This process represents, as it were, the inner preparation of the ovum for its natural destiny. Besides, there are organic changes, the end of which is the ejection of the mature cell from the ovary. For this, nature chooses a way to be found also elsewhere, when foreign matter that has penetrated an organism is to be removed. In the case of the ovum, however, this happens without inflammation and destruction of tissue : the surroundings of the foreign substance are liquefied, so that it will finally be swimming in a bubble. The melting and liquefaction of tissue continues in the direction of the surface of the organ. The bubble develops progressively into a little ball, which bulges towards the interior of the ovary, and which, under its thinning top, contains the ovum that is to be expelled. When the bubble has reached about the diameter of a hazel nut it bursts; the ovum is washed out with the liquid and received by the funnel-shaped entrance of the oviduct. This is called ovulation. According to Knaus-Ogino, this is the determining factor of the so-called 'safe period' in marriage. Such a free ovum remains alive and capable of fertilization at the most for twelve hours; it passes through the oviduct, which is approximately seven and a half inches long, in about a week.

The maturing of an ovum is directed by the secretory activity of the pituitary gland. Once ovulation has set in, there appears a new organ in the place of the collapsing wall of the bubble; this is a small gland with interior secretion which, from its yellow colour, is called the 'flavine body' (Latin *flavus*, yellow). This has a double task. First it has to stop the maturation and release of other ova through its secretions into the blood; secondly it must prepare the uterus for a possible reception of the ovum in case of its being fertilized. For this purpose the mucous membrane of its surface must be softened so that the ovum may be more easily embedded in it, and beneath the surface all materials necessary for the further growth of the fertilized ovum may have to be made ready, in case it should arrive there about a week after ovulation. For this purpose the lining of the uterus will be transformed; its mucous membrane is thickened, it is furnished with blood vessels, glandular ducts and other essentials. In short, everything is most efficiently provided for the embedding of the wandering ovum, so that it may find all that is necessary for its growth in its first maternal abode. These processes, too, are directed by the flavine gland.

If, however, the ovum has not been fertilized—that is to say, if it has not been embedded after its week's travel and arrival in the uterus, and hence has failed further to stimulate that gland—this will perish. It will decay, but at the same time all the preparations of the uterine membrane are obliterated, since, for the time being, they are serving no purpose. The mucous membrane shrinks, and beneath it bleedings occur which separate it more and more from its foundation. Finally the whole lining will be expelled. This is the moment when menstruation begins, which therefore involves not only bleedings but also ejection of whole pieces of tissue, so that the interior of the uterus, having lost its lining, has become a bleeding wound, as it were. Afterwards the normal mucous lining is gradually restored and the periodical process begins anew.

If, however, fertilization and hence embedding has taken place, the flavine gland will be preserved and will direct, in connexion with the secretion of other glands, the manifold processes needed for pregnancy and birth.

If the mother or the teacher is familiar with this marvellously planned waxing and waning in the female organism, she will tell her child these things reverently, and will in all simplicity point out the workings of an order which men can only have received from the divine Wisdom. Even the child will understand how wonderful it is that throughout the time of its full vigour the body of woman should prepare itself again and again for the possibility of motherhood, no matter whether this possibility will be realized or not.

The global view of medicine, which considers man in his psychosomatic totality, would suggest that these processes serve to revive and preserve motherliness. Woman's creative power has deep foundations; but it would be a mistake to see it as something merely biological. Body, soul and spirit are intimately connected, and penetrate each other in such a way that the higher sphere is served by the lower. The ultimate meaning of motherhood is to be able to protect and care for others.

MATURING SPIRITUALLY

Between the thirteenth and seventeenth years of her life the young girl is still not fully developed. Just these years are difficult, though not so much for physical reasons. The difficulties are spiritual and psychological; they spring from the novel experience of a change in her existence. So far the child has experienced herself as part of her family, her form, her group of playmates. Now she is detaching herself from these roots and discovers her own interior world as well as the difference between herself and her surroundings. These new discoveries, alluring and threatening in turn, are twofold. There is first the world outside, which so far has not been experienced as a living opposite, but as a framework of life that was taken for granted. Secondly, there is her own self with its powers of judgement and decision, which is something entirely new. The growing woman is becoming conscious of her own spiritual personality. Her memory is enlarged and perfected, she thinks more intensely, her imagination becomes bold and creative. New talents appear, enthusiasm and a hitherto unknown idealism provide spiritual adventures.

Remembering our detailed description of the physical development, it will easily be grasped that the spiritual and intellectual consequences of the change from child to young girl must be immense. This process of growth sometimes brings to light childish faults : obstinacy and recalcitrance, moodiness and excitability, boasting, vanity and conceit. Yet suddenly the child will come out again in her affectionate trustfulness and warmth. Such are the characteristics of the thirteen- to fourteen-years-olds, who are so difficult to guide. Sometimes one will have to make ample allowances and let bygones be bygones when a more tractable phase is reached. It is unwise always to hark back to faults that have been overcome.

After the first stage of maturing, the soul of a girl resembles broken-up soil: everything is topsy-turvy, weeds will be lying side by side with good seed. Uncanny questions begin to arise from within; whence has she come, whither will she go?—she is mysteriously becoming aware of the fullness of life in her own womb, and of the strength of man under which the woman becomes weak.

All this expresses itself outwardly in a lack of interest in her former activities; in revolt against the family, neglect of her normal duties; in a word, in a kind of helplessness in various directions. Patient understanding and protective kindness that is ready to remove dangers will be a better policy than active interference.

Once the activity of the germ cells has regulated itself, the first tension will be solved, the girl will 'grow together'. Often a pure interior life will bring forth hidden treasures, growing beauty and womanliness will soon show themselves. It will quickly become evident whether the development will go in the direction of coquettish fickleness, unmanageable truculency or quiet, maidenly development. There will be hardly any physical difficulties at this time; the troubles attacking the girl are psychological. It will scarcely be necessary to emphasize how important at this time is the protection of a solid home, the example of a balanced mother and the guidance of a revered father.

Just in those years parents ought to know exactly with whom their daughters associate; well-directed youth groups where they can safely 'let off steam' will be a great help. Suitable companionship, amateur theatricals, efficiently run holiday camps—all these will provide lasting experiences capable of counteracting inner upheavals. If these activities aim at fostering the ideals of truth and goodness, they will be important factors in building up a sound feminine personality. Even now the womanly abilities and qualities should be aroused and fostered, and the girls should be consciously encouraged to care for others; for unless this is done, we shall bring up selfish little hussies unable to resist the second danger period in a girl's life, which occurs about the seventeenth year. First they will succumb to their craze for vanity and pleasure, and soon to worse things that may have irremediable consequences.

At this time the girl will usually have chosen her career; often she will even earn her own living, which will sometimes lead to her complete separation from her family, though she may still live at home. Even our secondary school girls ask today mostly the same two questions as their other contemporaries: Shall I be able to earn enough, and am I soon going to have a boy-friend? The average modern girl between sixteen and eighteen differs greatly from the girls in her grandmother's days; the expressions 'teenager' or 'flapper' suit her well. In her grandmother's time the question of taking up a job was raised only tentatively; the girl belonged to the home and was educated almost exclusively for this. Today the subject of a profession is much discussed, and domestic work is even avoided. Romantic ideas about one's vocation have given place to selfish and materialistic considerations. The end in view is to earn enough to be able to afford as many luxuries as possible, not to find fulfilment by giving oneself to others. Even the characteristically feminine professions that involve personal demands and relationships are often considered above all as means of making a living.

Today we are producing no counterpart to the youth movement during and after the First World War. Youth has lost its ideals—of course through the fault of the grown-ups, who have deceived it with slogans and ideologies incapable of satisfying the needs of the young. Consequently they have learned to mistrust the ideals manufactured by the adults, and content themselves with a sober view of life that is mainly concerned with self-preservation. Moreover, the childhood of many young Europeans now reaching manhood has been terrible enough. It has been spent in air-raid shelters or on treks, in refugee and concentration camps, in constant fear and want, haunted by innumerable terrifying experiences. Often their parents were unfortunately unable to give them no more interior than external support.

After all, if youth is without moral restraint, this only reflects the attitude of their elders. It is hardly surprising that young people should try to break away from unsatisfactory and quarrelling parents and to be independent as soon as possible. It is equally understandable that, after years of terror, they want at last to 'live'. Having experienced as children the sombre reign of death, they now want life all the more, and they find the intoxicating fulfilment of this desire in sexual satisfaction. This explains why they are so easily seduced and why love is degraded to physical pleasure; it is the reason for their insatiable thirst for parties and sensations, as well as for their instability. We should not forget one thing: it is through our fault if young people should show no particular interest in shaping the future. We should also remember that the ways of our grandmothers have been considerably changed, because our whole view and manner of life has changed. Technical progress makes itself felt even in the changed way of housekeeping of an ordinary family. It is the duty of the grown-ups, not, indeed, to deny the practical advantages of technical achievements, but always to stress their intellectual foundations and to point out that intellectual work must take the first place.

Our young girls, too, have their finest possibilities between eighteen and twenty-four; they, too, are the future, like every new generation. It is true, they display on the whole a strong instinct for self-preservation which expresses itself as selfishness, desire for power and a craze for pleasure; they are more matter-of-fact than former generations, and an early eroticization of life in general will certainly lead to an undesirable solution of this problem, or to a staggering disillusionment and consequently to a devaluation of conjugal love.

AWAKENING OF SOCIAL CONSCIOUSNESS

Physical precociousness and knowledge of life are frequently matched by intellectual and spiritual immaturity and void. Here we have to begin, sparing no effort. Sport, nature and art offer sufficient points of making contact with young people of either sex. In the case of girls, who are interested in life and naturally attached to persons, it is comparatively easy to induce a healthy view of life. It is necessary, at this age, to deal with the question of human contacts on a plane that is above mere momentary satisfaction. In a case where religious motives are at first ineffectual, it is certainly permissible to adduce high moral principles if they are presented as personal responsibility in a sound social order. For this is the second main educational task: to train young people for community life in a wider sense. This will, of course, be easy where the family is intact. But if a young girl comes from a broken home, it may only be possible to make her understand the importance of the family for which she may one day be responsible by way of the larger community.

The professional ethos will have to be derived from this social consciousness, if it is really to be rooted in the personality. It may therefore be concluded that the fundamental problems of young girls, true partnership and a satisfying profession, may both be solved on the basis of membership in the social community, so that they will not become mere isolated egocentric activities. In fact, youth must be confronted with the question of serving mankind. Our young people's lack of interest in anything beyond a career is terrifying. This is especially true for Germany, where the political lying propaganda of the Nazi régime has produced an understandable lack of enthusiasm for the concerns of state and society. Even though the young people of today were then but children, the memories of the past are too powerful; besides, women are not, as a rule, greatly interested in politics. And it would seem very ill-advised to introduce the unhappy divisions of party policy into the school. This is not the aim of education; in this respect much will have to be changed.

LEADING TO A WIDER OUTLOOK

We should begin early to broaden the horizon of girls, too, and to guide them away from petty utilitarianism to neighbourly love and sympathy. At the age of puberty, hearts and minds are susceptible to all that is good and noble. For it is the time when the hitherto unreflecting child begins to taste the bitter-sweetness of his own humanity. This human sympathy should not be vague and sentimental, but open to all that is genuine and true; nineteenth-century idylls, for example, are out of the question. Our youth has gained its knowledge in war and distress; but this awareness of the dark side of life does not shut out from their hearts longing for beauty, purity and truth, the feeling that there is also nobility in man. This nobility is shared—in principle—by every human being whatever his race or nation. Education should therefore be free from racial and other prejudices and guide young people towards all-human responsibility. Thus it would become possible to rouse them from their indifference to moral and political ideals.

Of course such a world-wide view cannot overlook the fact that there are communities and national groups closely associated with each other, and that identical forms of life will be found only in small units living in the same neighbourhood. Though it is normal and desirable that these should be cultivated, it remains important that the young girl should learn to look beyond her own small circle; there will be many opportunities for this. After all, it is part of the divine world order that men and groups of men should be united in a world-wide community. There is no question here of egalitarianism; on the contrary, the young woman should learn to respect the difference of her neighbours. Nevertheless, the powerful impulse that springs from the first awareness of one's own self should be made socially fruitful by learning to understand also the self of others.

At this point of a girl's development it will also become evident whether old maids are in the making or warm-hearted, clear-headed women, capable of finding a way out of the unsatisfactory human situation of the present. The period of adolescence should not be considered unimportant or useless as regards the so-called ends of life. In these years all may be gained or lost. Nor should adults ridicule the seriousness with which the values of life are approached in these years. Today playful superficialities are certainly quite uncalled-for in the education of girls.

Educational errors in the years of adolescence account for the strange fact that, though women are in the majority, they tend to isolate themselves, and will, in later years, suffer from loneliness. Then it will be too late to integrate them into small groups, the contemporary form of work and recreation; for the woman over forty is set in her ways and difficult to change. Between fifteen and twenty-five all possibilities are still open, and in these years her interest in public life should be particularly cultivated. A profession alone will hardly satisfy a woman, especially if her personal inclination has to be subordinated to financial considerations; and waiting for the uncertain prospect of marriage will make her dissatisfied and unstable. Many women who do much useful work complain constantly that they are 'of no use at all'. They are incapable of independent intellectual activity or of working out their own view of life.

It may well be asked why so many youth groups in existence are so little concerned with social and political science. Religious zeal is rare, and if it is artificially stimulated it will only produce sham results. It would be better to acquaint the bigger girls with youth legislation and the principles of home-making. It would also be profitable to teach them nursing, babycraft, library work, the differences between social work and private charitable activities, the obligations of the individual to the community and so forth.

Since girls have a more personal attitude to things and people, it is very important to bring home to them the difference between a personal act of charity and mere emotion, especially as they will often during these years pass from a general 'crush' to a first flirtation without a sound psychological foundation. At this time it will also be necessary to remove the definitely hysterical characters from the group, or at least from their undesirable leading positions.

There is such a thing as service of mankind, which is a big word that needs to be rightly interpreted. Law and personal rights must be recognized, judged and, if necessary, fought for. Their responsibility as citizens should be explained to the girls and illustrated by impressive examples. Educational duties, protection of life in the womb, marriage as an institution and as a mystery, are subjects of immediate interest to growing young women. The purity of monogamous marriage can be preserved only if it is respected also by the unmarried, for good marriages cannot thrive without an appropriate social climate. It is a high art to interest oneself in vital questions without oneself solving them in the concrete. By doing so, adolescent girls will learn to look beyond themselves and to enlarge the narrow horizon for which women are often rightly blamed.

Three important points have to be kept in view in modern education. First, in order to master technical progress on the human plane, individuals need qualities which in former times were not so essential, namely independent judgement capable of making decisions and shouldering responsibilities. On the other hand, it is equally unthinkable that the individual should separate himself from the community. This, too, is a consequence of technical emancipation which requires team work. At the turn of the century the term 'social', in its political signification, was still restricted to the lower classes. Today it is at the centre of all vital questions. If we would educate our youth, and this includes the girls, in accordance with the needs of our time, we shall have to teach them to grasp and keep alive the tension between individual and community in the right way. The third point elevates the first two to a higher level and will deepen the young people's sense of values. It is a very important concern needing serious reflexion to save them from the poison of advertisements, propaganda and slogans. The ideal of peace, so near to woman's heart, should be presented to the girls from the highest spiritual level. They should be convinced of the human dignity that belongs to everyone, regardless of the power and greatness of his country, independent of nationality and race. There are human duties incumbent on all, that give a right to respect as well as self-respect to all who admit them. It is the task and mission of youth to serve truly human ideals, to recognize and to live them. Youth, especially young women, should help to conquer by their efforts in word, deed and thought everything that divides nations, races and groups, and thus hinders them from fulfilling their common destiny. Girls should realize their own kinship with all human beings, and know themselves responsible for everyone they meet, in the widest sense of the word. Only thus can they launch out into a wider sphere of life, where their healthy thirst for activity will be given new outlets, so that also those who will later remain unmarried will be able to find a satisfying fulfilment. It is quite frightening how indifferent many young people are to all that lies beyond their own person, such as the national community and its wellbeing.

But this should not prevent us from doing all we can to rouse their hearts and minds during these impressionable years to the ideal of humanity as the highest end of national education. Man, and man alone, is conscious of right and wrong; this distinguishes him from the animal. This consciousness must not be allowed to lie dormant, or to operate only within the narrow sphere of self-preservation. It is true, girls will assent without difficulty to the idea of international peace; but this will have to be based on the proper intellectual foundations. The traits common to all peoples should be emphasized in the lessons, and attention should be drawn to the silent heroism of so many pioneers of culture and scholarship.

The teaching of history, especially, should be adapted to the girls' mentality in order to lead them towards activities that will be fruitful for the community. Women are easily attracted to personalities; they should become acquainted with a St. Catherine of Siena, Newman, Florence Nightingale, to name only a few. If we would train them to live as responsible members of the community, we must train them to be fully human, to penetrate society with their whole personality, thus making it into a true community, and to sacrifice even their own personal predilections for this end.

DEVELOPMENT OF WOMANLINESS

The conscious emphasis on human values in the education of girls can be effective only if they are placed within a feminine context. The school curriculum is overburdened with subject-matter that has little connexion with life; in the education of girls in particular much will have to be done to adapt this material to the special needs of women. In some schools there are domestic science classes, but in those schools designed to prepare for the university these subjects ought not to be neglected. If a girl grows up in a large family, she will automatically take her part in the household duties. Nowadays, however, the formative power of the home has so largely deteriorated that it falls to the task of the school to activate the domestic virtues through the appropriate school subjects. If a certain measure of homecraft be assured in elementary and secondary education, special university studies will scarcely be a danger to sound womanhood. By this we do not mean to limit woman's horizon to a few domestic functions; we only admit their necessity. In order to value and accomplish them properly, we need today energetic guidance and, what is even more necessary for the growing girl, personal meetings with exemplary feminine personalities.

RELIGIOUS RIPENING

Without a religious foundation, desires for self-sacrifice, devotion to a person or an idea and the longing for truth, beauty and goodness will be vague and 'in the air'. And even a general religious foundation will not be able to form a character unless it be deepened and developed to personal familiarity with God. For only in this communion will the ultimate meaning of life be revealed, which can never be mere resignation, sacrifice and a narrowing of one's nature, but the joy of being united to God. From the psychological point of view it may indeed be questioned how far young people are capable of grasping ultimate religious foundations, apart from exceptional vocations. However, these questions can neither be asked nor answered from the psychological point of view, nor can they be solved by merely rational considerations. Yet one thing is certain : psychologically sound religious people have a very reliable sense of life which will show them the limits that are above as well as those below.

Sound piety will show more clearly than lack of faith what can be attained. For the unbeliever is more one-sidedly centred in his own ego and cannot really understand why all his desires should not be fulfilled. Now, desires that do not arise from a higher spirituality concern in general the satisfaction of sensual longings, of avarice and pride, and an undisciplined person can store up much of these. The believer, on the other hand, will see himself first of all as a creature whose possibilities are not unlimited; further, he will know that he is imprisoned by original sin, yet delivered from it and redeemed towards a higher goal. This religious support is a very valuable factor in the individual life, as is also the expansive power of a truly religious woman. If a person sees only the external mechanism of life at work, he will gradually lose his inner resilience; for he regards too much the external things. The believer sees things differently; he seeks God in the depths of his soul, nourished by faith and the Sacraments. Thus he will gradually come to see things with the eyes of God; the old humdrum activities are made new, light from above will shine on the daily round. It is true, struggle and cares will remain, and even sin will not simply be done away with; yet all will become transparent in the light of deepened friendship with God. Whatever life may hold, there will always be hope, and this can be sensed in a young girl who has real faith. She will become a guiding light to others, though they may not be able to say why.

Living in harmony with God is not a matter of emotions, nor will it normally express itself in sudden illuminations. It is the fruit of religious ripening, and if this has reached the inmost mansion of the soul it will move everything from there; whenever it ventures forth to work among men, God is going with it, as it were. Through this inseparable, living interpenetration of nature and grace the world is changed; the felt harmony of a person united to God endows everyday life with a different quality. It is like a miracle, like the crossing of the Red Sea. The rushing waters of complications and entangled affairs are divided, and one of God's people passes through, leaving behind him an indescribable trace of God's brightness. 'The world' does not know what has happened, but it has looked up for a moment; and during this moment it has forgotten to think of its own advantage, and this is already much. It is quite true that faith has external effects, and there is no reason to condemn our youth wholesale. Besides, about the eighteenth year there may occur a lessen-

ing of the religious interest, which may finally establish itself
interiorly about the nineteenth, when it often will deepen in an
astonishing way. Generally speaking, girls normally have a moral
sense and affirm without questioning the moral law, because it is
a law of human nature. The healthy woman will live in harmony
with the laws of life. If much of this has been destroyed in times
of unrest, it can certainly be restored by a sound and understanding education.

In this connexion the building-up of religious youth groups
will be very important. Gradually the organization of the Catholic
Young Workers is sure to be extended also to other groups. It is
essential to let the young people themselves solve problems of life
by their own efforts. It would be advisable to have less entertainment and give more time to serious questions of shaping one's
life. Besides, there should be informal meetings for reading and
conversation. Another point is the religious indifference of so
many homes. Cardijn's principle—"Everything through lay initiative, nothing without the chaplain"—is certainly valid for
every feminine youth group. It is essential for the young girl to
get to know priests as advisers and trustworthy friends, rather
than as onlookers at games and entertainments. Experience teaches
time and again that vital questions have to be worked out by
the young people themselves. Solutions presented all pat and
taped by adults will produce only the sham certainty of a 'nice'
upbringing, which looks pleasant but will easily be defeated by
serious situations. On the other hand, a good team spirit and purposeful activities will produce surprisingly satisfactory results.

BETWEEN GIRL AND WOMAN

EXPECTING TO MARRY

A PESSIMISTIC attitude towards youth is certainly not invariably justified. There are enough young girls—and, given a reasonable upbringing, their numbers will increase—who will not throw themselves into the arms of the first-comer, nor find it quite normal to yield to a man's urging to give him 'everything'. Girls should not make themselves cheap. Those who may find our attitude surprising have a distorted view of life. It is not much use advocating the purity of marriage without a readjustment of one's whole philosophy of life. At the risk of repeating something from the introductory part, we must stress in this connexion particularly that everything in the world is ordered by God. He directs all, He has made all, and all is of such importance to Him that He wishes to bring it back to Himself, for man comes from God and returns to Him. Apart from this Way, none other will lead to a goal but only into the desert, if it be not altogether a blind alley.

Man is made of flesh and bone. This can be cut or sawn asunder and investigated under the microscope. In this state he is mere matter. But in the body it all forms an organic whole, pulsating, breathing, growing and decaying. This is living nature, conscious of sensations, of pain or well-being, of desire or satiety and much else besides. Beyond this, man can name what he sees, can judge the things and persons that come his way, is able to say Yes or No in his decisions. Precisely this is his dignity, since he is a spiritual being.

The whole human being is to be found only in this triple composition. Whether this be man or woman makes no difference, the human nature is common to both. But most people mistakenly content themselves with the middle layer; according to them man would be living by his instincts. Nevertheless, the order is graduated from the higher to the lower; the lower layer is absorbed by the higher, and the highest rules the whole. Thus man governs the microcosm that is himself. This is the destiny that

God has allotted to him. In the same way man is to rule the larger world around him.

Now, as regards marriage, people attract each other spiritually, psychologically and physically. What is essential is the mutual delight and esteem in the spiritual order, which is invisibly present when two people meet, and should therefore be very clearly felt before the senses are allowed to have their say, for where they are clamouring the whisper of reason cannot make itself heard. Though it may sound horrid in the ears of lovers and engaged couples, indissoluble lifelong marriage must be based on reasonable considerations.

For if man has yielded to the urge of the senses without pacifying them in a suitable marriage, it is a law of fallen nature that the intoxication will first increase rapidly and then cease very quickly. The union between man and woman is a profound mystery, which may easily lead to catastrophe if God's angels are not there to veil its depths. Unless both firmly intend to be faithful, to refrain from brutal egoism, and rather to give to than to possess each other, this experience will lead to anarchy. If we live exclusively by our senses the effect is the same as that of looking too closely at a portrait which, if viewed from the right distance, gives the impression of a successful artistic achievement. But if we come too near, we may see every single stroke of the brush, any minor break or error of contour. The unlimited satisfaction of the sensual appetite will leave behind an incredible loneliness and void that are truly terrifying.

God has, indeed, intended magnificent surprises for man— marvels of beauty, loveliness and harmony. But they are given only to those who will not taste the forbidden fruit. Paradise is reserved for those who can wait and obey. The others will be met by the angel with the sword, though perhaps only much later.

No doubt young people will meet innumerable temptations if they would keep themselves pure for marriage. This is true; but unless men have to fight for their ideals, they will suffer from arrested development. Moreover, life in general and marriage in particular require much self-control, even in quite different spheres. It is an excellent thing if young people are used to that; for there can be no sound family life without discipline. Much self-restraint is needed if children are to be brought up properly. Nervy parents incapable of giving their children the right education are often victims of hasty marriages and will later say : "If I had only known my husband—or my wife—before as I know him —or her—now." Are these, then, trial marriages? some people may ask. They are, but only because one has tried the wrong things. Character, way of life and hereditary characteristics have been disregarded, because the couple have never met in a normal, sober atmosphere. Half or wholly forbidden love-making does not produce a tranquil happiness, but flashes through body and soul, exciting blind passion. But, it may be asked, if people are not suited to each other in this, how can they be in other things?

Now, in the order of love the physical capacity is only one step. Above it are the spiritual and psychological capacities; and defects in the lowest sphere are mostly symptoms of faults in the structure of the personality. It would be wiser first to direct one's attention to the other signs, which will never be wanting.

A healthy girl with a fresh mind and soul will always be attractive to a man of taste and intelligence, even though she may not have the measurements of a beauty queen. This latter kind of valuation is based on the principles of a cat or dog show, it will never size up the real beauty of a woman. For this begins in the heart, forms the body and again returns to the heart. Therefore the centre of the soul is the 'seat' of love. There it must never be allowed to die, for it is from there that, in the course of a long married life, it must always be renewed. It is strange, whatever man has been given for his pleasure and recreation will become stale, and is bound to change from a truly human enjoyment to an automatically used tool, unless it be constantly replenished 'from above'. Freely to enjoy one another—especially in marriage—is something quite different from doing so 'when nature demands its rights'. The demanding will mostly be done by the man, though not in harmony with his whole nature, but merely in obedience to the interplay of glands and hormones. It would often be much more in keeping with the nature of woman if he would tenderly care for her, in order to make her feel that he appreciates and values her.

Men are really sometimes stupid. They will assert their 'right', the necessity of relaxation, the fact that 'they are like that'. Now this is not quite correct. It would be truer to say that they have 'become like that'. The underlying reason for their behaviour is a lack of restraint or, more charitably, 'general nerviness'. They have never had to control themselves. Mother passed over everything, she spoilt her boy and stuffed him with sweets, never said No, and so he got used to always giving in to himself. Tough life may knock off some of the egoist's edges; there will be enough left for a wife to contend with. Yet the woman will bear her burden in silence—at least in many cases.

CHOOSING A PARTNER

Strictly speaking, education for marriage begins at birth. It is important into what kind of a family the child is born. If it is harmonious, with the mother as the natural example of the girl, everything will be easy; for in such families the children will receive a good general education. Now it is true that education for, and expectation of, marriage are two different things. The latter begins when the child develops into a young girl, and never quite ceases, unless celibacy is deliberately chosen as a state of life. The woman naturally desires the most handsome, chivalrous and bravest of men. It is, nevertheless, a fact that those men are often most successful with women, whether experienced or not, who only fake these virtues and are actually easy-going and superficial. Drink, instability and shady business transactions are three evils that are often hidden under such attractive manners that a 'nice' girl will frequently choose just such a person. As soon as the girl appears, the young man will pull himself together; he may even feel capable of making a new beginning, because he imagines this woman to be his 'destiny'. He will, indeed, give up one or other of his bad habits, or even free himself from them all by one big effort. These fellows attract particularly the deeper characters among the girls; for they give the impression of being above the average, often have artistic leanings, are pleasant to talk to, well-mannered and generally cut a sufficiently dashing figure to resemble the ideal of a girl's dream. Films and literature, moreover, contribute their ample share to present weaknesses as virtues and praise vices as if they were heroic deeds.

A man is incapable, however, of suppressing his inclinations throughout his life. Only years of systematic training and reformation will produce the basis for a stable character. We need not dwell on the tragedy of being married to a drunkard, though we would advise young girls not to make light of it if they learn that their fiancé likes the bottle. We are thinking of another weakness.

Many men cannot get used to being perfectly faithful. There may not always be actual adultery; but frequent slips of this kind will damage a marriage more surely than some sudden outbreak of passion, of which a man truly repents. Other men, often even the same, are unstable in their work. This will result in financial difficulties which may seriously threaten the matrimonial peace. But how could the young wife have known this? The man seemed so nice at first and made such a good, solid impression. In these cases it will often be found that the couple became engaged after a very short acquaintance, that the girl was hardly introduced to the young man's family, and that the time preceding marriage was not devoted to a serious examination of oneself, one's partner and external circumstances, but to pleasures and travelling together. Thus, of course, the most essential factors can be overlooked; that is to say, the capacity for faithfulness and constancy, self-control and charity.

It should further be noted that eccentrics often develop only in middle life, long after the marriage has been concluded. In any case, inhibited and very introverted and over-shy people are not particularly well suited for marriage. If one recognizes in the future partner early indications of stiff formalism, pedantry and stinginess, it would be advisable not to marry him; for these traits will hardly be improved by living together. Moreover, if two difficult people come together, the children will usually carry a heavy hereditary burden.

Girls without any maternal instincts or domestic abilities will rarely become balanced wives and mothers. It is true, in favourable circumstances outside help may sometimes make up for missing talents. There are men who will prefer taking up domestic burdens to giving up the woman of their choice. But these are exceptions proving the rule.

Another cause of matrimonial friction is a kind of immature, somewhat unwomanly motherliness which may lead women to disregard their husbands while almost persecuting their children with exaggerated tenderness. A woman must have a healthy and positive attitude to intimate married life; if this is lacking, it will be very difficult to mend matters later.

On the other hand, it may sometimes happen that a woman well suited for marriage only made a mistake in the choice of her partner. This will occur mostly in cases of unbridgeable differences in social standing or age.

Women may often be attracted by weak men and 'milksops'. They imagine that it will make them happy to be needed by a man whom they can mother and who will appreciate their tenderness. Such men are sons with an exaggerated mother fixation, who for this reason can never properly grow up. In married life they will want their wife to be exactly like their mother, and everything should be precisely as it was at home. In such marriages 'his' mother has a very big say; she will be jealous, disparage her daughter-in-law and try constantly, whether consciously or unconsciously, to keep her son for herself. In such cases, too, it will be difficult to achieve a harmonious marriage.

By contrast, domineering men will often fall for the 'little girl'; they love having a childlike wife whom they intend to 'form'. There need not be much difference in age; but a difference in social standing will almost certainly be fatal. She is simply the playful little kitten, very charming, very sweet and bewitchingly childlike; whereas he knows the world and its hardships and would like to build 'his own world' with the 'little wife' at its centre. After the wedding things will look very different. She has no idea of the requirements of everyday life, she is too spoilt, perhaps even too stupid, to adapt herself to the world of her husband. Marriage, however, can never be a kind of training college for the spouses. They will certainly help each other to mature; but a lack of education cannot be made up later. These discrepancies will lead to deep-seated annoyance and aversions, which will be the more corrosive since they will remain unconscious. The motherly, domesticated young girl is sometimes married the moment she leaves school, and will then quite simply reach maturity in union with the man she loves; but this will never happen in the case of the silly and superficial teenager, who has not yet a fully developed personality and is therefore incapable of giving herself to another. Sometimes it seems, indeed, as if a woman could find herself only through a man; but in such a case the change will be brought about by the love, woman's own particular faculty, which the man was able to kindle.

The individual human being is imperfect and limited, whereas human love is a spark from infinite creative love; therefore it desires to find in the other what its own nature needs for its fulfilment. Fundamentally the general attraction of the sexes for each other and the particular love between two individuals rest on this unquenchable longing for wholeness.

In our view, this is a desire for the sacred whole, for total salvation. In the case of exceptional characters with a strong capacity for sacrifice, we may concede that another's need can be a motive for their love. In general, however, experience shows that 'pity' is no very durable basis. For man is primarily destined for happy fulfilment. It is true, two can become one only if both are ready not simply to make allowances but even painful sacrifices. But these sacrifices are meant to produce a fuller and richer 'we', not to bleed one to death in order to preserve the other in his former selfish way of life.

A frail, crippled body may be animated by a wonderful soul. The sacrifice involved in serving this body may then lead to the enrichment of both, even though many desires may have to be sacrificed. But this is an exceptional situation needing two heroic human beings with high aspirations; it is not possible for the majority of those destined for marriage.

We should like to add a word on class distinctions in the choice of husband or wife. Strong characters are capable of overcoming anything; but people should soberly examine themselves in this respect. Generally speaking, differences in education and social standing are obstacles to a perfect community of life; for in marriage one cannot keep at a distance, but has to share everything. Similar habits, which spring from a similar background, are the cement of everyday life, whereas the different customs of another cultural milieu may actually have explosive effects. A marriage will gradually deteriorate if the manners of one partner come from a world far removed from that of the other. Of course both may yet be happy if their hearts are in harmony. Nevertheless, it will be difficult in the long run to share the same table if manners are different. Even far less obvious differences of behaviour may fray one's nerves; therefore people should examine themselves carefully before binding themselves for life. Marriage needs good manners, else it will remain something like a bivouac. However, it is better that neither should have had a proper education than that only one should have had it.

Certain women will always have a weakness for younger men. But they will run a risk, though a number of happy marriages of this kind may be adduced to prove the contrary. As a rule, it will be best if the man is four to six years older.

In order not to be misunderstood, we would add some explanations. Our over-civilized age has refined many needs and developed new ways of satisfying them. In proportion as our senses have taken possession of the outside world and as the machine has replaced the work of our hands, our instinctive reactions have been blunted. By this we mean the spiritual faculty to act in a fully human way; in this particular instance to choose the right partner so as to perfect one's own being, and not merely to gain external security. To do this, a normally maturing woman will scarcely need the services of depth psychology.

From the very beginning human persons have been related to other human beings and the sexes have been destined for each other. A fully matured person will long for a partner; the well-developed normal woman will desire a husband. Marriage is regarded by a healthy, normal person, and certainly by a normal woman, as a permanent, lifelong union. She will not need to have her acquaintances medically and biologically examined in order to ascertain which of them is suited to be her husband. Later it will be found that married couples are complementary in 'type'; but it would be against all sound feeling to base the choice of one's partner on tables and blue-prints. Either one is capable of choosing or one is not.

Hence we should be misunderstood if anyone were to use these suggestions as one uses a cookery book, attempting to compose, as it were, a menu for one's life from it. It is a consequence of the psychologization of life—itself a consequence of its mechanization—that people are satisfied with mere recipes. Modern medical psychology, whatever people may make of it, is in the first place meant to cure diseases. It is impossible to regard every impertinence, ignorance or doubt as due to disease, or to ascribe every stupidity or misfortune to a deviation from the pattern of life or to a psychological trauma.

Every human being is destined to reach maturity, be at its zenith and decay, no matter whether he broods over it or not. Nevertheless, it will be a good thing sometimes to think about the connexions, though one should not let oneself be hypnotized by 'cycles of psychological problems'. As has already been said, the general insecurity of life and the suppression of fully human, including spiritual, faculties will frequently result in twists and maladjustments. Here a methodical analysis would be necessary. If somebody is interested in this psychological approach, it would yet be wise to supplement it from the cultural and philosophical spheres, in order to avoid one-sidedness.

CONFIDENCE WITH OR WITHOUT RESERVATIONS

Owing to a lack of mental maturity, or under the stress of war- and post-wartime shocks, many a girl may have become entangled in experiences which she was soon to regret. Here, too, we can give no 'recipe' of behaviour, but we would urge such women to consider whether it would be right to win with a lie the man with whom one intends to share one's whole future. If a young man has the healthy desire to marry an innocent girl, he will certainly not remain indifferent if he later realizes that he has been deceived. Such a girl is either lacking in courage, and will for this reason be easily inclined to lie, or she will generally have no sense for truthfulness. This is doubtless a human failing. If the husband should be unable to forget that his wife did not live up to his ideal, this may result in serious obstacles to a harmonious marriage. It would be better to part beforehand rather than to suffer a whole lifetime from such frictions.

Of course cases of rape, as may happen in wartime, leave no spiritual stain. Such a girl will have remained pure in heart. Nevertheless here, too, frankness is indicated. Many men find this hard to swallow. We admit that it is somewhat narrow-minded to be unable to forget the past, but such an attitude cannot be changed. A person who can never forget should not be involved in a situation where complete forgetting is the only choice.

One cannot insinuate oneself into love by stealth. For love is a primeval power; it is not a composition of ingredients to be analysed, to which one need only add some others in order to make everything function according to plan. Love is a gift from above, radiating from one's own heart which, in its turn, receives the rays of another. Pettiness may spoil everything, as may also such a faulty beginning that refuses to give away some stain in one's own being. If one risks being frank, one will gain in any case clarity on the attitude of one's partner.

It should go without saying that a woman, too, has the right to a man's purity. Though just on this point popular opinion differs. Nevertheless, an opinion, however widespread, need not necessarily be right. If a man preserves his strength for marriage, this proves how greatly he esteems woman in general and his own wife in particular. Moreover, he has the courage to swim against the stream. For such a man marriage is not a tentative venture or a plaything, it is his 'great chance', as it is of course also that of his bride. It is a sign of softness and estrangement from nature that men should not be asked to practise self-control. It is true, this latter view has been held by self-satisfied and unperceptive men at all times and in all climes. But the fact that pure marriages are healthy will always be a striking argument for the opposite opinion. These marriages will develop into families with many children, for here sexual power is valued as what it is primarily meant to be; that is, power of procreation. It is true, even in the plan of creation, not every conjugal embrace can have been meant to produce a child. Nevertheless, this natural incapacity is quite different from the case when two people embrace only after having first prevented conception. Here man limits the course of nature in order to give rein to unlimited indulgence of his instincts. But to act in accordance with human nature means exercising one's will and observing moderation. The tyranny of the instincts can never be regarded as a completely human line of conduct. This problem, too, or rather above all, cannot be separated from the whole, which is man and his conception of the world.

3

THE MARRIED WOMAN

THE CLIMATE OF MARRIAGE

THE principal theme of this book necessitates a discussion of marriage. We might even add : whatever the subject of conversation, nowadays one always comes back to the problem of marriage. Because it is so often unsatisfactory, the very existence of marriage as an institution is being questioned. The crisis of marriage has become a commonplace; more precisely expressed, we are faced with the problem of marriage in a time of crisis. The decisive point is probably that the structure of marriage itself is opposed to modern life. For this life is being lived at a fearful speed, while marriage is stationary. The landmarks of modern life are sensational experiences, whereas those of good marriages are peaceful expressions of an interior attitude and the various stages in the development of the children.

Our modern exaggerated stimuli produce an urgent need of satisfaction which, hastily enjoyed, in its turn produces new desires. Man wants ever more experiences, by which we do not mean only sexual ones. The over-valuation of 'concrete experiences' causes the sense of an authentic spiritual orientation of life to atrophy. Now, marriage is part of such an authentic, spiritually determined life; for the love that causes men to decide on it is essentially spiritual, since it desires not some fleeting pleasure but a lasting common life. Moreover, marriage itself cannot become 'concrete experience', only the conjugal act can be that, and this, again, is not 'marriage', but only the expression of the perfect union of soul and body. Marriage as such is actually opposed to modern man's hunger for experience, for the richer the matrimonial life the poorer it will be in excitements. Now, since both partners are often hankering after just these excitements, they will live too much on the surface; even if this be done together, they will miss the essence of married life. This is the new spiritual birth 'in the flesh' of matrimony. The new event is the view of the world as a pair. If husband and wife love each other, one will see things with the eyes of the other. This will result in a peculiar completion of one's fundamental view of life; a bridge is formed that leads from the spiritual union in marriage to union with all creation, of which the physical union is the centre. If the marriage is built on spiritual foundations, this physical union becomes a border-line experience; for the other cannot be completely 'embraced' or comprehended, though both have given themselves completely.

If a marriage is built on mere 'experience', its sense-element is reduced to sexual sensuality, hence it is liable to be blunted. On the one hand, sensuality should not need to be ever more keenly stimulated; on the other, it will not profit a marriage if satiety causes both partners to abandon the intimate conjugal life altogether. In the first case the physical self-giving is degraded to mere sexual satisfaction; in the second love may well fizzle out. In either case, the world shrinks to its normal dimensions; the 'miracle of love' has lost its power.

The tearing hurry of life, the constant preoccupation with externals and the unnatural conditions of life in general do not create a favourable 'climate' for marriage. Marriage itself, the current between the two partners, may well be dynamic; compared with the world outside, however, marriage as a whole is static. In a good marriage nothing 'happens'. The natural differences between man and woman constitute the charm of life together; if a marriage is too closely connected with the exciting world outside, the peculiarities and differences in character may well lead to friction.

It will hardly be necessary to analyse the misery of war and post-war conditions. Marriage and the family are interrelated; the former was certainly more secure when the social order rested on the latter. Today the family is no longer an active part of public life; together with matrimony, it has become a private affair. On the other hand, however, the individual is being very strongly attached to the community, and as 'living in the mass' is on the increase, this may be even more the case in the future; hence there is the danger, noticeable even now, that the matrimonial home may be no more than a place for feeding and sleeping. The community makes so great demands on man's time and energy that it is hardly possible still to speak of a proper common married life.

It is also due to technical progress that far less things need to be 'home-made'; one can buy everything ready-made. Hence one rarely works at home; it is only a place of rest. Now, this rest is by no means happy recreation but complete exhaustion, inert languor. Without it one would not be able to stand the pressure of work during the week. And this total exhaustion actually rules out healthy relaxation, which consists precisely in the cultivation of capacities that are left unused in one's professional work.

When discussing the conditions of a stable marriage, people like to play off the marriage based on rational considerations against the so-called love-match. Now on this subject we would observe that the former used to flourish in a climate generally favourable to marriage. In those days there still existed a hierarchical order of society, in which matrimony as an institution had its definite place and the foundation of a family ranged high in the scale of objective values. Besides, we would remind the reader of what we have said before on the home as a place of production. The individual had his stable position in society; no one dreamt of demanding to be specially defined as a 'person'. Everyone recognized a system of values, and behaved, or at least tried to behave, in accordance with it; if he violated it he thought it only natural that he should be held responsible.

The so-called love-match comes at the end of a development. It is based not on a hierarchy of values, but on the desire of the individual. In the meantime 'personal existence' has come to the fore; nowadays no woman will be simply a 'woman', but a 'feminine personality'. Less store is set by the value of an object in itself; the way it will affect the individual becomes the standard of desirability. Thus it gradually comes about that man will no longer submit to certain institutions, least of all if this should involve sacrifices; but the institutions themselves have to give up some of their principles in order to adapt themselves to human circumstances. In former times the percentage of people suited or unsuited for marriage was perhaps not very different from what it is today; the difference is that the 'personal attitude' was less important then than it is now.

In addition, the position of woman has actually become different, owing to the changed general situation. She is no longer only considered a woman, but within the framework of our technical civilization she is being used quite without regard to her sex. Apart from the fact that many activities are today no longer carried out in the home, women themselves have to work to a great extent outside it. They are proving every day that they are a very useful help and complement to men even in spheres far removed from marriage and family.

This may certainly have a detrimental effect on marriage, which will suffer not only if one denies women equal human rights, but also if one forces them into an unnatural equality with men. It is a subordinate question if the wife who has a job will be unable to make a success of her marriage for external reasons. What is essential is whether her husband will give her her rightful position in the home, or will twist the patriarchal pattern of marriage into making her his unpaid housekeeper. On the other hand, there is an at least equal danger that the wife has been spoilt by her increased efficiency and financial independence through her own earning, and hence will look upon the matrimonial partnership as a kind of competition, with a view to becoming herself the head of the family. This equation of the male and the female parts in marriage actually lowers the honour of the wife, which consists in her perfect devotion and loving surrender to her husband. For thus the marriage will be ruled by the power of the heart in secret, symbolized by the veil. The true wife will want to reign only in the realm of love, by keeping her family united and giving joy to her husband, so that he will be able to protect his home from outside dangers and prove himself its true head. Family customs and family happiness depend on the woman, whose power rests on far deeper foundations than can be legally defined. Juridical measures, as they are being applied today, will certainly not be able to stem the decline of a marriage.

The emphasis has been considerably shifted since the wife, who was once supported by religious sanctions, has been replaced by the legally protected marriage partner, who is assured of equal rights and may even be called upon to provide for the children. Thus the woman's rôle as a mother is changed into that of a father, responsible for external support and protection. Now we do not mean to depreciate the heroism of thousands of women, who may support war-crippled husbands and children or for other reasons have become breadwinners for their families; the admirable energy of many women who have become heads of their households should not be belittled. Nevertheless, these are exceptions due to emergencies, which contradict the original vocation of the sexes.

The dignity of woman is lessened even more if she is degraded into a temporary companion. If this is supposed to be a sign of her equality with man, it really means that she has been divested of her mystery. Whereas the bride is led to her husband hidden by the veil, the 'partner' advances towards him unaccompanied. If the choice has been made chiefly for interior motives, the partnership will become a life-long companionship provided the external conditions are favourable. This kind of cohabitation will receive its meaning, not from a higher sphere but from itself. The economically superior woman will not complement man but supplant him. Thus the masculine power will consume culture rather than create it, and the emancipated woman will indeed be in full view, but not actually effective in her own feminine sphere. Here the friendship between man and woman is no longer spiritual, nor will the fullness of its tension become creative. Rather, it is hemmed in by utilitarian safeguards, and thus degraded to a useful instrument. The charm of spiritual exchange between man and woman is thus changed into disillusioned sexual satisfaction.

The consequences of this kind of relationship are far-reaching. Love loses its enchantment, and this in its turn leads to spiritual stagnation, which shows itself in the boredom of so many contemporary couples, who no longer know what to do with each other. From there it is only one step to cruelty and selfish greed, because unveiled love is neighbour to hate.

If, after the full experience of companionship, the woman is left alone, it will be difficult for her to find her feet again. She will look for someone else, and will find him if she has enough to 'offer', and she will have to do this all the more the older she gets. Behind each of these episodes there lurks the spectre of the loneliness of a generation whose idol is she herself, the independent woman. And finally she will find herself broken. For the caricature of the wife will naturally make too great demands on her partner; the friendship will die, because the 'thou' is made into an absolute, for the 'companion' who has lost her bearings can recognize no other value than 'concrete man'.

DEMANDS THAT CANNOT BE SATISFIED

The demand for the absolute places a great strain also on legitimate marriage. Since only 'experience' is considered valid, for many people the meaning of life consists only in 'man as an experience'. As soon as this experience vanishes, all is empty and meaningless, a nothingness that is itself experienced as fear. In this fear men cling to each other, and this leads to exorbitant demands on the other, who is expected to offer absolute security. The general lack of confidence increases in proportion with the demand; its formula is: "I have only you." The more deeply distrust of oneself and others has eaten into the men and women of an age, the higher will be the expectations with which they approach their fellows also in marriage. Thus human beings will be alternately adored and reviled. Now, this unconquerable mistrust of men constitutes an interior obstacle to marriage and is responsible for the fact that today many marriages have already become generally unstable before breaking up externally and in detail.

No doubt we are at present experiencing the contradiction that the problems surrounding man are legion, while at the same time the individual becomes more and more submerged in the mass and hence destroyed in his humanity. Millions have been sacrificed in the war, and thousands are still being uprooted, transferred, detained in camps and scheduled for forced labour. Even in the normal social, economic and political life the individual loses his significance and becomes part of the mass.

The dignity of man seems an empty formula. Nevertheless, everyone is intimately concerned to escape being merely part of the mass. In order to assure himself of his own worth, he makes immeasurable demands that are incapable of fulfilment and can only lead to self-destruction. Contemporary marriage is marked by this unreal demand which, in the words of Paul Claudel, sees not only woman as "a promise that cannot be kept", but man in general. This will invariably lead to disappointment in marriage and accusations against each other. In point of fact, this attitude makes impossible demands on each, since it is part and parcel of human existence to realize man's limitations.

PRELIMINARY REMARKS ON LOVE

Love, too, belongs to man's nature; without it man would not be man. It is the root of marriage, which is not just an ordinary contract concluded by two parties; for the decision to marry is preceded by love. This is to say: when a marriage is about to be concluded spontaneous love becomes a love bound by a contract; this adds a moral aspect to it. Since all human institutions can be considered from many angles, marriage, too, becomes a subject of legislation, economics, ethnology and so forth. Thus it may happen that its human side is overlooked, and ordinary people are frightened by a multitude of 'problems' quite unrelated to their personal life.

Men can scarcely be expected to be encouraged to marry if this is only presented to them as a task and a duty. For love is intimately bound up with it. To prevent misunderstanding, we would explain that by love we mean the appreciation of value. I like this person means : I discover a value in him, or he is the value that I discover. In this case a woman is given an entirely new direction by her love for a certain man. And so we have arrived at what may be called the climate of marriage, which is essentially created by the woman. It would be hopeless, indeed, if we could do no more than affirm that our age is unfavourable to marriage. Apart from the shortcomings both in contemporary circumstances and in human beings themselves, it should be emphasized for the sake of justice that the capacity for love is part of the nature of normal women, as we have emphasized in our introductory remarks. Now we think it important to make this fundamental fact our point of departure. Rules on the choice of a partner, on the community of interests and of milieu are but crutches that may be thrown away if one loves. We read in matrimonial advertisements : "I am a lover of nature, looking for someone with the same interest" ; "Sports-girl seeks partner with a view to later marriage" ; "Widow with building plot wants robust gentleman in his fifties who would like to build." Perhaps it would not be a bad guess to see in such cases a helpless longing for love that finds no other expression. The decisive point is that someone should have the courage to love. For our contemporaries suffer from a regrettably diminished capacity for love, which is being squandered and split up into a thousand channels.

A harmonious marriage is not based on identity of profession, hobbies or frame of mind. The heart of the matter is that two people are united with each other in love. Every normal person will see this love as an insoluble union of spirit, soul and sense life. At a certain stage of human maturity the capacity and the desire for love are evenly balanced. It is not at all so that the maternal instincts a woman possesses in the depth of her nature will already be fully developed when she begins to long for a husband.

DEVELOPED AND UNDEVELOPED LOVE

Capacity for love and the desire to give are by no means identical. In every normal woman there is a longing for tenderness that wants to be satisfied. She will be able to give only in the measure as she herself has received; for one can only give what one has. Children who have enjoyed no parental love, or only little of it and at odd intervals, will find it difficult to give love to others when they have grown up into mature women. They will first of all want their own desire for love to be satisfied. In the first section of this book we have mentioned the psychological readiness to receive; now this will have to be satisfied before a woman will be prepared for self-giving and sacrifice. This means that she should store up joy, that she should let herself be enriched by the treasures of art and literature, nature and social life. In this way she will develop and preserve a feeling for true values which will help her unhesitatingly—or sometimes perhaps after some uncertainty—to recognize the right partner when the time comes. But how this is to be done cannot be described without making nonsense of love as a primeval power of the spirit—for the particular something that distinguishes one human being from all others defies description.

Sometimes one might almost say that all this talk about marriage obscures love. Hence we would defend the love match, on condition that love be not understood as a mere intoxicating feeling that leaves both spirit and heart unsatisfied.

Through love a woman receives the world of her husband and her husband in his world. The transforming power of married love creates a 'milieu'. It is right that a woman should take the name of her husband, for in a good marriage she will enter his sphere of life to brighten it with her individuality. A woman should not expect her husband to understand her as well as she understands him. By living with him she will soon know how to treat him, when to encourage and when to restrain him; for a woman normally understands the character of others by intuition; she needs no systematic studies for that. The man, on the other hand, will have to penetrate her world step by step, from the outside. A wife should consider herself 'understood' by her husband if he is happy in her presence, and likes her manner and the way she makes a home for him. She will feel herself appreciated if she can turn to him with the fullest confidence without fearing any barrier whatever between him and herself. The man, for his part, will learn the wisdom of the heart in the mirror of her being; he will recognize the polarity of all created things, and through the mysterious power that draws him again and again into the feminine sphere, he will dimly apprehend the invisible cultural support woman gives to our thoroughly visible civilization. He will realize through his wife the necessity of humanizing its soulless forces and the charm a personal approach is able to cast over our workaday world. A woman's love generously poured out in marriage will reveal the primeval truth that one half of created being is irrevocably feminine. Man will respond to this with reverence and chivalry. If these are completely absent, this will be due either to serious defects of character and upbringing in the husband, or to mistakes on the part of the wife, who has not yet learnt to release him from interior strains and stresses.

In the first case hardly anything can be done. The second needs infinite, never-despairing patience on the part of the woman. Marriage is not an educational institute for husband and wife: the training will have to be done in a roundabout way. If a husband belongs to the category of tactless, narrow-minded egoists whose only complaint is that they have always been too well off, and who take it for granted that they are the masters of creation, a woman will sometimes have to make it clear to him what mature manhood really involves. But this task may need years or even decades. A woman has gained the mastery if she does not take every display of brusque masculine egoism as a personal affront. The worst she could do would be to make scenes, for this would only make him more obstinate; patient hope and the firm conviction that his behaviour is not meant as a personal insult will be the best way of dealing with the situation. If a woman loses her self-confidence too easily because her husband fails to express his appreciation of her, she will become nervy and despondent, so that no contact can be established.

Frequently, however, wives will blame their husbands for not loving them enough for no reason at all. Such women may either be simply immature and badly brought up, or suffer from deep-seated uncertainties, as we have mentioned before when discussing the exorbitant demands made on marriage. Formal declarations of love and faithfulness ought really not to be demanded; they can easily be deduced from ordinary behaviour. If we want to unveil mysterious depths unduly, we may easily upset things. For such demands may call forth exaggerations which may then change into hypocrisy, and later result even in lies. Moreover, some men are constitutionally incapable of expressing their feelings, and may hide a deep and genuine love under awkward and even rude phrases. Here a woman must learn to distinguish.

Very sensitive and emotional women will often suffer because their husbands are so very matter of fact; they fail to show tenderness even in the intimate married life, are always dry and serious, and never unbend sufficiently to be gay and playful. Such behaviour may hurt a woman so badly in the beginning of the marriage that she will withdraw, without perhaps even quite admitting to herself that she feels offended. Nevertheless, there are unmistakable signs of this: she will keep her husband at a distance and react coldly to his approaches. The woman 'does not want to' when he wants to. This is one of the reasons why many marriages break up. First a man will give in, then he will go his own ways. This does not necessarily mean that he will go to another woman, but that the common married world disintegrates into the separate world of man and woman.

It can hardly be said that faithful and blameless husbands are necessarily imaginative lovers. They take what they want, while perhaps thinking all the time of their work. This need certainly not imply a lack of esteem for their chosen companions. It is simply the masculine lack of appreciation of the unique charm of intimacy, the symptom of a self-centredness that will often remain unconscious. Without actually realizing it, many a man behaves as if he thought it the most natural thing in the world that his wife should find her whole *raison d'être* in his personal well-being. Now, it is not simply so that a woman has more time for the inner sphere of life, she actually lives in it; while the man may remain outside even while he holds her in his arms. This will perhaps not be his attitude during the honeymoon, though it may appear even then, in that everything depends only on his mood.

Now, it is true that adaptability and intuitive gifts belong to women rather than to men, and love will make a woman clear-sighted. Hence she ought to recognize even the hidden possibilities and shy delicacy of her husband. Instead of feeling hurt and withdrawing, she ought to lead him gradually to respond to her desires and to become sensitive to a woman's feelings. For this it is indispensable, of course, that she should frankly admit that a woman does feel. To deny this would lead to strain and error.

The capacity for producing posterity is given to man as part of his human nature. The requisite instincts are not automatic, as in the case of animals, but they will normally come into play when the right partners have met, and more particularly when the play of love has begun. Just the preparation for this is often so serious and heavy-going that it produces inhibitions and a misplaced sense of shame in many a well-bred woman. For its immediate realization love must be accompanied by love-making. On this point women should thoroughly examine their conscience. They should ask themselves whether they have really done everything to make it easier, or even possible, for their husband to approach them, whether they have taken enough trouble and thought to teach him in a quiet hour to see a little further. There are books and films available to help, though this must be done discreetly so that a man may not feel inferior by comparison.

STAGES OF LOVE

What attracts people to each other in the first place cannot be explained, and often not even expressed. It is the bloom of love, but not its whole essence. It is the pleasure one finds in one another. Women especially are able to state very firmly: "I do like him, or I don't like him." But what exactly it is that attracts them is far more difficult to make clear. It is not some detail in his exterior or his character; it is the whole or rather the whole man. That is to say, the woman has mentally apprehended what makes him lovable. One chooses the man who complements one's own nature. Immediate harmony and understanding will result in a Yes to the other, who will suddenly—or gradually—come to fill one's heart so exclusively that it is impossible to feel the same for anyone else.

So far everything is perfectly clear. Heart and feelings are united in appreciative love, which is the normal prerequisite for marriage. If pity or cold calculation should take the place of this appreciation, the spiritual and psychological motive for a true union will be missing. For this appreciation is not a fleeting sentiment or the reflexion of entranced intoxication, it is a fundamental knowledge in the depth of one's being; hence something ultimate that cannot be analysed. This, of course, cannot apply if a woman is a stunted personality, living on the surface and following merely her lower instincts. If such be the case, her capacity for love will also be stunted, and with it her surest guide in the choice of a partner : the unerring affirmation from the centre of her being. It makes no difference whether a woman has so far been acutely conscious of her own personality, or whether she has been led to this only through her love for a man. The ego becomes capable of decision even without having much reflected on itself. The more sensitive a woman is to values, the more difficult it will be to gain her love ; on the other hand, the greater the interior riches of the other the more guarantees for fulfilment in marriage.

If love is to lead to marriage it will not be satisfied with esteem and enthusiasm. It desires that the other should also love ; more, it wants to be as near as possible to him in a perfect union. This desire is indispensable for married love. It results from the harmony of the finest and deepest impulses of soul and body, and is directed towards that goodness and beauty by which the divine image is expressed in man. It is natural to enjoy what is recognized as good not only from a distance, but to want to draw it towards, even into, oneself. Love desires profoundly to be united, to give and to receive one another, and to exchange one's treasures. Conjugal love includes physical desire ; it would be a mistake to deny this ; and if a woman feels aversion for that she does not love perfectly. On the other hand, sexual desire without the love of the heart is no full married love, either.

Yet conjugal love has a third aspect, which is charity. This is the summit of love, to love the other so as to help him to reach his human perfection. This is that love of benevolence which always seems somewhat pale to us. We have lost the deepest meaning of the word, because we modern men find it difficult to disregard ourselves. For this is the giving, the 'serving' and 'saving' love which is wholly concentrated on the other. We would add at once : concentrated on the other in a higher sense, not only with regard to his well-being, but for his salvation. Naturally this religious element of conjugal love cannot be cultivated where religious faith is lacking. Without this, love, as has already been stated, will easily make demands that cannot be fulfilled. For only by virtue of this last element will it be possible fully to realize that even the best companion has weaknesses and imperfections, that he is threatened by dangers and has his lucky and unlucky 'stars'. The woman who loves maturely will strive to fashion the common life so that her husband will profit from it interiorly, even at her own expense. Being prepared to renounce oneself for the sake of one's husband is the most delicate point in married life.

When this subject is being discussed two mistakes are frequently made : it is either pooh-poohed or avoided altogether. On the other hand, a one-sided presentation of this highest form of love alone will produce discouragement, besides being not quite true to reality. For full conjugal love is not consumed, but constantly renews itself until it reaches that self-forgetfulness which will unreflectingly put the other first. Thus in the course of married life the heart will always be open and ready to perceive the joy, the peace and the happiness of the other as if they were one's own.

Nevertheless, nature may be so stunted as not to admit such a kind of love. This will happen to people who lack the impulse to leave their own little selves; their love does not radiate, it always remains within its own circle. Empty, narrow-minded and dissatisfied people have no store of confidence and will not risk anything. Longing for completeness, they want their partner to give them even the share they themselves ought to contribute to the perfection of marriage. So they will become dissatisfied, jealous and actually insatiable. For one cannot only 'draw' from marriage, one must also 'pay in'.

Frequently, too, egotistical matrimonial love may be due only to immaturity and bad training. Spoiled young girls have coveted false ideals and escaped into a dream world in which they want to remain. As life is being viewed so largely from a psychological angle, the image of man tends to become two-dimensional, being reduced to reason and vitality. Relying on merely rational knowledge, people imagine that they must needs satisfy their instinctive sexuality. But this view is based on a human error. For it denies the activity of the living human heart, which sees more deeply than mere reason, and rules even sexuality with unerring logic. "Sex is certainly difficult. But we are meant to cope with difficult things ; everything serious is difficult, and all things are serious. . . . Physical passion is an experience of the senses, just as is pure sight or the pure feeling with which a beautiful fruit fills the tongue. It is a great, infinite experience, which is given us, a knowledge of the world, the fullness and radiance of all knowledge. Evil is not that we should receive it, but that almost all men abuse and squander this experience by using it as a stimulus and a distraction for the fatigue of their life instead of making it a means of recollection for its highest moments. Would that man should be more humble in the experience of this mystery with which the earth is filled even unto its smallest things, that he should bear it and realize how terribly serious it is, instead of taking it lightly. For he should reverence his own fertility which is but one, whether it appear to be spiritual or physical" (R. M. Rilke, *Letters to a Young Poet*).

We have lost simplicity, and with it the sense of the sacred. If we possessed that, we would see through the ramifications of life into its insoluble mystery. It is this, that the love of God is "poured forth in our hearts", and that ultimately every earthly movement of love reaches down to this ground, even though many are not aware of it. Thus love surpasses, strictly speaking, its partner and is directed to God, just as the love one receives ultimately comes from Him.

WOMAN'S PROBLEMS OF LOVE AND SEX

It is the general view today that unsatisfied instincts are apt to cause illness, though it is not always clear what one means by instinct. Taken in its narrowest sense, the term denotes those impulses that man has in common with the animals; that is to say, the instincts of food and sex. Here we are only concerned with the latter. Now one important characteristic of the instinct is too little known; this is its double structure. For each instinct is complemented by a counter-instinct or check. A well-known scholar has pointed out that the check, too, belongs to 'nature'. We do not know, however, where exactly in the organism such instincts are situated. It is just as wrong to locate 'sexuality' in the endocrine sexual organs as it would be to place it in the spinal cord or in certain parts of the brain. Sexual disturbances may occur also without any physical foundation, and we know that the sexual instinct may be transformed for psychological reasons. Moreover, the function of the instinct and its complementary counter-instinct depends on temperament and the constitutional peculiarities in general, as well as on outside factors such as surroundings. If all this be taken into account, it becomes clear that an instinct cannot be located in a particular part of the body, that it cannot 'press' or send 'bad fluids' into the blood if it is not released. It is true, physical impulses are necessary for the final release of the instinct, but the whole structure of the instincts is intimately dependent on general factors which, in the case of man, include spiritual data. Man's essential characteristic is the union of body and soul; consequently psychical states will produce physical reactions, but also vice versa. Now, owing to insufficient knowledge and a defective education, many people are quite ignorant of the motive power in the centre of their being. On the other hand, we would not deny that there is such a thing as a strong sexual constitution. Nevertheless, most people, whether they have this or not, make no effort to give their life a spiritual orientation either in general or in this particular direction. In any case, sexual needs are being greatly exaggerated, and the possibilities of mastering them are definitely under-estimated. Certainly this requires discipline. If one is used to giving in to one's other impulses, one will do so also in this. People do not fall ill because an instinct has not been satisfied, but because circumstances have offered unworthy opportunities for love.

To give an example. If a widow has relations with a married man who can only rarely make time for her, it is quite possible that the interior strain will make her ill; but this will not be caused by the too infrequent sexual intercourse. In this sphere cause and effect are often being mixed up; the physical instincts, taken out of their human context, are given an importance which rightly belong to the psychological motives.

Naturally a woman, whose whole personal structure tends towards marriage, the 'born wife and mother', will suffer from being alone. But she will never effectively heal this wound by a merely sexual relationship. Such a woman can become whole only in a perfectly secure situation; or else she will grow into a higher form of life, when she will be shown an ideal that promises a new, perfect fulfilment through giving up certain partial satisfactions.

Temporary abstinence, by the way, may be recommended in every marriage in order to preserve the tension and attraction between the partners. It seems also very important always to keep in view the whole purpose and organism of marriage, and not to build it simply on the sexual intercourse, however regulated. After all, the intimate marital relationship is only the consequence of the Yes that husband and wife have said to each other with a view to building up a common family life, and not the other way round, that a marriage should be the result of a 'smoothly functioning' sexual relationship. Sexuality does not rule man; man regulates it. A woman, especially, can hardly do without har-

mony in all spheres of life. Her spiritual understanding urges her
to give in to her husband also in physical matters. If the senses be
indulged without restraint simply for their own sake, sexuality will
be marked with the seal of transitory mortality, even with the
painfully felt thorn in the flesh. In marriage it is elevated into a
community of life and destiny through the hope of the child.
Where this hope is quite genuine but economic considerations
make it impossible to receive the blessing without planning, there
the tender love of friendship will enable husband and wife also
to choose the times of sexual intercourse. Where the meaning and
goal of marriage are not endangered, because both have the right
attitude to it, the proper way to intimacy will always be found
again. But a marriage will be a failure from the start if people
enter upon it because there are days when a woman cannot conceive—in other words, if a child is not wanted. If one wants only
'legalized intercourse' but no real marriage, people will be hypnotized by the 'safe period' and lose love for the sake of technique.
The stations of this way are often frictions in the most intimate
sphere, general nerviness and finally the breaking up of the marriage. Here, as always, fear is a very bad counsellor. The mutual
surrender should not be made in the shadow of the fear of a
child, but in the light of genuine love. It is, however, too little
known that mental discipline does not weaken the buoyancy of
the heart, but on the contrary gives it its proper measure. The
mature Christian who truly cares for the Church will learn to
master the psychosomatic tension of her marriage, and thus be
able to cope also with the unfortunate obstacle that straitened
financial circumstances may place in the way of building up a
family. Where, on the other hand, there is no overriding principle,
but everything is directed towards the fulfilment of selfish desires,
no other motive will, of course, be recognized apart from that
which satisfies one's egoism. In this case, however, people should
not be surprised at their own increasing nerviness and irritation,
which may even result in general disgust with life. For there are
also retarded consequences of false ideals. To sum up we may say
that, apart from pathological states, sexuality will become a problem in itself only where parts of the human whole are stunted.
Women, in particular, do not, as a rule, suffer from a starved
body but from a starved heart; and this void cannot be filled
merely by hygienic measures.

FORMATIVE POWERS OF MARRIAGE

Married love contains a great deal of human formative power, which both affects its surroundings and draws from them. This power does not depend for its increase on the existence or the number of children, but solely on the strength of the will to marriage. This is, indeed, clearly expressed in the child, but is latent in the whole life of husband and wife, though far more in the latter, since a woman, as we have noted before, is less easily detached from herself than a man. Therefore the task of shaping the married world falls to the wife rather than to the husband. Now, marriage is not simply an ideal or a slogan, but the institution by which human love is to be realized in accordance with nature. Hence if this be done without hindrance it will benefit also the possibilities of love that are to be found around it.

From the Christian point of view, this is the missionary vocation of marriage. It is the island of responsible love in the ocean of a vague longing for love that is ignorant of its own true goal. Besides, every marriage offers a woman the opportunity to fulfil her own being, even if her husband fails to live up to all her expectations. But to understand this we shall have to leave the narrow view of popular conceptions and consider marriage from the spiritual angle. Properly applied hygiene may, indeed, effect the smooth working of sexual relationships, but it will not be able to create a truly perfect marriage. If marriage is to reach its fulfilment, it must be open to every creature's infinite need of assistance, which is to be achieved through loving care within a strictly limited circle. For the longing for love latent in innumerable seeking, erring and despairing human beings is somehow focused in conjugal love.

A woman who is 'known' and pacified in marriage—pacified, because she is 'known'—has been redeemed into that permanently effective and secret motherhood of which perhaps the unmarried woman, too, may be capable. But the latter will have to go only by her own feelings, whereas the wife will be given infallible signs of it through the experience of conjugal love.

A woman who finds the natural difference of the sexes confirmed by marriage will be inescapably aware of the limits of psychosomatic understanding. Thus she will gain a sober view of life and content herself with what is attainable. She will be rendered immune against unreal fantasies and insatiable enthusiasm, which, after all, only centre round themselves. Marital companionship shows how much one can gain for oneself by always being concerned with another. Moreover, it provides the unique knowledge that there exists a spiritual union beyond the limits of psychosomatic understanding. Even though this knowledge cannot be subjected to psychological tests nor gained by psychological recipes, the experience of spiritual understanding, nevertheless, carries with it the certainty of infallible faith. Again, this is not so much a question of philosophical agreement or of the same cultural standards, though these may facilitate understanding. It means to be attuned to the other, to see with his eyes and feel with his feelings. Since, nevertheless, one's own individual being continues to exist undiminished, this experience will enrich oneself immensely. Besides, fully developed married love has something of the inexhaustible comprehension and breadth of the spirit, so that the individuality of the other acts like a picture screen reflecting all that corresponds to it.

To understand others intuitively is probably a feminine rather than a masculine gift. Hence a woman ought not to weary of entering as far as possible into the world of her husband and making it her own. The will to understand and accept what the other has to offer will create a good basis for unswerving faithfulness, though it may seem at first as if the one who does the understanding were at a disadvantage. Yet in marriage the heart has to take its risks and to be ready to take things on trust.

We should not forget that most men are caught up in a highly rationalized social and economic system, and hence have very little practice in speaking the language of the heart. Besides, 'home-making' also in a metaphorical sense is pre-eminently a feminine task. A woman may be an excellent housewife and yet fail to understand men. Today love is largely broken up into love-making, eroticism and sexuality; hygienic and technical instructions are often over-estimated; and the human being as a whole is the loser.

Now, just in this large sphere faithfulness should make its home. By this is meant the ready sympathy and penetration that will quickly catch the mood of the other, and which are so essential in marriage. Men feel the protection and peace of their home very clearly, though they may not have the gift to express their appreciation in words. Nevertheless, his four walls will normally not mean everything to a man, who is generally much taken up with his work. So it might seem as if he did not notice his pleasant home. Nevertheless, this is so only in appearance. For if the domestic peace were disturbed the whole man would be upset. A good life will be accepted with quiet gratitude, but will hardly call forth much comment.

The respective parts that nature has destined for man and woman in marriage cannot be allotted differently, even if the wife should be forced by material circumstances or impelled by irresistible inclination to take up a job. In such a case there may, indeed, be a certain division of labour in the household; yet even so the powerful efficacy of conjugal faithfulness ought not to degenerate into faithfulness to one's profession.

THE CHILD AND MARRIAGE

Unless marriage is seen as a storehouse of sound humanity and the partnership itself as a responsibility, parents will not be able to provide the protection necessary to give the family security. The plain fact that the end of marriage is undeniably the child is now no longer considered a matter of course, because our technical civilization increasingly estranges us from simple natural conditions. We no longer make a water-wheel, place it in a brook, run a mill with it and grind the corn into flour—an action which, though it is made up from several components, does not surpass a man's imagination. This is something quite different from the technical construction of an electrically run establishment of the same kind. The layman cannot see from the designs of the engineer how the modern mill will eventually work. Our understanding of nature has first to be guided through all manner of artificially constructed channels before it realizes that it is in the presence of well-known forces that are used in a new way.

Thus also personal life has taken on new forms. The 'apparatus' of a complicated social structure has invaded even the most intimate spheres. Innumerable decrees have to be taken into account even when concluding a marriage. The external difficulties of the common life often make so many demands on one's strength that little is left to look beyond them. Besides, war and emergency measures have accustomed us so much to provisional situations that cannot be altered, that through this, too, the sense for the 'real thing' has been weakened. The increasing popularity of sects and prophecies shows that many people feel there is no use in planning far ahead.

External and internal insecurity prevent men from taking a broad view. They are incapable of seeing farther than their nose; fear and distress make it impossible for them to want anything more than to get over the momentary difficulties. One thinks in circles and cannot make a fruitful beginning.

People fail to realize that from outside no more can be done to solve the great human problems than to prepare the ground and suggest a certain direction that may lead to their solution. But the actual task of coping with them must be left to the individual. A nation can recover its health only through its members; the beginning must be made with father and mother, who supply the 'material' from which the nation is fashioned.

There are married couples who are completely wrapped up in each other and yet stay alone throughout their life. They are sufficient to themselves. To make this love truly human an essential factor is lacking, which is self-forgetfulness. A love that bears in itself the infinitely fertile creative urge of the free human spirit cannot limit itself by being so exclusively given to the other that it must fall back on itself. For a couple love selfishly if they are so attached to each other that the outside world ceases to exist for them and their love fails to grow into the desire for the child. It is quite possible that the aforementioned factors of liking, desire and charity may all be evident, but not for the sake of the other but, lastly, for the sake of one's own personal security.

Such selfishness will be punished at the latest after the death of one of the spouses. Then the survivor will no longer be able to cope with life alone. But even before, such people will often find no peace. They are constantly afraid of losing their happiness; even the shortest separation will produce panic. Thus they will become over-anxious, and even indulge in superstitious fears, surrounding themselves with queer rituals in order to propitiate imaginary gods. For they are unconsciously aware of a guilt. A person who wants only to have and never to give, that is to lose, perverts the meaning of human life, which is not to keep and to hoard but to give and surrender so as to create anew. What is new in a marriage—even though it may itself contain immense powers of spiritual creation—is the child. Now, it is irrelevant whether the child is actually given; the essential point is that it should be desired.

All mature love wants to overflow, to share and to give, in such a way that not only another self may receive, but something new may come into being. In the psychosomatic unity of marriage this new being is, of course, the child. If, then, the meaning of marriage is the loving union of the spouses, and if the child thus produced is the fulfilment of its end, a marriage that consciously excludes the child has missed its meaning. For here the motive power is not a giving love but a calculating love deprived of its end. In the course of years the characters of such couples will imperceptibly become twisted; they will grow narrow, cramped; in short they will become stunted. Naturally childless marriages have their share in producing an aged population and imposing social burdens on the children of others, since every working member of the community contributes to the upkeep of the older generation. Just those people who live quite by themselves will often be proud of 'needing' no one; but this is not altogether true.

On the other hand, there are 'born mothers', women who are quite evidently dissatisfied as long as they have no child. They marry for the sake of children, and for this reason may even neglect their husband. They at least need not reflect on the end of marriage. In the case of such women delay, caused, for example, by waiting till the home is adequately furnished, will often have bitter consequences; the husband may die early, and a child would have consoled the young widow.

RIPENING TOWARDS MOTHERHOOD

Despite woman's natural inclination, we must admit that, generally speaking, she has to ripen towards motherhood, and this does not always happen by itself. Gertrud von Le Fort is right: "The child is not only born by the mother, the mother is also born through the child." Motherhood means the beginning of a new period in a woman's life. It may sometimes involve a crisis comparable to that of puberty or the change of life. The wiseacres will say when they hear such statements that in the time of our grandmothers such problems simply did not exist. People would marry, have a number of children and bring them up. To this we would answer: A large percentage of these children did not survive the baby age; besides, even in those days many women were unable to cope with their duties, only these difficulties were not so generally discussed. Further, we would refer to what we have said before on the growing technical civilization, which has caused estrangement from our natural tasks. The question is how to harmonize human dignity with the tenor of our time.

When the woman develops into a mother this transformation involves the sacrifice of former rights, just as adult life will often entail increasingly dehumanized routine duties. Thus there are oppositions between inner and outer progress. The development of the personality—and becoming a mother means precisely this —demands highly personal achievement; whereas this is not always required by one's daily work. Now, every man and woman of our time needs to learn the right balance between their own inner world and their surroundings, hence it has become much more difficult to cope with life in general.

What demands will the new task make on the mother? First and foremost she will need to free herself from all conscious or unconscious particular desires regarding the expected child. It will be God's gift, even though it has been formed from father and mother. It ought not to be awaited with preconceived ideas, for example that it must be a girl or a boy. Some parents fail to realize their own disappointment when the child turns out to be different from what they had expected; nevertheless, it will be expressed in their behaviour. The mother, for example, will not admit that it is like such and such a relative. If it does something wrong or is obstinate, she may say : "That the child has got from my husband's brother"; or even "from my husband", if she does not like him. Such behaviour is unworthy of a mother. In fact, personal desires and fears may easily hinder the maternal development. Selfish mothers will have nervy and difficult children.

One virtue is extremely important for a mother, though certainly difficult to achieve for many a harassed wife today. This is infinite patience. It is a special kind of patience, which involves not only bearing with the child and just tolerating it, but bending down towards its own rhythm and tempo. This does not mean fooling about with the children. But one should not constantly rush a little one and add a "quick, quick!" to every command— not even in thought. Otherwise the children will be torn in all directions; failing to obey their mother's wishes, they will at first only appear obstinate, though they are really helpless; only later will they really become obstinate.

To adapt oneself to the child also needs courage; not, indeed, the bravery of smart behaviour, but the affectionate courage of protective motherhood. This is nourished by patience and faithfulness, avoiding the limelight of sensation. A mother may never desert her child or laugh and sneer at its needs. A child is not yet capable of understanding irony, and cannot grasp the meaning of a humorous correction that is not meant literally. It is a grave mistake to make fun of the child's small world which it must take seriously, because it seems comic in the perspective of the grown-ups. Indeed, eternal values, above all confidence in the mother, may be destroyed by such behaviour. An experience of this kind may produce a crisis of confidence in all the important spheres of the child's life, which may after many years end in disgust with life or atheism. It is an important quality for a mother to have the courage to adapt herself to the ways of the child, which may even be a challenge to her own lack of spontaneity.

The last and hardest demand made on a woman, especially if she is 'wholly a mother', will be to be ready to let go. The birth of the child is only the beginning of this process, which accompanies the whole life and has for many a mother of this century reached its tragic end when her child was killed in a war. If she desires the healthy development of her son or daughter, she will be well advised to foster his or her independence even in infancy. Those mothers whose one and only interest in life is their child are not the ideal, though it may often appear so to the outsider. These are the overfond mamas who will not let their children out of their sight for a moment, and sometimes see them to school till they are ten or even twelve years old. This exclusive maternal love hides not infrequently unfulfilled desires, interior insecurity and aimlessness, a festering fear of life.

The problem of the only child is important also from the point of view of the mother, who will concentrate all her love and interest on this one child. She clings to it—though it would be better the other way round. Such children will develop into sons and daughters who find it very difficult to found their own homes. If they marry nevertheless, they will be haunted by a sense of guilt and never quite let go their mother's apron-strings. It will easily show in the sons, if they could not develop into real men; they will then once more choose their mother in their wife and want to be spoilt. The daughters, on the other hand, will fade early by the side of their mother; and it will seem as if the shadow of her despotic love had never allowed them to blossom.

We would advise all mothers to extend the range of their interests wide enough to let the child remain their first but not their only concern in life. True maternal attachment will grant freedom without losing its intimacy. Now, only a person with a rich interior life will be able to grant freedom, and the education of mind and heart will bring these riches. Hence a girl will not lose her educational assets, even if she does not use them throughout her life.

We would not gloss over the fact that many women make their daughters pay for their own disappointment in marriage. Many become mothers not through the man who was the love of their youth or one who resembles the ideal of their earlier years, but through one quite different, who corresponds very little or even not at all to this image. In these women there remains a void. They will experience conjugal love but not Love; intimacy with their husband will not make them really happy. This is not the place to discuss all the causes or interior motives from which such a situation may arise. We would only say that such women will gradually arrive at the firm conviction that marriage necessarily leads to disillusionment and will want to save their daughters from a similar fate. It can easily be imagined what kind of sexual instruction such mothers will provide; it will certainly not be of the right sort to prepare their daughters for marriage. Besides, the mother will miss no opportunity of warning her daughter against it.

The practical result will be that the children of such mothers will be given a distorted view of the natural processes. But since their own nature will develop and demand its rights, they will be subject to incomprehensible tensions, which result from longing desires and physical maturity on the one hand and a gloomy picture of sexual relationships on the other. From these, serious inner conflicts will arise in the child which may lead to a permanently twisted mentality.

To such mothers especially their child is their one and all. If their husband dies, they will try almost to absorb their son or daughter for good. They leave their children no freedom, are anxiously trying to have them always with them, and do everything in their power (though mostly without realizing it) to prevent them from marrying. In this they are guided by a twofold desire : first they would save their child from the dangerous and painful experience of marriage; secondly—but this can only gradually be made clear to such mothers—they would compensate themselves for the loneliness of their own married life by a belated companionship with their child.

THE IMPORTANCE OF A HARMONIOUS FAMILY
LIFE FOR THE CHILD

It is probably generally known how important a harmonious
family life is for the sound development of the children, though it
is far less clear how this is to be achieved. Above all, external circumstances are overrated in comparison with the internal ones.
There are many women who have not yet found their interior
balance, though they may be living in comfortable circumstances.
They are unstable and superficial, and themselves too little convinced of the importance of their status as mothers of a family. It
is true, their children are not lacking in anything such as clothes,
food and a home; yet something essential is missing : the family
has no calmly beating heart, its members are not conscious of their
unity. Such mothers will not be much good at occupying their
children. They may indeed see to it that there is always 'something
going on'; they may arrange for all sorts of lessons and are concerned how and where their children spend their days. But they
educate them far too little through their own personality; their
children have too little opportunity to learn what is true, good and
beautiful through their life with their mother. For the mother
should unite the family and draw it to its centre, which is herself.

The family, and hence the sound development of the children,
is even more gravely endangered if there are tensions between
the parents. Nervous diseases of the children are nearly always
caused by conflicts between the parents. It makes little difference
whether the children have witnessed scenes or whether the parents
have always controlled themselves in their presence. Children are
very sensitive to the harmony of their parents, and often have a
sure instinct for the disturbing intruder, even before the worst
happens. Unconscious conflicts of the mothers, or some psychological disturbances which they cannot overcome, have a particularly baneful influence on the children. In order to help them
effectively, something will also have to be done for their mothers.

Apart from grave frustrations in the intimate sphere of married
life, a woman will sometimes also be painfully disappointed in the
character of her husband. Perhaps she may not even have any
opportunity for talking about it to a trustworthy and discreet person ; for outsiders will often judge only by appearances and refuse
to believe her.

Perhaps with a little tact the wife herself might be able to exercise a favourable influence on her husband; but she may be too deeply hurt, and simply incapable of quietly bearing with this or that defect. His slightest *faux pas* will infuriate her. In such families there will be a permanently thundery atmosphere, which will badly harm all their members and have a very undesirable effect on the children. A woman should examine herself carefully on this point, and strive to correct faults that may have developed. It is quite true that many women are considerably more capable than their husbands; they may be more industrious and persevering, even more successful in business. But they will destroy all the good they could do by their restlessness and their mania for lecturing and nagging their husbands. Much would be gained by a little patience. The children of such a marriage will then be torn hither and thither between father and mother, not knowing which side to take. Such discords experienced in youth may produce a psychological trauma that can never be perfectly healed.

Children who suffer from the bad temper of their parents will not be able really to forget themselves completely when they play. Yet the play-world of the child is important; it forms a sound basis for life and will one day become a treasured memory. Now, it is just the joy of playing that forms the character; it enriches the soul and will foster a true love of brothers and sisters that will last a lifetime. Happiness in one's life and work cannot be gained from outside; it is a gift, the fruit of a happy childhood, and this is largely the responsibility of the parents.

On the other hand, if children have always been oppressed by matrimonial quarrels, if the first experience impressed on them has been that father and mother are seldom or never 'nice', they will be greatly hampered in their development. Deceitfulness and cunning often originate in a child's need for defending itself from the uncontrolled outbursts of the grown-ups. In these circumstances brothers and sisters will not share a common joy; they will become fellow soldiers in the premature battles of life, boon companions casting dice for the favour of father or mother.

Such children will have been cheated of a vital experience, in that they have not been given a true picture of man and woman. For they should not come to know them as representatives of sex, but of life as a whole. For man's rôle in the world is different from that of woman. If the child is to develop in a healthy way, it should learn this fact in and through its own family. It will always go to the mother for help, who should always calm, pacify and console it in its sorrows; whereas the father will guide its first steps into the world outside and provide the link with the freedom that lies beyond.

Spiritual receptivity and a developed emotional life are an essential part of man, who should be able to grasp intuitively such important facts as the redemptive power of loving patience, the increase of vital energy brought about by the appreciation of beauty and purity, and similar associations. The mother who devotes herself to her child in the right way will herself provide such indispensable education, and so lay the foundation of a sound mastery of life, including the knowledge that restful relaxation, recreation and a *dolce far niente* are part of a healthy life. Sometimes it is the fault of the mothers if their grown-up children are cramped and a prey to a constant feeling of emptiness which results in a tortured craze for ceaseless activity.

In the same way the future personality of the child will grow out of the right experience of the father. Conscience and responsibility, freedom, happiness in work and purposeful activity will develop as they should if the father makes his children familiar with life.

Parents should know, however, that they must grow with their children. Family life will change when the children grow up. Daughters who are developing into young women should no longer be treated like little girls, nor youths like small boys. A lack of insight in this respect may lose parents the confidence of their children and lead to incurable ruptures, as a result of which both parties will grow bitter.

The mother of a daughter who is changing into a woman will once more take leave of her own childhood. At this moment she will have to make yet another sacrifice, by giving up possession of the whole soul of her child. For the daughter now discovers in her own centre a sphere into which even her mother may not penetrate unasked. Above all, the children should be made to realize that they are being trusted and left free to follow their own interests. For how are they to face the dangers of life if their parents give them no opportunity to grapple with them while father and mother are still there to protect them? Unless in these years a mother be able to stand back and tolerate new features and unexpected developments in her children, she will have failed in her task.

It is only natural that parents should want to see their own ideals and hopes fulfilled in their children. Yet it will often happen that the children are different and turn towards other objectives. Provided these be unexceptionable, parents ought not to disapprove of them because their vanity is hurt. They will do their children no service if they remove all external obstacles from their paths but remain themselves the main obstruction, refusing to budge an inch. If a daughter, for example, should want to join a group of young people with similar interests, she may fail to achieve her purpose because she stumbles, so to speak, over her mother. If she wants to marry, the mother may even constitute an insuperable obstacle, because she does not want to retire into the background. Thus the wheel has come full circle : for the mother is partly responsible for the good marriage of her daughter (and also of her son). If we would help future marriages, the family climate should be such as to allow the children to develop into independent men and women.

MENTAL ATTITUDES UNFAVOURABLE TO MARRIAGE

To make a success of marriage, education and self-discipline are needed as well as knowledge of one's own character and of other people, else it will be impossible to choose the right partner. It is also important that both should be able increasingly to develop towards each other, and should be aware of the limitations of all human beings. From this knowledge one ought also to draw the right conclusion : we can hardly expect to enlarge the limits of another, but it will be possible to extend one's own a little.

If a person is willing to set to work on himself and anxious to remove the hard shell that encrusts him, he will be mentally and psychologically suited for marriage. This is essential. Marriage is not an educational institution; that is to say, one should not expect to be able to correct in time things one dislikes in the other. This would be a grave error. If one feels one cannot bear with the other such as he or she is, then there can be no union for life. Nor is marriage a nursing-home. Difficult characters and twisted attitudes are by no means the same as the anæmia of young girls for which one can prescribe marriage.

It is no less a fallacy to assume that exorbitant or perverted sexuality can be completely put right by marriage. This will often be only a symptom of deeper anomalies which may later appear in other forms. No one can be so transformed by marriage that the dark depths of his nature will simply change into *joie de vivre* because another person is sharing his life.

Before entering on marriage one should also be clear about the fact that the natural merging into one another has its limits. If women regard the physical intimacy not as the foundation but as a tiresome adjunct of marriage with which they have to put up, they will not have sufficiently understood that marriage is a form of the common life, and so will not achieve its full development. The term foundation should be understood quite literally; it is, indeed, not everything, but it is an important element. The emotional and spiritual edifice is certainly indispensable if marriage is to bring all its possibilities to fruition; but only strong and rich characters will resign themselves completely if harmony has not been achieved in the sexual sphere.

Women who satisfy their husbands in this, but are either unable or too lazy to follow him elsewhere, must get reconciled to the fact that they will be left out from part of his life. The 'total' community of married life may even be over-estimated. On the other hand, frigid women who submit only grudgingly to their 'duty' ought not to be surprised if they lose their husbands completely. This means not necessarily that the husband will become unfaithful and seek his satisfaction elsewhere, but that without the physical accord the harmony of life will be lacking.

THE RELIGIOUS SIGNIFICANCE OF MARRIAGE

Nevertheless, we must not overlook the fact that even in marriage the visible reality is but a section of the whole. For only if it be viewed in the absolute setting of eternity will it correspond to the spiritual and psychosomatic nature of man, the first of these components pointing beyond itself. Sanctity and indissolubility of marriage derive from man's origin and goal: he comes from God and goes to God. Man always belongs to Him who has created him in the freedom of love; and he resembles his Creator precisely in his task of propagating mankind.

This freedom in giving also belongs to the sanctity of marriage. Men are not forced into it. The marriage contract is based on the well-considered, freely pronounced Yes of the partners. This contract is distinguished from a mere legal formality by the mutual love from which the decision to marry has sprung. In the Catholic Church marriage is a sacrament which the spouses confer on each other before witnesses and before God. It is a *sacramentum con-*

tinuum, a continuous sacrament by which the whole married life is sanctified.

Certainly love and marriage involve a risk, for the partners must give each other more than they actually possess. Human life has its tides, its vacillations, its times of dryness—in short its destiny. In sanctified marriage the vow of faithfulness is made to God at least as much as to one's partner. It is a profound consolation that the whole, life and marriage, is guided by divine Providence. The spouses stand not only before their Creator and Father, but before the Triune God of love, and through grace even within Him. The various phases of the mystery of the Incarnation have their share in shaping married life. There is no complete resurrection as long as men live; this must always be accomplished through the Cross. In marriage one partner may be the cross of the other; for even if the marriage is not without its human fulfilment, it need not be completely fulfilled in this way.

Everything may break up: the affection for one another, the common life, the possibility to understand each other even a little. Yet the Sacrament will be, and remain, a source of grace, if one accepts it and submits to it by resigning oneself to the life that is not, humanly speaking, fulfilled. There is no such thing as a meaningless or religiously empty marriage. How many other marriages may be saved by one's own perseverance. For much good will and self-conquest have invisible effects that cannot be measured. Not everything can be proved by statistics and arranged in files. Every bride and bridegroom are animated by the desire to remain together; they would be indignant if people were to doubt their honest intention to spend their whole life in each other's company. Nevertheless the Church is considered inhuman precisely because she emphasizes this deeply human desire and surrounds it with safeguards. Trust is an essential factor in love, which will degenerate without it. Where religious faith is lacking, faith in men has also been shaken; external safeguards are introduced in the place of interior support. Now, the possibility of divorce is actually opposed to the peaceful ripening of marriage; because it will be used as a threat to intimidate or infuriate each other at the slightest provocation. Where this is used as a weapon, the prospects of married harmony are poor indeed.

The situation is very different in a marriage that rests on faith, where the Sacrament constitutes a rampart that prevents the

couple from being blown apart even in a storm. It is the greatest
mystery of believing existence that faith itself will constantly
release inexhaustible revitalizing energy. Contrition and penance
are two fundamental religious factors which exercise their re-
generative power also in marriage. Their dynamic force will be
quite different if it be truly religious, for then it will bring about
restoration and forgiveness. Let us take a case of adultery for an
example, supposing that the wronged party is not religious yet
capable of forgiving. This will be a generous and beneficial act;
yet it will remain a purely ethical, individual performance. Besides, the human reserves will be quickly exhausted unless they be
replenished 'from above'.

If a person is only staring terrified at the indissolubility of
Catholic marriage, he is still far from the region of faith and its
all-embracing beauty. The marvel of the Church's faith is its
universality and the realization that we are members of the
Church. The vital exchange between God and the Church is
present also in every sacramental marriage. Hence if the true believer thinks of marriage he will not see as it were the closed door
and the irrevocability of its undertakings, which are negative; he
will see his Church as a mysterious union between God and
human nature, the birth of the Church from the side of Christ,
her motherhood and her union with Him. From the theological
point of view marriage is hidden in the Triune God through being
embedded in the Church; hence it is removed from petty changes
and given sufficient time and strength to bring forth even more
fruitful love.

In this view marriage is not an experiment with a doubtful
issue; it is seed designed to spring up. For the first-fruit of marriage is not the child but the marriage itself. As it has been concluded within the Church, it is also the concern of the whole
Church, which shares in the responsibility for it. This may be a
spur, but also a judgement.

As has just been shown, only the sacramental marriage preserves its social character. Today these things are being much
discussed. If a new social order is mentioned, what is meant is not
the 'mystical Body of Christ' but an earthly reality. Marriage as
the cell of hierarchically ordered life is certainly important also
in this sense. But its importance will probably be in no way diminished, if one remains at the same time conscious of the place of
marriage in the Kingdom of God, refusing to leave this aspect

out of one's sight. For if married people use the graces of their state in the right way, turning towards the Holy Ghost with a living faith, they will be able to release powers that will serve society also outwardly. Christian married couples will be responsible for achieving the proper balance between individual and community, which a future collective society would certainly have to derive from the Christian order.

No doubt the rationalization of life and the increasing importance assigned to technical progress, psychological research and political activities are responsible for breaking up the unity of man. This specialization penetrates even into the private life of the individual; else it would be impossible to stress instinctive being on the one hand and spiritual being on the other. Marriage, too, has become involved in this process of division that affects all departments of life. It has been brought far too much into the limelight nowadays, and its different components are being made conscious in a rather objectionable way. It is hardly possible for a young person to retain his natural attitude, and be brave enough to risk married life, if he has first to ask himself whether he is biologically, characterologically, sociologically and perhaps even metaphysically suited for it.

Even if one has gained such partial knowledge, which is in fact no more than an accumulation of certain scientific facts, one is quite capable of entering on marriage just as unprepared as without it. The capacity for choice depends on the spiritual and psychological maturity which is gained by general education combined with self-discipline. The physical precocity of modern youth precedes their psychological maturity. If, for example, a girl marries only to escape from a disorderly home, such motive will offer little guarantee for a favourable issue. The lower moral standards and the greater emphasis on erotic factors which are held to be partly responsible for broken marriages are themselves consequences of the crumbling unity of the human being. We should therefore consider man from the ontological point of view, and lead him back to wholeness. In the same way marriage should be shown to be planning for a common life, through which two spiritual beings are not only added up, but are united into a new creation. If the individual life is complemented by the right partner, it will gain a new dimension, which is the other side of the world, and so the full cosmic harmony will be achieved by finding the 'we' in the spiritual as well as in the psychosomatic sphere. Through the demand for lifelong faithfulness this 'we' will gain its concrete reality, for this is the meaning of marriage. Love which is formed within the sacred bond of marriage has its meaning in itself, it does not receive it only through the child. On the contrary, the child is not the first expression of the meaning of marriage but its confirmation. Conversely, the vow of faithfulness loses its meaning if it not only fails to intend but actually excludes the child.

This is so, because the spiritual desire for love which is continued in the physical union remains fully human only if it results in genuine surrender. For the man this means neither to hold back nor to squander his pent-up strength, but to let it bear fruit; whereas the woman will surrender herself in the willing expectancy of physical motherhood. Thus the love of husband and wife will result in something that transcends them; that is to say, in the child. Nevertheless, this loving union between man and woman is the profound meaning of marriage which is perfect in itself; it does not need the child to justify it.

NATURAL AND SACRAMENTAL MARRIAGE

Only a lasting and indivisible sexual union within the framework of a lifelong community is worthy of human beings. The German name for marriage, *Ehe*, meaning union, indicates its permanence. This tallies with the concept of marriage found in the natural law, and presupposes an essential difference between man and animal. If, as stated above, man be taken as a spiritually directed being who may be expected to decide freely what to do and what to avoid, his sexuality, too, will work in a way different from that of animals. Whereas the animal is wholly subject to the promptings of his sexual instinct, in man this is integrated into his personality, by which it is responsibly directed. More, owing to the psychosomatic unity, man has no adequate means of satisfying this instinct outside marriage. Now, it is true that at this point the notion of man is enlarged into the self-transcending being that is made for God. The purely natural man with all his faculties well-ordered at his disposal does not exist. Man as we find him is weakened by original sin; and we may just as well admit that he is hardly or not at all able to govern just this strong instinct, if he is no longer aware of his true spiritual and religious destiny, but considers only bodily existence as wholly human and remains satisfied with that.

But if we know that human nature is wounded by original sin, we shall be equally familiar with the consoling doctrine of man's redemption through the sacrifice of Jesus Christ. In this context the help given by a religious way of life becomes very evident.

It is true, there are strong natures able to master life, at least in their own opinion, without God. They forget, however, that they did not invent their own principles, but that they have inherited them from the Christian spirit of former centuries, which, though under different names, is still alive in our civilization.

Sexual power is most surely not only mastered, but preserved in marriage, with the help of religion. Therefore the sacramental marriage is the marriage *par excellence*. This order has, of course, to be accepted as divine and derives its guiding principles from the Scriptures; within it the respective positions of man and woman in marriage are firmly established.

Christian marriage always works, provided it be truly Christian. The Church regards it with that large-hearted wisdom which she always shows to man, because he is a creature endowed with reason and free will. The Sacrament consists in the words by which the spouses signify their will to establish a community of life; that is to say, in the marriage contract. This is the highest value in marriage, from which springs the grace necessary for its own, and later the family's, well-being. The Church acts only as witness, leaving her children to take the first place in their freely willed communion of life. Thus the Church stresses the responsibility of Christians as well as their trustworthiness. It is not their mutual love that constitutes the Sacrament, for this love might be indefinite and vague, but the clear, unquestionable will to lead a common life. Yet the Church, too, is needed, for her witness is important since the union will have consequences reaching far into the future. The simple Yes of two people forms an insoluble union. Two baptized Christians have placed themselves at the disposal of God's Kingdom in a new way, in order to serve Him through their natural, earthly powers.

Nevertheless, the union of the spouses resembles the union of Christ and the Church. The man stands in the place of Christ, the woman signifies the Church. Christ is the head, the new Creator; the Church is the body, the new creation. All this the Church places in the hands of the spouses. They receive no new character, no special consecration fitting them for particular liturgical actions; yet they receive something new, namely the power of realizing God's order of love in life. Thus the sacramental marriage is a potent factor within the scheme of salvation; this is its deepest meaning. Seen from this angle, the 'subjection' of woman to man is not humiliating for her; it expresses itself as a harmony between the two partners. For the loving woman will divine the desires of her husband and 'incline' herself to them. On the other hand, responsive and sympathetic women usually succeed well in gradually introducing their husbands to feminine ways and desires.

In any case, the Catholic sacramental marriage is a permanent union of bodies as well as of life and love, with a view to producing and bringing up posterity. Yet this first end of marriage is not the only one. The secondary ends, which visualize the mutual integration of life and the regulation of sexual love, belong definitely to the essence of marriage, even though they cannot be arbitrarily separated from the primary end. Moreover, marriage has been elevated to the dignity of a Sacrament and endowed with all the graces belonging to this form of life. If one is not only a nominal member of the Church but lives in her spirit, one will appreciate the protection and security this view of marriage affords. Vital questions become simpler whenever one tries to solve them according to a view of life guided by eternal principles.

INDISSOLUBILITY AND DIVORCE

In principle and according to divine law, marriage is a lasting and exclusive community of life. The state, however, claims the power to dissolve it also in its bond by a legal decision, and thus to clear away the obstacle to another marriage. Even the mere possibility of a divorce is to the disadvantage of the woman, for normally she will be hurt most when the marriage breaks up. The legal position is such that even if the woman is the innocent partner, her financial situation and capacity for earning are taken into account; moreover, if her husband marries again, the claims of his new family will be given first place. Many women do not know that the right to a divorce because of faults (adultery) of the other partner is lost by condonation. This is supposed to be the case if matrimonial intercourse has taken place, even only once, after the other's fault had become known. Though this may have been permitted only reluctantly, it is still considered as 'condonation'; only if it has actually been enforced will it not be reckoned as such.

After the divorce the wife retains the family name of her husband; but by a declaration at the registry office she may resume her maiden name. According to the law, the husband may forbid his divorced wife to use his name if she is the guilty partner.

A divorce will always be painful and bring in its wake not only much turmoil and agitation, but also bitter human disappointments. Experience teaches that there is no advantage in making it easy; for then slight divergences, instead of being overcome, will quickly lead to complete rupture, and insignificant lapses from fidelity will result in irrevocable estrangement. People are taking too little account of the fact that there are no ideal human beings, and that every new acquaintance will first show his good qualities, and reveal his faults only under the magnifying-glass of daily intimacy. Children will hardly ever survive unharmed the 'change of parents' following divorce and remarriage.

Here, too, it is evident that modern men set very little store by their solemn promises, and that spiritual values, of which pledged troth is one, count for nothing. For the love that is sealed by the marriage contract is a higher good than the passion which may suddenly spring up in the heart for someone who has entered one's life later. It must be admitted that love can err, and a completely wrong choice may result in an indissoluble marriage. This marriage can be a torment. And then someone else may turn up whom one knows without fail to be the right one. Certainly it will now be felt impetuously that marriage has become a prison to which one is chained by the dead letter of the law, and that the new, living love demands that it should be broken.

To this argument we would answer that what obsesses us temporarily is not true, if it only seems so in the personal opinion of the person concerned, without being rooted in the unequivocal universal consensus of opinion. The right thing to do, indeed the only right thing, is to keep one's freely given, contractually pledged word even in adverse circumstances. In the sacramental marriage, moreover, unalterable religious destiny has also a part. A human mistake may, indeed, have been made even in connexion with the mystery of salvation, but the religious destiny bound up with this mistake was certainly no error. Naturally faith does not preserve us from becoming unhappy in the sense that essential parts of our existence may remain empty, which means, in the present case, that marriage may not be harmonious. Nevertheless, the externally visible course does not indicate what will happen interiorly. It is nowhere written that only happiness of the heart, satisfaction of the senses and 'harm'-lessness of the soul will lead to perfection. Indeed, a happy marriage may sometimes so limit the human horizon that it will, in certain cases, need a partially unfulfilled longing for a person to remain open to 'higher things'.

Certainly, man is destined to realize, not destroy his own self. Yet tears shed in secret because marriage is full of silent suffering may moisten the soil of prayer; the outstretched hand that fails to touch the other may yet find the Hand of the Father. The willing heart may be rejected by its partner, yet if it knows itself understood by eternal love, it will be filled with incomparable wisdom. Surely not every bud is bound to open, nor every flower to be plucked or every fruit to be eaten. Strangely enough, today the conception of suffering joyfully accepted is quite foreign even to Christians. Saints, resigned in faith, have bowed to God's will; whereas we resign ourselves unwillingly, imagining our wilful demands to be due to us as a sacred right.

Men of today find it hard to wait, though the wars have often cruelly compelled us to do precisely this. Yet if a man goes off quite suddenly and unexpectedly—as may sometimes happen with men about fifty—the woman will find it very difficult to get over the insult. This is quite understandable; but important decisions should not be made in the midst of catastrophes. Besides, it is unwise quickly to give up a marriage. It may look as if the man were tied to another woman for good, and it may even come to that. Nevertheless, if a hope be fed by religious hope, it will have great power. The right thing to do will be to wait, firmly convinced that in the end all will come right—though this 'in the end' may even mean beyond death. But normally we do not think thus far, and perhaps we need not even do so. The important question is whether we are still able to wait at all. We tend at once to be completely upset if something important goes wrong. Time and again we are caught out by the fact that we are totally implicated in the immediate situation. To all intents and purposes we have lost the relation to the vital roots of existence which derive neither from the present nor even from ourselves, but have been 'given' to us. We fail to hear the theme that is sounded in distress, calling us to ascend from a lower to a higher form of existence. Often the need of the hour is simply to wait, to learn to understand and not to pull out the spiritual root of love. Yet only too frequently we allow hasty first reactions to drive us to decisions which later can no more be undone.

THE CHANGED SITUATION OF WOMEN AND ITS BEARING ON MARRIAGE

Marriage being a form of life, it is not enough to know about it in theory and to consider it from various points of view. It is an important question whether it has been affected by the changes of time and is, perhaps, no longer as fully valid as it was. As we have shown, its essence as a lasting union between man and woman for the purpose of living together and raising a family is valid for all times, hence not subject to change. Yet in the present century the position of woman in society has changed considerably, and this is no doubt largely responsible for the subversion of marriage. Women have won the battle for their place in the professional world by the side of men; they have at last been admitted to the same higher education; they have the political vote.

No less a person than Pope Pius XII himself has on several occasions referred to the co-operation of women in public life. In his allocution to the International League of Catholic Women's Organizations of September 11th, 1947, he says: "Your allotted task is quite generally to work that women may become ever more conscious of their sacred rights, of their duties and influence, whether this influence be exercised on public opinion in matters of daily life, or on the public authorities and legislation through the right use of their civic rights."

It is hoped that the desired public co-operation of women will achieve the protection of marriage, a right family order and the mitigation of hardships in public life. There is no question of dethroning men in order to establish a matriarchal order; nevertheless, history and the general development have shown that women, too, have their place and an active part to play in the shaping of life. This new activity will naturally bring about a change in them; they will increase in knowledge, self-confidence and responsibility, and will be able to make their own decisions.

Above all, their share in professional work has taught them better to judge and understand men. Because women have become enlightened, they will now make other demands—in the good sense—on marriage than before. They know enough of the world of men not to let themselves simply be excluded from it. Men can no longer put them off with a curt "You don't understand that", and treat them as a piece of furniture, albeit the most valuable and useful one.

Women have acquired a standing in the professional life to which they are entitled by rights, no matter whether they actually practise a profession or not. They have made good by the side of men; in an emergency they have even been able to replace men. Moreover, the economic and domestic life has been changed by technical progress. Today a household is no longer the same as it was in former times; the work of the housewife has changed, and will probably go on changing even more.

So it is an unalterable fact that many—though not all—women are no longer completely satisfied with domestic work. There are excellent wives and devoted mothers who are yet not particularly good housewives. It is very questionable whether they should be simply condemned *en bloc* for not sufficiently caring for their home. Since other professions besides the domestic ones have been thrown open to women, a number of them will show themselves more gifted for those and will also be able to achieve success in them. Surely in our so largely rationalized economic world it is not necessary to let a household go to ruin only because its mistress can do something else better.

Domestic work is increasingly being recognized as a separate profession. This means not only that it can be taught and learned, but also that it implies a special suitability. Once housekeeping will have been brought into line with other feminine professions and the domestic staff will have the same rights as industrial workers, we may well believe that supply and demand will be more evenly balanced than at present, while this profession is still so little recognized and organized. Then many problems of wives with a profession will be more easily solved than they are now.

We are fully aware of broaching difficult questions. Yet we are of the opinion that one cannot put back the clock. There will always be isolated cases of patriarchal conditions, yet these will not be very numerous in future.

There are 'born housewives'—that is to say, women who are really content only if they can care for a family—whose maternal instincts can only develop in the way indicated by nature. On the other hand, experience shows that women who are living only in the narrow circle of their family are by no means always the best companions and the wisest mothers.

From a not merely superficial point of view, we may say that during the last fifty years women have greatly gained externally as well as interiorly; they have given the world much capacity for work as well as power of love. On the whole, women have become better groomed and more graceful; they are surer in their bearing and think more deeply.

We cannot escape the impression that men are still so much perturbed by the development of women into independent, responsible personalities, that they have so far been unable to find the right way of treating them. Chivalry must be transformed to suit the 'awakening of woman'. The times are past, it seems, when wives were regarded, above all, as ornaments in a show-case. Nor should it be forgotten that in those days prostitution was rife, and highly respectable men had no scruples about dividing their love in this way. Then, social standing and financial security played a more important part than a woman's own personality. We have learned in the meantime that such securities no longer exist. Fortunes have melted away, and family influence depends on many very changeable circumstances.

Since marriage, however, is not a spiritual community in a vacuum, but needs rooms and tables, clothes and money, material foundations are indispensable. These will best be provided by a person who has both her feet on the ground and uses her hands to provide the necessities of life. Today the job of a woman will often take the place of a dowry.

MARRIAGE AND PROFESSION

Nowadays it seems to be the generally accepted opinion that a girl should be trained for a job. We have presupposed this as self-evident in our section on the young girl. Normally, too, this training is taken seriously, and not only regarded as a period of waiting for a better time, when the young girl will marry and give up her other work. Woman's vocation is certainly to become a wife and mother. But here it is the same as with other vocations: before they are realized, there is no certain sign forthcoming which would guarantee that the person is destined exclusively for this particular calling. Even though, as will be shown in a later chapter, a woman's life is certainly not completely fulfilled by an average job, yet there is hardly one that, if morally unexceptionable, would make her unfit for marriage. It is also a fact that girls who before marriage have worked only reluctantly, are by no means better wives afterwards. Perhaps they have unconsciously harboured the desire to be provided for, fearing the inevitable struggle for the daily bread.

We would emphasize yet again our conviction that a woman can be completely fulfilled by her vocation of wife and mother, and should be, if she has recognized the value of a healthy family life. If she remains interiorly empty, though she has a husband and children, she has missed her vocation. It is quite a different question what claims the duties attached to this vocation will make on her. These will vary considerably; they will not be the same for a townswoman as for a family living in the country, and depend, moreover, on the age of the children. As long as these are small the mother should be completely at their disposal, if this is at all possible. But once they are sufficiently grown up, so that they will spend a large part of their days at school or in some other educational institute, it is difficult to see why the mother should not resume her profession. To achieve this, however, women ought to take the initiative and insist that part-time work should be made available to them in far greater measure than this has so far been done. In this way more people would also become wage earners.

What is new in our present world is, no doubt, its greater uniformity and unification, due to technical progress. As men draw closer together, they have also become increasingly similar in their customs. We would even go one step further and assert that men and women have become more similar to each other in their way of life. This does not mean that women have become more masculine or that their femininity is to be disparaged; on the contrary, the more conscious a woman is of her special gifts, the more important will be her influence in the one-sidedly masculine technical world. All will then depend on what kind of women those are who are destined to bring men the 'feminine element of culture'.

Professional experience has one great advantage for marriage, in that it teaches a woman to understand a man's overpowering interest in his work, to enter into his joys, disappointments and desires, and to realize his concern for her when he tells her about it all. Further, a mother who has herself once chosen a profession will be better able to give advice to her children than one to whom such problems are quite foreign.

All this, however, has no bearing on the question whether marriage and profession are compatible and whether such a combination would be desirable.

If a woman is conscious of her great responsibility as mother of a family and wants to make a success of it, she will choose the profession of housewife in her own circle as *the* profession, or rather she will have been chosen for it, if this be *the* external form of an inner vocation. This will depend on the size of the household, the economic circumstances of the husband and domestic ability.

Nevertheless, a number of women may serve their families also in another profession, provided they love the family and sincerely desire to care for it. It is supremely undesirable that a married woman should take up gainful employment only for the sake of getting more out of life. For then the family will suffer from her selfishness, though such women will hardly become more 'family conscious' without a job.

No doubt marriage plus a job may lead to overwork, and there will probably be many cases where this actually happens. If her work leaves a woman no time at all for her domestic duties, and if she has no support from her family, her job may, indeed, harm her marriage and her home.

But apart from this, the possibility of a profession for women may give security to marriage and freedom to love—not of course 'freedom for free love'—but the opportunity for man and woman to meet on equal terms. A married woman of high moral standing will gain many human and ethical assets that are of the greatest importance in the present crisis of our culture, and which will counterbalance many inevitable drawbacks.

It is true, the professional training retards the final maturity of women, who will be ready for marriage at a later age than formerly. But surely this need not be regretted. Greater maturity and independence need not make a woman more 'emancipated' or 'masculine'. Certainly, in the technical age which is, however, our vocation and our destiny, we live farther away from 'natural nature', as Guardini has it, than other periods of history. All nations and races are being increasingly amalgamated into a cultural whole. There is no possibility of turning back; we have to go on. It seems willed by Providence that just at this stage feminine spirituality should be released into the world.

In accordance with the increasing industrialization, in future women's mode of life will probably move farther and farther away from that of their sisters who lived in the time of family businesses and small peasantry. In these patriarchal conditions which are often considered ideal women were definitely harnessed to man's professional work; the only difference being that this took place within the domestic surroundings. Today a farmer's wife has indeed her children near her, but she cannot devote herself only to them, since she will normally have to put in a good deal of work both in the house and on the farm. Since consumers' goods are now almost exclusively produced in factories, man's place of work is no longer in the home, and this situation will become even more general as the industrial centres continue to expand. Besides, complicated technical production will make a man's workshop so different from his home that women will be wholly excluded from his world unless they gain some insight into it. The happiness of future marriages will certainly depend partly on a woman's understanding of her husband's professional milieu.

Professional efficiency and technical knowledge may, however, harm a marriage if they cause the motherly functions to atrophy and induce a woman to avoid motherhood intentionally.

Some women want not only to be sheltered when they marry, they also try to avoid any responsibility, and like only to be provided for and to be fussed over. For it is also possible to marry in order to escape from life. Naturally this discussion is meaningless in the case of a mother who has brought, say, eight children into the world—she has certainly not escaped from life.

But not every mother will have eight children. If one has only two or three, and later goes back to her profession—if possible part-time, as has been suggested before—this should not be taken for objectionable independence. Perhaps straitened circumstances may thus be relieved; the woman's salary may allow for improvements in the home which, in their turn, may save much of her energy. Surely the harassed housewife who is never allowed to take off her apron is not the only ideal of a good mother.

There is no doubt that certain women can combine marriage very well with a job. Indeed, there are some whose marriage would be much less satisfactory if they did not have one. Through their work they have learned to control themselves and to fit in with other people. This will profit the marriage, in which they will also know how to serve the whole; and they will fulfil their motherly duties the more contentedly because, despite their marriage, they know what is going on in the world outside. Daughters of mothers who have had a profession sometimes possess astonishing reserves of strength, because they have, so to speak, learned to battle with life at their mother's breast. Such women will bring to their professional milieu the feminine element of motherliness and will be no less satisfactory wives and mothers.

Others will give up their work when the first child arrives, and only resume it when the children can do without their constant care. Yet others will relinquish their job for good when they marry; but it will have enlarged their horizon and given them more understanding of a man's life outside the four walls of the home; and these are undeniably great assets.

We would not be blind, however, to the misfortune of those women who have been forced—whether by their husband's inefficiency or through some other hardship—to take up employment without being equal to this burden. Where profession and household cannot be made to fit into each other, and where both are so exacting that they add up to two full-time employments, the double responsibility will indeed be too much. If anything is to be sacrificed here, it must be the job for the sake of the family.

In general, a profession, at least the one for which a wife has been trained, does not seem to have bad effects on a marriage; for such a woman shows herself capable of standing up to great strains. The woman of our matter-of-fact time is certainly no longer the same as her sister of a hundred years ago. The language of the heart has, indeed, become less exuberant, but not the heart itself. Even though we express our feelings less effusively nowadays, they are nevertheless strong and deep. Many responsible people certainly strive to find a style of life adapted to the modern world without betraying eternal values; they will shape the true marriage of the future.

THE YOUNG WIDOW

We ought not to forget the tragic situation of the young widow, especially the war widow. Some widows have been married only for a very short time and have then been left alone with the child. It cannot be denied that the experience of marriage, however short, normally produces such a change in a woman's existence that she cannot return to her former life, even if she should have remained childless.

Memory may only too easily idealize a very short happiness and the life together, though the beginning may actually have held great promise. In any case, her situation will be extremely difficult. A widow represents maturity, which she will, indeed, need for the education of the child. But the firmness of the father and the tenderness of the mother, which would quite naturally have developed in marriage through the mutual love of the parents complementing each other, will now have to be provided by the young widow alone. Often she will seek support from her mother. The older woman, however, will too easily forget that things cannot become again what they had been before, and that it is now no longer the daughter, but the grandchild, who is the immature and irresponsible being. Even if the daughter should tend to be dependent and undecided, it would be a grave mistake if the mother were now simply to take the lead and lord it over both daughter and grandchild. The former would sooner or later lose her vitality.

The problems of life cannot be solved by blueprints but only on the basis of sound principles. The young widow needs interior strength particularly to prevent her from succumbing to two possible temptations. The one is to dwell on one's sorrow and repeat incessantly: "Why just I?" This will soon so stifle her as seriously to endanger her balance; she will be weighed down by an unhealthy disgust with life. Gradually the preoccupation with her spoilt happiness will become so intense that inferiority feelings and envy of everyone else will combine to produce deep depressions. Tortured by bitterness and discouragement, the widow will look only at herself and so quickly lose contact with her surroundings. People will call her difficult to get on with. It is an old experience that a totally negative attitude to life blights all growth. In fact such a woman will gradually develop into a misfit and knock against all corners. Naturally this is not a healthy atmosphere for the child, who will come to reflect the unrest of its mother.

If it is bad in such a case to be wrapped up in oneself, it is equally so if the young widow wants to forget at any price, and for this reason entertains intimate relationships with men which cannot, or are not meant to, lead to marriage. Here the case is similar to that of the divorced woman. The child will know that its mother's 'friend' is not its father. This will produce tensions, the damaging results of which will perhaps appear only much later.

The best way for the young widow to bear her fate will be first to face the new, hard reality of her loneliness. Here, as in all other vital questions, what matters is the point of view from which one looks at life. If a woman is entirely enmeshed in material things and unable to look farther than her own immediate concerns, if she admits only tangible causes and effects, widowhood will seem meaningless. But if her standpoint is above palpable facts, if she is used to ask for the meaning of things, she will regard this state, however much renunciation it may involve, with far greater inner security. It makes a great difference whether dark hours will sometimes find us dejected and unable to cope with obstacles, or whether we have from the beginning written off all happiness and find a bitter satisfaction in noticing and always remembering every adversity. Such an attitude will drain one's vitality and dry up all good impulses. 'Destiny' has its zones, which are left to be shaped by one's own efforts; and this is what matters most. If we always grind the grains of dreariness and sadness in the mill of our memory, we shall soon be victims of melancholy. Thus force of habit, exaggerated reserve and mental laziness may produce evils that need not exist. If a child depends only on the mother, who must also replace the father, there should be enough to do to leave no time for brooding. If life has to be lived alone, it will offer many stimulating suggestions even apart from one's work; they will only have to be followed up with a little interest. But we will reserve this subject for the following chapter.

4

THE UNMARRIED WOMAN

HER LIFE IN THE PLAN OF PROVIDENCE

IN older books dealing with feminine problems the question of the unmarried woman is treated only cautiously and doubtfully; they fail to do her justice and are prejudiced. This is probably due to the erroneous nineteenth-century view, according to which man was simply a 'natural being' with physical functions designed to perpetuate the species. From this point of view love, too, is narrowed down to sexual relationship, and the woman who is denied this form of love is viewed with suspicion. Only in this century have women taken their place in the professional and public life; and so the woman who builds up her life by her own work is a new phenomenon. But she is not always rightly appreciated. We will not decide whether her work is regarded without prejudice, not in its unimportant aspects, but in responsible positions. Generally speaking, the unmarried woman is still viewed with suspicion and under-estimated in her human qualities. After thirty the *Fräulein* (Miss) often ceases to regard this address as an honourable title. She will be ashamed, lose her self-assurance and begin to be doubtful about her own human dignity. Nevertheless, she ought to be convinced not only of this, but also of ranking equally with the men she meets at her place of work. Men and women not only supplement, they even depend on, each other in many spheres. The advantages of feminine influence are gradually becoming ever more apparent in legal and administrative posts as well as in the widespread social organizations.

POSSESSING COMPLETE FEMININITY

Reality teaches that the human being achieves wholeness through man and woman. They complete each other naturally, not only when they form a family but also in the whole social structure. Man and woman experience the world differently; its total picture emerges only through the different impressions of both.

Repeating some statements of the first chapters, we would emphasize that all that has been said there of woman as such remains fully valid for the unmarried woman. A man thinks deductively, he desires to give shape to his constructions; whereas a woman thinks with the powers of her heart, and what emerges from her thought will be the product of her love. This may take different forms; it may show itself as an inclination for a particular profession, as attachment to her milieu, or express itself in a noble idea or a spiritual friendship. Human mediation will certainly be a potent factor in realizing her ideal conceptions, but this should not be a hindrance. For women, whether married or not, are meant to enrich life through their particular gifts. This is a most important feature of their growing participation in our increasingly technical civilization. It can hardly be a mere coincidence that women, with their great gift for personal relationships, should have been placed into the very midst of our soulless and complicated economic apparatus.

The first need for the professional single woman is to become sure of herself and take herself seriously. She should know that she is no mere bundle of emotions. Even though she accepts values first of all with her heart, nevertheless this is not to be a lifebuoy drifting in the sea of her existence, alternately drowned in feelings or knocking against the plank of a wreck. Woman is a spiritual being; though differing from man in structure, she is interiorly independent and bears responsibility just as he does.

It is essential for her to hold her place in the world of men; for hers is the beautiful task to help to pacify it. If the unmarried woman is conscious of this vocation, she will not feel frustrated in the fulfilment of her womanhood, but she will regard herself as wholly a woman with the particular calling to the single life. We know only too well that these things are more easily written and read than lived in practice. However, many men regard women, especially if they are capable, as competitors; and when there is a question of filling a responsible position, preference will normally be given to a man. Woman's professional equality is not yet functioning without friction.

We would note in fairness that this point should be pressed especially by those whom it concerns most; that is, by the professional women themselves. It is not our task to discuss political and economic questions. But who is to be interested in women's activities and influence unless women themselves? Many have not yet

found the right attitude to themselves and agree, at least unconsciously, with those who regard them as 'underprivileged'. Quite
a few highly respected, gifted women with a good income and independent position almost despise themselves because they have
no husband, and actually imagine that all difficulties would be
solved if they were not compelled to remain alone. These women,
however, fail to consider that married life has also its Cinderella
side; and strangely enough, talented single women have mostly
little aptitude for this rôle.

The happiness of the unmarried woman depends on professional ability and experience, for they show that she is equal to
the demands of life and fills her place adequately. Nevertheless,
we would not like to maintain that her work will fulfil her life
completely. This may be so in the case of certain specially constituted women and in particular professions. Generally, the work
will be the way towards a fulfilled life; but not this life itself. For
some it may afford possibilities to organize their existence according to their liking; others will find in the fulfilment of their duties
a measure of satisfaction which will help them to overcome the
poignant emptiness in other spheres. There are those for whom
the spiritual meaning of life is sufficiently real to convince them
that their existence among men will be of value for others. Akin
to them are the women with a pronouncedly religious attitude :
their faith forbids them to doubt that their life is the 'right' thing
for them.

In connexion with what has been said above about the maternal energies, we would mention here that readiness to conceive is
the structural law of woman's nature. The married woman
realizes it in physical motherhood and every mature woman in
motherliness, a fact of which unmarried women are far too little
conscious. The feminine soul and spirit yearn to conceive; this
is a need which their life should satisfy. Nevertheless, a woman is
not simply born motherly; she only becomes so in the harmonious
family, because the masculine energies exercise their influence on
her. Every woman becomes a mother in the large sense by assimi-
lating spiritual and cultural treasures; this side of feminine education is particularly essential for the single woman. The highest
and most universal aim of the education of girls is to train them
to be motherly. All other powers derive from this. Hence being
a mother is the basis of womanhood, whatever the actual state;

for both the woman who is physically a mother and she who is not draw from the same well.

Here one point needs to be considered. The motherly energies are, so to speak, above marriage. Yet the maternal destiny of the wife is different from that of the unmarried woman. We may even say, there is no substitute for physical motherhood; moreover, the childless wife is different from the childless spinster. At the same time, we repeat what has been mentioned in the first part: motherhood is in itself a parable. A profession is no substitute for marriage, as little as are the innumerable sacrifices and charitable or social good works which unmarried women are frequently encouraged to undertake. They should know that certain natural gifts remain unused. They will go a different way, though not without bringing their womanly gifts into play, apart from utilizing their general human endowment. It would mean casting away the good with the bad if, in the case of unmarried women, we were to speak of unfulfilled destinies. On the other hand, it would also prevent a woman from building up her life serenely if everything were to be concentrated on self-sacrificing motherliness. The result of such an attitude would be a breathless effort to cover up a defect, instead of fully accepting the reality of the single life and using all one's powers to give it form and meaning. A marriage does not only depend on the 'presence' of man and woman, but surely also on their capacity to 'meet', which is linked not so much to sex as to character. Neither can the selection for marriage or celibacy such as fate decrees it today be rightly equated with suitability or its reverse. Providence seems to decide it according to a plan that is not always clearly visible to us. In the case of outstanding women it makes no difference at all whether they are married or not. Their influence depends solely on the harmonious development of their feminine humanity. Readiness to conceive also means willingly to turn towards one's neighbour, in one's closer proximity as well as in a wider circle. Moreover, conceiving is protecting, holding and keeping together. We have already indicated its importance in the rationalized technical world of man.

Such readiness to conceive shows itself clearly in the receptivity of the heart, in this mysterious feminine gift of attracting and sheltering others. Men have colder hearts; much joy and sorrow passes unnoticed by them, because they are hardly interested in the living thing as such.

Nevertheless, a direct and personal approach has its serious defects if it is combined with narrowness; it will then appear as pettiness, officiousness, love of gossip and intrigues. Hence a woman should enrich her heart and keep her mind alert before devoting herself to special tasks; else this will result in much distress. The single woman must go in for physical culture and sports, she needs a comfortable home, relaxation and beauty culture. If a woman is the heart of a family, her own well-being will be reflected in the happiness of those dear to her; but if she lives alone, she needs the 'mirror on the wall' to tell her that, though she may not be the most beautiful of all, she is yet a good-looking woman. This is important; for the sacrifice of physical motherhood does not mean completely to give up the physical fulfilment of one's womanliness. Here people often will make mistakes. A woman is not a 'loose person' given over to unseemly lusts if she spends a free day enjoying a Turkish bath, massage and a hairdo. It is nowhere written that women of strong character may not also look nice. Part of a woman's fulfilment consists in being attractive. This belongs to her nature and destiny, and women who insist on denying this feel, in fact, unable to compete with their prettier sisters. Hence a visit to the theatre in festive surroundings may sometimes be just as important as the social and charitable works which are so often recommended to single women as a substitute for a family. The healthier the development of an unmarried woman's personality, the less will she let herself be cheated of her feminine charm, which in its turn will call forth the true chivalry of men. Levelling the differences between the sexes as a consequence of a wrong kind of progress will falsify natural data and do no good either to women or to men. If women demand positions only in order to show that they can fill them just as well as men, they overreach themselves and their femininity will gradually degenerate. Then they will give nothing to men and will gain for themselves only sham successes, because their natural powers have failed to enrich anyone. On the other hand, the more they mature intellectually and spiritually into feminine personalities, the more they will be able to add to the various departments of life essential aspects that have hitherto been overlooked. The more securely they rest in themselves, the less they will have to fight for their rights; they will one day simply be given to them. It is true, we cannot say that this development is almost complete; on the contrary, professional equality of men and women may exist on paper, but in reality it is not always quite evident. In any case, the achievement of this end will largely depend on the true maturity of women and on their ability to stand up for themselves. A woman must see and accept herself as a feminine human being. If she does this only in her profession, as a politician or a neutrally creative person, suppressing her particular feminine characteristics, she will easily take up wrong attitudes.

MISFITS

One of such misfits is the type of the 'emancipated woman', who will no longer receive and expect, but demands—not, indeed, human fulfilment, but the conquest of the world and all its positions. But if a woman wants to make conquests of this kind she jettisons her readiness to conceive and her whole feminine destiny. Having severed herself from the productive powers of earth she will, in the end, give over her body to lust; having abandoned the natural feminine desire for an interior life, she will seduce man spiritually by turning him away from serving his work to mere enjoyment of material things. Thus, in the words of Gertrud von Le Fort, "her wrong surrender becomes ultimate refusal". This is shown by the sterility of our culture; its symbol is the woman who panders to lust, but does not give all-embracing love. She wants to possess at all costs; the stations on this way are disturbance of marriage, intrigue and pleasure even to intoxication. She chooses and again rejects men, fashions and motives.

Such deviations from the true picture of the single woman result in restlessness, dissatisfaction and escape into irrelevant occupations, unceasing rush and changing 'affairs'. The collapse will come when the desire for conquest no longer finds any objects. Confronted with her own emptiness and the experience of utter loneliness, such a woman will receive a fatal shock from which there is no recovery.

Another species of the unmarried woman who fails to understand herself is the timid old maid. This type shows symptoms of repression that result from anxiously avoided opportunities in every sphere.

We should not forget that the balanced unmarried woman represents the absolute value of human freedom and the eternal significance of the person. To our contemporaries devotion to the community is more important than the individual personality.

Now the community that offers values is not the amorphous mass; it consists of persons. The professional woman is a symbol of the individual representing the community; more, she represents eternal spiritual values. Now these considerations need to be studied more deeply in order to be understood; but this does not mean that they are not valid.

After discussing the effects of consciously suppressed womanhood mentioned above, we now turn to the even more evident consequences of its unconscious repression. This expresses itself as emotional self-abandonment in the place of loving surrender. This is a pathological form of feminine love. Such women let themselves be sucked dry, usually by one particular person, though they do not admit that to themselves. Gradually they will become completely dependent on the existence or non-existence of this relationship which they deny. Such an unfortunate woman no longer receives all that enters her life in order to give it back, enriched by the treasures of her heart, but will shut out life except for the part that unites her to the object of her affection. Thus she passes life by and limits herself to a narrow choice. This attitude will necessarily result in stunted growth, which is much more dangerous than to resign oneself to the indivisible remainder, which actually exists. As has been said above, we think it would be dishonest to present satisfaction in one's profession as the panacea for the unmarried woman, for this would not be true. The mere job that assures one's livelihood leaves much to be desired. Even where inclination and talents find a satisfactory outlet, important human spheres will yet remain untouched.

TIMES OF CRISIS

If the single woman is really a woman, sufficiently conscious of herself, she will sometimes have to sigh for 'him'. Even the natural curiosity what 'it' is like can hardly be completely mortified. Moreover, it is part and parcel of life that hours of despair should come. Then the only thing to do is to 'grin and bear it'. Every state of life has its own sufferings. At the end of her twenties a woman will face the first crisis of loneliness, in her mid-forties the second.

This latter is much graver than the former; it coincides with the beginning of the change of life (with which we are going to deal separately), which often affects the single woman far worse than the married one. There will be sudden breakdowns, acute attacks of fear caused by loneliness, accompanied by physical symptoms. Something signalizes to the emotions rather than to the rational consciousness : You have lived and blossomed in vain; the great chance will come no more. In the case of believing Christians this state of mind will sometimes be accompanied by the frightening realization that religion offers no help; here, too, they have waited in vain for, let us say, 'the great encounter'. Now this will happen even to mentally and spiritually healthy women, well-versed in the experiences of life. They have coped with things until now, they have done their bit and are still doing it. Yet something snaps at the moment when the female organism begins to change. They realize that this is a farewell, even an anticipation of the terror of death. Now everything will depend on this, that the disturbance in the foundations of their being should lead to the great transformation, by which the soul will fully mature and achieve the supple wisdom of those who have already thrown some of their encumbrances overboard.

This is also the time when daughters who have always had their mothers beside them will be faced with external changes. They will suddenly be left alone, either freed from a lifelong tyranny or deprived of their only human support; often both will be mixed up together. Some sort of clubs are urgently needed for such unfortunate creatures, where they would gradually lose the acute feeling of loneliness, which will be only too oppressive within their own four walls. There they would be able to talk without restraint and to enjoy an adequate social life. We need places of recreation where shy, timid people can find rest and relaxation without being crushed by their fear of life. For our generation suffers less from an excess than from a lack of vitality.

SIGNS OF OVERSTRAIN

In this connexion we would mention the nervous exhaustion of the woman who is permanently tied to her job. Work in modern conditions in whatever capacity is extremely exhausting, since it has mostly to be done in a welter of noise and at top speed. Recent research has shown that there are natures whose automatically working nervous system, providing the inner organs, glands and vital centres, tends to be easily affected in such circumstances. This nervous system is related to psychological states and moods. It causes well-being or the reverse, according to whether the harmony of its parts is left undisturbed or is upset; but it has also the unpleasant characteristic of being greatly influenced by favourable or unfavourable external conditions. Irritability, moodiness and lack of self-control are first indications of an injury to this apparatus, which is diffused throughout the whole organism. Later mere sensibility will turn into torturing hypersensitivity. In this case a time of complete rest and a systematic building up of the nervous resistance are indicated.

Inability to concentrate may be due to the nervous cause just described; if so, it will respond to proper rest and medical treatment. But it may also be a symptom of escapism. This will be hard to understand, especially for those who are conscientious and keen on their work. Though they have the best intentions, their mind is yet never quite on the things they ought to do, and often even want to do. By way of explanation we would recall the 'ocean of consciousness' of which we have spoken in the general part of this book. All sorts of things with which people cannot properly cope, that annoy, worry or pain them, are not just 'gone' and dissolved into thin air if they are angrily brushed aside; they will be moving on, deep below the level of consciousness and even exercise a profound influence.

It is quite possible to have resigned oneself to the fate of remaining alone on the bright surface of reason, and yet still to rebel against it in the dimly lit depths of the heart. Such a 'double life' can exist, as experience proves again and again. In the emotional sphere this will result in restlessness and sorrow, in confusion and distress. We would also mention that feelings in the organs can exist independently of one's mental attitude. Even the best, purest and most sheltered people are capable of dark sexual desires. If they are inexperienced they will be frightened and full of scruples. Now, such feelings should on no account be equated with 'evil', the conscious negation of purity. This kind of thing worries many thoroughly good women; yet it is nothing worse than bodily nature making itself felt.

It is too easily forgotten that man is neither a being governed merely by instincts, a bundle of emotions, satisfied by purely earthly ideals however noble, nor entirely intellectual and spiritual, destined to heap virtue upon virtue in order to enter the heavenly beatitude in a state of absolute perfection. Eternal life cannot be gained apart from fickle human nature, and mostly only through turning towards our brethren around us.

To accept one's humanity such as it is, in the form of the

special destiny reserved for each of us, includes also the acceptance of the destiny of the unmarried woman, with all its light
and shadow. We may sometimes be hard pressed by vital forces
which we have always to hold down; but this does not mean
that, because here essential energies are left unused, they will lead
to a twisting of the whole personality. A twist is a false general
attitude to life, produced by a natural disposition and by influences of childhood and milieu. To be unable to make reality,
such as it is, the basis of a solid existence will then become a hindrance in life. The instincts are only part of the whole personality.
Experience proves that marriage is by no means a panacea for
this; for after a time, difficulties will again show themselves even
in marriage, though they may appear in a different context.

FLASHBACK TO THE TYPES

People often ask whether married or unmarried women are
the more 'valuable'. Now, this question confuses orders of value
and combines incompatible points of view. If a vital problem becomes a topical subject, it will always be spotlighted and hence
be seen out of proportion. This has happened also here. For one
thing may be good, and yet the other may not be less good. It is
certainly true that the majority of married women are more
'average' than those who remain alone. The reason for this has
nothing to do with differences in 'value', but with psychological
dissimilarities which are quite independent of good or bad and
only suggest different personalities.

The first obstacle met with in this respect is just this concept
of personality. It is used in many contexts and may crop up in
the philosophical, the scientific, psychological and the quite un-
specialized characterological spheres. Hence it can mean something quite different in the different contexts. Here we understand
by *person* a being with an intellectual and spiritual sphere, endowed with an inner world that is conscious of its ego and capable of understanding itself and of pronouncing judgements. Personal existence is given to man as part of his being; he develops
into a personality in the course of a process which, strictly speaking, ends only with death. This process will be sound if one's own
character blends with the stuff that life provides from without
into a harmonious whole forming one's destiny.

The relation between one's own character or introversion and
extroversion has led to the typology elaborated by C. G. Jung.

We have given an account of this in a preceding chapter, and would here only repeat briefly : a person is extroverted if his attitude to reality is chiefly objective, and introverted if it is subjective ; that is to say, metaphorically speaking, if everything that approaches him is passed through the filter of his own individuality. Life is truly lived only if both the experiencing ego and the experienced event are properly proportioned.

It is easy to understand that, according to this psychological classification, the majority of women suitable for marriage will be extroverted, because they make contact with the world and men more quickly. Wholesale judgements on entire groups of people are expressed mostly from the point of view of extroverts, who form opinions more easily. Average equals extroverted. If seen from this point of view, more 'average' women do, indeed, marry. Those for whom it is hard to come out of their shell, and hence to make friends, will have more difficulty in finding a partner.

For this reason there is a greater percentage of introverted or, to use a different expression, of out-of-the-ordinary women among those who remain single. From their point of view the other, extroverted ones, are ordinary, boring or superficial. Hence it is understandable that certain representatives of professional single women think themselves justified in attributing a greater inner value to themselves, while maintaining that intellectually and spiritually indifferent women are more easily married. Now adaptability is of great value for marriage, while the single woman needs it less.

On the other hand, a highly intellectual creative personality may perhaps achieve great things in her own sphere of work and yet be less capable of making a success of her marriage ; not because she is too good for it, but because she is less willing to serve, as a really good wife and mother should. Again, a pleasantly motherly woman who works efficiently in her home and family will, despite excellent conditions, perhaps not be very successful when she has to work for her living, not because she is too 'stupid', but because it is against her nature.

These considerations suggest the idea that there really will be a greater number of sharply individualized personalities among the single than among the married women. In a good marriage the wife will adapt herself to her husband, and change her self-will into willingness to serve her family. This is a process which fulfils rather than destroys feminine nature. Seen from without, such women may perhaps show no 'marks of distinction', while one who has been formed by her profession and a single life will probably have many.

What attitudes and qualities may we expect in a single woman, who corresponds fairly obviously to the introverted type that is shut up in itself? We would once more note in passing, however, that the living human being is never a type, but that certain of its features will fit a type. The strongly introverted woman may have a rich creative imagination, but will be unable to express it; she will find it difficult to make herself understood by others. She will be strongly influenced by subjective factors, and will find a way to another human being only hesitatingly; her feelings will be delicate and easily hurt. It will be hard for her to open herself, even if she urgently wants to do so. She will brood over things a good deal and often fall a prey to introspection, while being extremely sensitive to criticism from others. Experiences of importance to herself, especially praise or blame, will go deep and affect her for a long time. To this will be added the unfortunate tendency to take all setbacks personally.

Clearly life with its difficulties will be hard for these vulnerable, mimosa-like natures, many of whom will be shy of social life and over-anxious. In associations of single women there will always be many of this type. Their great advantages are that they are reliable, exact, thorough and gratefully attached once they have given someone their confidence. They find it difficult to unburden themselves, and since they are well aware of this incapacity, they appreciate it the more if people try to understand them. We should therefore make every effort and exercise much patience and delicacy to achieve this, because we ought not to infer an empty interior from a plain façade. These single women often do much hidden good, putting to shame many a noisy organization by their silent generosity.

We would now turn to the extroverted woman, that is to say, the one who has both her feet firmly on the ground. She will easily adapt herself, and deal squarely both with her work and with other people. She sometimes tends to express her feelings rather too gushingly, she will bear disappointments and failures comparatively easily, not be given to futile introspection, and quickly be satisfied with herself. Extreme representatives of this type will readily enthuse over this, that and the other, and are by no means immune from sudden changes of temper. This is their weak spot. In the sphere of religion this enthusiasm may express itself in a vague emotionalism that feeds on the æsthetic aspect to the detriment of its inner core. Models of virtue will be ardently venerated rather than faithfully imitated, and pleasant religious feelings will feign a degree of intimacy with God that has not yet actually been reached.

The positive characteristics of these women are their capacity for unprejudiced appreciation, energy and an evident interest in ideas of value and their realization. On the other hand, they will be tempted to attach themselves too strongly and too quickly, a tendency which will produce emotional catastrophes that may affect their whole circle; they will also be inclined to follow their heart rather than their head. Types of this kind, too, will not be lacking in any community.

LONELINESS AND ITS REMEDIES

We will now say a word on the question of associations of single women. In the first place, it is a universal human characteristic that the individual should seek society. Now a haphazard agglomeration of people is not yet a society. This requires order, resulting from this, organization, and, above all, a common goal. Our complicated economy contains the most diverse professional associations; they are important, since they look after the numerous external interests of the individual. Professional women will certainly belong to such associations; but they will scarcely help them to overcome their loneliness. This is naturally the main problem of all unmarried persons regardless of their sex. It has never been proved that unmarried men cope better with the problem of loneliness than women; though a man will more easily find partial or pseudo solutions. Excepting the case of priests and religious, if a man remains a bachelor he will in some way differ from the average man, either because he is a genius or because he is a neurotic, or both. But he will more easily be absorbed by his own talents or by his objective interests than a woman, and will be better able to associate with people occasionally and for special purposes. Women, on the other hand, are more easily absorbed by their human relationships and only occasionally attracted by objective interests. The more 'human' a man or a woman is, the more distressed they will be by their own limitations, but the more they will also be elated by the vigour and gifts of their own *and* of the other sex.

Unmarried women have many associations at their disposal,

serving various purposes, which may be humanitarian or political, scholarly, artistic, devoted to sports and games; finally also religious. Yet they will not join them as single women, but as people interested in one or the other of these subjects. Many will, indeed, thus be well provided, being attracted to others and rescued from their isolation.

Others again will not really feel at home in these associations, though they may be grateful because they offer a stimulating change. These might be advised to try associations of professional women, though the international ones cater more for the professional interests and less for the 'single woman'. Nevertheless, they do justice to the feminine individuality. We have in view such organizations as the International University Women and the International Association of Professional Women, both with national and regional sub-sections. Apart from these, there are several societies according to the various professions. We would also mention the large foundations that are closely connected with the new educational opportunities open to women and their changed position in society, dating from the turn of the century. We are not, however, going to give a summary of the question of feminism, but presuppose the recognition of women as personalities in their own right. We would not so much make society aware of the importance of women and fight for their rights, but encourage them to be themselves and oppose their self-depreciation, which exists at least unconsciously.

The former method must also be used, but it will have little effect if women do not understand themselves, and, as is often the case, fail to take their own professional organizations seriously. Just those among them who suffer most from loneliness make least use of the institutions that are already available for their protection and advancement. In any case, they persistently deny—at least unconsciously—their own right to exist. They simply will not admit that there are, and probably must be, single women; they attach no importance to their own fundamental human value.

The single woman seeks not so much to be esteemed and recognized as a worker and member of society, she wants to be called and loved as a person, and also to love and give herself. If we penetrate to the roots of the sufferings that stem from a loneliness hard to bear, we shall find time and again that at decisive periods of their life these women have been lacking the love and care they needed, or had to be content with a caricature of true love.

What they should have is a small group where they are understood and appreciated, where they can talk intimately and be together without the paraphernalia of big 'events'. In a word, we have in mind a kind of women's club with members of similar state and interests, which will offer opportunities for recreation without any other motive than escaping from the oppressive atmosphere of one's own four walls into happier and more homely surroundings. For no 'organization' can meet one's most secret and personal desires, and no 'movement' can give peace to the heart.

Nevertheless, a right appreciation of oneself is not to be achieved by reason or will alone; it must flow from the conviction of the dignity of the intellectual and spiritual human being. It is almost a kind of faith, and where this rests on religious faith it will become the foundation that carries the whole life. Yet the mysterious fact remains that knowledge and conviction, even honest efforts, cannot always be transformed into happy existence; it is difficult to say in what depths or heights the faith in one's own worth should be situated, by which forces it should be nourished, so as to make its transforming powers consciously felt.

One thing is certain : if one nurses self-centred prejudices and sees only the dark sides inseparable from the circumstances, events and complications of one's life, one will never come to realize one's own possibilities, an achievement that is akin to joy. It is a sign of maturity to accept one's fate as it has come to be. Things are as they are because they were meant to be like this. The meaning of life is to fill the place that has been assigned to us, and in which we must also be 'neighbour' to others. There are hundreds of small tasks waiting to be done, which should not be overlooked. Whole libraries are covered with dust, talents remain unused, social contacts are neglected, simply because some unpleasant dissatisfaction with ourselves discourages us from making a start and keeps us turned back on ourselves. Hosts of false judgements will result from this preoccupation, and soon the ability to see beyond ourselves and be attuned to the world outside will be altogether lost.

Religious people looking towards the eternal goal ought not to have such difficulties at all. Yet even they are not proof against the depression which the solitary life often produces in women. There are, however, many religious associations which will help to foster the awareness of the end of life and point out practical ways to achieve it.

An essential point of many humanitarian and almost all religious institutions, recommended especially to those who live alone, is to find fulfilment in social and charitable tasks, and to forget oneself in devotion to the needs of mankind. Today religious associations of the most diverse kind normally combine character education and the building up of the spiritual life with work that transcends one's own self by serving one's neighbour. There are so many various opportunities that really every intellectual and spiritual inclination should be able to find what it needs. Women can associate themselves only very loosely or undertake strict obligations; they may be asked to assist only occasionally, or join in activities needing constant or frequent attendance. The Church especially has great sympathy for the unmarried woman and endeavours to help her to find her place in the world. In the Secular Institutes, which we shall discuss in another section, the religiously minded woman may even take vows while living a free professional life in the world.

Such communities, however, are possible only for strongly religious women; they will not help those of a different type to overcome their loneliness. The difficulty is to relate one's personality to another, for man is made for conversation. There can be no substitute for this, and monologues are not even an emergency solution, they are nothing but an emergency, and will always lead to singularity, not to fulfilment. The longing that wants to transcend self is mistakenly thought to point only to another human being capable of satisfying it completely. But this is not so, even though it might be assumed to have been proved by passionate love that has actually found its fulfilment. Fundamentally, the longing extends into infinity, for it derives from man's own limitless spiritual possibilities. Hence only the religious person related to God can achieve complete fulfilment in another.

Now many people have no idea of the religious 'structure' of man; hence they seek the absolute where it cannot be found, and pass by opportunities for partial fulfilment. So they continue to seek without finding, because they know not the goal. It is, nevertheless, essential to realize that little will be gained by shutting oneself up and forcibly suppressing the desire for another. For this will not lead to a balanced way of life, but probably only to painful self-destruction.

Experience shows that partnership does not give a woman all she needs, quite apart from the fact that no human being can ever satisfy another perfectly. Very feminine women will miss the object of their motherly care even more than a husband. Here the much recommended social work will be found a real help, though it needs much sympathy, ready to understand other people's ways. Many unmarried women of a less feminine type suffer consciously only from the lack of a companion, which is itself only a consequence of their less developed motherliness. They fail to find what they want, because an important feminine trait, though not wholly absent, is not sufficiently conspicuous to attract men. Hence their desire is not so much inspired by a woman's love of caring and making a home as by their longing to see their own being and qualities appreciated and intensified. But a man wants a woman to give him, above all, peace and security; therefore he will pass by a girl who is too exacting. Now, the repose he seeks he might perhaps also find in a woman who appears cool and less compliant, if he were able to satisfy her spiritual and intellectual demands. However, men want not so much to be stimulated and amused; they desire in the first place peaceful receptivity.

A mother knows how helpless creatures can be; she will support, give and care, without troubling too much whether the objects of her love are worthy of it. She will not constantly rub up against the defects of others, but hide and mitigate them. One might almost say it the other way round : wherever there is need for help, motherly women will be found to be.

From this it follows quite naturally that a certain type of single women will attract many others. Quite a respectable number of professional women are by no means disconsolate 'wall-flowers', but themselves walls for innumerable weak and insignificant flowers unable to cope with themselves. The more naturally such a woman has become the centre of a circle, the more spontaneously she gives herself to its members, the more affection will be given back to her. Loneliness will certainly not be a permanent affliction for her, even though it is part of human life that people should sometimes not only be seized but completely knocked out by the feeling of being forsaken. This is inevitable in this world of ours.

It will be futile to tell those independent women who are worried by their fate to join societies, take up hobbies or help other people. For just these women are not tormented by a kind of loneliness that can be cured, but by their own shadow. They are permanently weighed down by their 'passive balance', unable to rid themselves of the idea that life owes them something, even everything. Actually they themselves owe life the main thing, namely to face it, to meet it and to 'go to it'. They are prevented from doing so by constantly staring at their own dreams of desire and fear; like actresses on the unreal stage of their own sealed-off personality.

Such people will often aim at a kind of self-destruction that is not the right way to life; this can be found only in a self-forgetfulness that conquers the world outside.

Now, if we have an empty space inside, we shall never be able so to fill it up with occupations and duties as to leave no void; nor can one that is cluttered up with the wrong kind of 'furniture' be really filled by the right kind. A human being wants to meet another. Not everyone will penetrate so far as those happy ones whose solitude is shared by God.

DIGRESSION ON FRIENDSHIP

It often needs another human being to find God. But is there no other more intimate form of human relationship apart from married couples and the just-mentioned 'circles'? Today we speak much of love and marriage, also of erotic relations, but little of friendship. It is a fairly widespread opinion that women are incapable of friendship with other women; that, if they feel drawn to their own sex, this will lead to unhealthy, hence dangerous, relationships. We would not deny that there are pathological aberrations, even many of them, in proportion with the general state of psychological disease and lack of balance; yet we are of the opinion that friendship is not sufficiently esteemed. The reason for this is the universal materialism and life in the mass. Genuine friendship has been replaced by superficial good-fellowship, and personal relationships have suffered from the tendency of modern technical development to reduce everything to a common denominator. Cinema and wireless have become substitutes for conversation. To this must be added the lack of interest in objective values, and preoccupation of modern men with their own 'personal problems'. A last but not altogether unimportant obstacle to friendship seems to be the psychologization of the inner life. The need for self-expression is not met by a corresponding desire to receive; the dialogue between friends has largely given way to the monologue of confessions made to the psychotherapist. Even apart from actual medical treatment in the case of definite neuroses, modern men desire to relieve their own mind rather than to enrich it. All this is no favourable soil for friendship.

Though observation and description of psychological behaviour are indeed very illuminating for the expert, self-observation as an end in itself is of little avail to the layman. Unless one's own behaviour be correlated to general principles of conduct and the 'concrete' be placed within a spiritual and intellectual context, the individual experiences will not form a meaningful organic whole. Psychological self-representation generally uses interior or exterior experiences only in order to emphasize one's own ego. In the dialogue of friendship, on the other hand, the soul of the friend serves not only as an amplifier of what has been described, but will also supplement and even elevate it; indeed, the conversation between friends will itself become an experience of value.

Today friendship is little esteemed also for this other reason, that modern men think it is lacking 'completeness'. Legitimate conjugal love embraces the whole human being, spirit, soul and body, whereas friendship, being related only to spirit and soul, does not affect the whole man. Now just as genuine love can be realized only through self-sacrifice, so friendship, too, can exist only where men wish each other well, give to each other and forget themselves. Though friendship, like love, does not give possession of a human being, it affords nevertheless intimate exchange and the enjoyment of mutual understanding and service. Friendship is 'incomplete' also for this other reason, that it does not necessarily share the whole condition of life, though this does not mean that it is not worth while. Separate lodgings and different professions will not prevent people from perfecting their affection by sharing many experiences, though these will not develop into a common life. Sympathy is a feeling of affection which may suddenly be called forth by a meeting; yet not every meeting of this kind will lead to friendship. But if this does happen, it means that two people have realized that they have something to 'say' to each other, not in occasional conversation, but by wholly turning towards each other.

We appreciate in our friend the complement and elevation of our own being. Friendship should contribute to the perfection of the friend's nature. Hence, rightly understood, it exists in order to take people out of and above themselves. Therefore only those will be capable of a fruitful friendship who do not take their own self to be the measure of all things. If a person is afraid of his own emptiness and feels he must talk to somebody only to escape that, he has not yet enough of his own to establish a genuine friendship. This is proved by many superficial relationships; people may, indeed, be constantly together, indulge in all manner of activities and entertainments together, and yet be far from happy. In this way two unstable people will often pool their anxieties, their lack of balance and their unanswered vital questions. They will be attached to each other, unable to do without each other, and yet remain tormented and restless. Why is this so?

The popularity of psychology has led to the habit of observing and analysing people, of describing moods and physical states. This has been taken over quite unconsciously by individuals, who consider self-observation as something like their life's work. Thus individual cases become more important to us than the basic principles of human life. Now, the ultimate end of life is certainly not to be found in a thorough analysis of ourselves, which can always only be a means, but in the knowledge and recognition of spiritual values. These will no doubt be most fully revealed in generous love. Therefore it makes us happy if we have found someone worthy of love. This happiness produces a pleasant emotion, hence an increase of value in the sphere of spiritual feeling. It will, however, truly enrich our life only if it leads us to realize the good in and with the friend. This does not mean that we should produce great social achievements together, but that the relationship must be experienced and fulfilled in a way worthy of our humanity; it must be shared by the spirit, heart and senses alike and not consist only in an indefinite longing that is a craze rather than a healthy desire for love.

To round off this subject we would say already here, even though not all our readers may follow us thus far, that no love, and no friendship either, is wholly man-made. It has been placed in the soul by the Creator, who in His overflowing love has made man in His own 'image and likeness'. God Himself has given man this love that would constantly urge him beyond the narrow limitations of his ego, so that he should never weary of seeking the true, the good and the beautiful, in order finally to gain God, who is alone true, and good, and beautiful. For no human desire has reached its limits unless it has found God. It is true there are many important stations on this way, one of which may be friendship with another noble human being.

FRIENDSHIP AMONG WOMEN

Since women are spiritual beings and may be open to the manifold values of life, there is no reason why they should not be capable of friendship with one another. Sometimes this has been doubted. But perhaps this may be due to a wrong conception of man, as well as to the tendency of our times in general. For, as has just been said, this is not particularly favourable to friendship, which needs quiet development removed from the rush of everyday life. Therefore we would now recall some kinds of friendship among women. Perhaps those who have been, or still are, enjoying it, may fail to appreciate it in the right way.

There is, first, *the* friend of our girlhood, with whom we used to share everything. No calculating selfishness darkened the harmony of those days, which may even brighten our whole life. However, a friendship that loves to give presupposes a right education in childhood. Mere feelings will produce a proper attitude of mind just as little as good manners come to us from nowhere. Friendship is an attitude, or, in other words, an inner form of behaviour, made visible in external acts. Even children should be taught by example that two people can be united in heart and soul through friendship. This is easy in the case of friendship expressed through hospitality, which is the flower of civilization and also deepens private life. It will be a good idea to give a child the opportunity to treat a small friend as a welcome guest; thus the delicate plant of true frienship will be encouraged to grow. For it belongs to its essence to want to share everything, to gather riches not for oneself, but to spend them for the happiness of a larger circle. For the joy of young human beings will radiate well-being to others.

However, it must now be asked what will be the fate of such friendships when the first common enthusiasm is passed, when the venerated teacher no longer writes her name in one's album, and when, beside the shared joys of the gallery in the theatre, the individual ones of the dancing lessons make their appearance. This might bring about a loosening in the childhood friendships. For there are really women who are incapable of genuine friendship with other women. Such types will easily sacrifice friendships with girls to passionately desired relations with the other sex, or make them serve these latter. For example, the friendship with the sister of a young man is used to gain the brother; and if this has been achieved, the sister is dropped because it is undesirable that she should know one's secrets. If, however, she should be retained in order to provide an alibi, the friendship will have lost its bloom, and nothing is left but cheap matiness. Then there will be no end of whispering—a habit that knows no age limit. Such women will still continue to whisper with each other as ripe matrons, even though their secrets will no longer concern their first love. Later their gossip about their neighbours will be equally breathless and inexhaustible, because this, too, will have forbidden things for its subject. Women of this type continue to long for what is not permitted all their lives. It is quite evident that they cannot enjoy friendship.

Unfortunately this type is more noticeable than the harmoniously developed woman; therefore the prejudice that women are incapable of friendship with their own sex is understandable. Friendship between women is put to the test when relations with the other sex develop and are consummated in marriage, which in itself does not necessarily spell death to girlhood friendship. If the other one marries too, they will perhaps be separated by space, but the inner relationship may even grow stronger. If they meet again after a separation of years, during which only few letters have been exchanged, they will mostly resume their relationship as if they had parted only yesterday. In later years such a meeting will become a veritable feast; perhaps this girlhood friend will be the only one who has still known the other's mother, who died early, and of whom the daughter can speak freely only with her.

Then there is the unmarried friend who takes a deep interest in the married one and her family. Not every single woman views the family life of others with bitterness; many truly feminine natures fully accept their own lot and preserve their girlhood friendship without envy. In such a case the growing children will often feel deeply her love for their mother and the latter's love for her friend. Many girls have shaped their ideals after their mother's friend, the professional woman who found her recreation in their family circle, who shared all their joys and sorrows, and many a time helped the daughters discreetly and tactfully in their difficulties.

Nothing, however, is more unpleasant for a husband than if he has reason to suspect that another woman knows the intimacies of his married life. But these are aberrations, signs of stupidity and narrowness. The true friend will also be liked by the husband, and if she is generous and intelligent she will be a social asset to the home. But we should perhaps mention in this connexion that it is a law of life that it not only gives but also demands. Every state has its advantages as well as its drawbacks. The unmarried friend will certainly sometimes feel unwanted; in the same way the married woman, too, will have her hours of depression when, unknown to her friend, she will envy the other's freedom.

Women who know how to run a house generally form a social centre without wanting to do so. Young girls gladly look up to them, and will do the same even after their marriage. Lonely and unattached people, and those who have not found their feet in the world, like to be with them and reward their unconsciously given care with attachment and silent love.

Now, these are the same kind of women whom we have described in the first part. They have been leaders in their youth, and remain so later in life; there are many of these among the unmarried. Friendships between single women will naturally be largely determined by their mutual need for a complementary character. One of them will always be the leader, whereas the other will gladly take a more passive rôle—these will be the shy, clinging ones, who may sometimes even give the impression of being tyrannized, though this can be deceptive. Both sides may lovingly give to each other; only one will do so in a more active way, whereas the other will contribute her share with the gesture of expectancy, ready to receive whatever the friend has to offer. We may think, for example, of the housekeeper of a famous artist, who will be far more than a mere servant. Or take the faithful secretaries of women in leading positions; here it is easy to see how giving and receiving can be inextricably bound up with each other. Women working in collaboration, especially in the social, political or charitable spheres, prove time and again how productive such friendships can be. In fact, such common work will create noble friendships among women more easily than among men. It would betray a very one-sided outlook if one were to point only to examples of the opposite. Isolated cases of lack of harmony prove nothing against the majority of others. The religious Orders have at all times offered convincing arguments for the efficacy of friendship and concord between women. But of this we will speak later.

No woman ought to be ashamed of friendship with others of her sex. It is one of the finest flowers of humanity indicating that goodness, self-forgetfulness and loving care for others are powerful factors in life.

FRIENDSHIP WITH MEN

Like all other human relationships, a close friendship especially has to be marked by discipline, else it will degenerate into matiness, mutual exploitation and a mere occasion for amusement. If even a friendship between women must be safeguarded by moderation and reserve, this will have to be even more the case when it is a question of friendship between an unmarried woman and a man.

So we have come to the much-discussed subject of friendship between man and woman. The possibility of a 'pure' friendship is frequently denied. If 'pure' were to be understood to refer to two a-sexual beings who are not properly male and female nor react in such a way, we should indeed have to agree. But this is hardly thinkable, since the differences between the sexes are by no means restricted to the functions preserving the species, but show themselves in their whole attitude to life. Whatever they experience or desire will be marked by their masculine or feminine reactions. Thus understood there is, indeed, no 'pure' friendship.

If the idea be, however, that every relationship between man and woman serves an instinctive desire and is determined by sexuality, that there are, in fact, only sensual relationships, then we cannot share this view. Man has, indeed, instincts, but he is certainly not dominated by them. He should develop in the direction of regulating instinctive desires through his spiritual and intellectual personality. All depends on the guiding light he follows, whether he serves an ideal and accomplishes certain tasks, or simply lives from day to day intent only on his pleasure.

Man has no doubt been created for companionship. He wants to be spoken to, and to be allowed to speak himself. Moreover, everyone is prevented by his own limitations from being self-sufficient; hence something urges him to approach another. Mankind as a whole, too, is meant for 'complementation'. Community is not a sum of individuals, it is the interplay of the energies of all seeking to balance each other.

Not everyone is destined to find the one partner for life; this becomes quite clear in the existence of unmarried women. Yet they, too, need other human beings. Many are satisfied with slight contacts; some have happy family relations; professional women may often find fulfilment in the relation to their mother for the best part of their life. There are as many possibilities as there are destinies.

This, however, does not prevent even the single woman from having a closer relationship with a man, who may mean much to her heart. It should be noted, however, that we are speaking here of the mature woman whose life is determined in its main features. She has found her place and is satisfied with this. She does not feel disinherited because she is living alone; she has understood what just this life means for her. An eighteen-year-old girl, unless she be destined for a very special career, will not have finished with her plans and expectations. This would be strange, indeed. For her it would be very unsuitable to entertain a relationship with a man which for some reason or other could not lead to marriage. In such a case we should think a 'pure friendship' very unlikely. In the life of a mature professional woman, however, this appears possible. It requires, indeed, inner independence, energy and renunciation of the complete fulfilment of a woman's life. It is of course absolutely incompatible with disturbing or even destroying another marriage. It is always immoral to procure one's own happiness at the expense of another woman, and will never, in the long run, lead to interior peace. But friendship is meant to produce precisely this, with the help of understanding the other and wishing him well.

The most obvious case is that of a friendship grown out of common professional work. It must be admitted this often looks one-sided, in that the woman seems to be the one who does all the service. But here the same consideration holds good as has been applied to friendship among women; many women in a confidential position are fully satisfied with this 'confidence' as their share. Private secretaries of long standing take a personal interest in the life of their employer; their work satisfies them ultimately only because it is done for a person. It is, indeed, sufficient for them to be united to another only through their work. Surely this, too, is friendship? They are industrious, intelligent women who have gained financial security and are deeply attached to their employer's person and work. Are they all supposed to be unhappy because they did not become wives and mothers? The reality seems different.

If some women work harder than they need do, this extra is surely the service of friendship; of course, we have to distinguish whether an employer takes undue advantage of his employee, or if she herself adds more on her own account. The first case does not concern us here. In the second we have again to distinguish between its immature and its authentic form. We can hardly speak of friendship based on one's own decision if a woman will not admit her feelings for a certain man, if her exertions seem excited and her fussiness is still a kind of wooing. Such a woman is not at all satisfied with her position. Her selfishness, combined with her desire to be admired and thought indispensable, will result in crazy activity, which others realize to be the outcome of unfulfilled desires. Just these women will be scarcely conscious of their feminine desires and think themselves animated by purely altruistic motives.

If friendship is what it ought to be, namely benevolent love that wants to give, it must be unobtrusive. Conspicuous marks of affection, benefits breathlessly showered on the object of one's choice, always indicate that a person has not yet mastered the depths of her being. Only if she has accepted the sacrifice as painful will it be possible no longer even to desire physical fulfilment. It is a great mistake to pretend that the sacrifice of this is the automatic result of recognizing moral principles. If we are to make an absolutely valid order our own, we shall have consciously to open up the centre of our being. It is undeniably one of the positive results of contemporary psychology to have recognized this necessity. Spiritual decisions are certainly in conformity with human nature, but they have to be made. Everything depends on this being done without self-deception.

The restless busybodies among the professional women will drop their childish ways and become fully adult only if they admit with tears that their gifts offered on the altar of neighbourly love still savour a little of trying to conjure up the Prince Charming. This ulterior motive is generally noticed by the recipient earlier than by the giver, and this explains why so much eager activity of very reliable women remains futile. Here less would often be more.

These women imagine that they can always only give without desiring anything else. They are incapable of diluting their love sufficiently to make it acceptable to the other. But the average person cannot stand this sort of love, which will therefore be met with surprise, misinterpretation and misunderstandings. Its power is so great that the women afflicted with it will suffer even from its own reflection, as far as this becomes visible in the other. It is hopeless if love hangs in the air, as it were. For it cannot remain there, but will fall back on the lover and tear her heart. Such women experience this as failure; but, given the law of their nature, they have made no 'mistake'. They reveal the fate of 'useless' love. It is strange that love that aims straight so often misses its object; love should be 'played', it must simply happen in order to be bearable for the other.

Delicately constituted women, especially, who would not entertain a 'low' thought and imagine that their love is directed only to the 'neighbour' and not to the man, often suffer acute torments. Their sensual instincts have been taken out of their appropriate soil and become related to their spiritual and moral nature. Now, these instincts do not, indeed, change the direction of the love that ascends the heavens and wants to take even the 'neighbour' with it in its flight, but they fill the spiritual and moral sphere, so to speak, with their own ardour, and make everything heavy with a longing for consolation and peace. This can so oppress the sufferers that they feel they are dying of weakness, misery and frustration.

The situation will be quite different where the above-mentioned conspicuous and heavy-going love has been purified by conscious effort and transformed into a gentle accompaniment of life. Such a woman has accepted her fate with all its difficulties and defects, and is now really capable of selfless friendship. She has also admitted to herself that she loves her employer, if such be the case. She knows exactly how far this love will be satisfied; there will be the common work, the common service and the joy of being esteemed as absolutely reliable. There may occasionally be an hour's friendly chat, nothing more. Yet she will be happy to know that she performs her daily duties for 'the right man', and is sending the ray of her love through the prism of his personality, whence it will come back to her own heart broken into a hundred colours. For this marvel will ever repeat itself : love that does not contradict its own being cannot be lost; it will renew the one who gives it. It is, in its deepest aspect, the primeval power of the spirit, that becomes creative through recognizing and affirming worth, not in frigid separation but in community of heart and mind. A woman who loves in this way will know that the man for whom she works understands, more, esteems her. Even though the man's part in this kind of friendship is not very active, he will meet his assistant, in contrast with the aforementioned examples, with reverence. By this, apart from recognizing her personality, he will express his silent respect for her friendship and his own response to it.

It seems that mature women are lacking in courage for friendship with men. This may be due to the devaluation of spiritual realities and the lack of understanding for interior liberty, which is usually mistaken for emptiness of soul. It is a great boon to be on terms of friendship with a strong personality who scorns neither his own nor the other's dignity. Of course this will be most fruitful between spiritually alive people who are interested in objective values. After all, spiritual longing is no less vitalizing than physical urge, and there is no reason why, when growing older and more mature, one should not enjoy the one while giving up the other.

We would stress once more that the fulfilment of one's nature is more important than mere sexual satisfaction. A woman without feeling is a complete misfit, whereas a barren womb means no more than that an organ has been left unused, as happens in all departments of nature.

It goes without saying that we do not mean to recommend a kind of friendship with men which, while avoiding the 'one thing', would deprive a wife of her husband's affection. No good can result from a situation in which a man regards his marriage as a desert and the company of his unmarried woman friend as an enjoyable oasis. Here the only solution is separation before the marriage breaks up completely.

In these cases pity is often adduced as a motive for continuing the relationship. Now, it is true that pity belongs to love and softens desire into tenderness. However, in the situation in question pity is not very pure, but intimately linked to the satisfaction derived from the thought of being the freely chosen object of a man's affection, even though not its legitimate one. Oneself is not, indeed, the recognized wife, nor physically a mother, but has been able to oust a wife and mother. Here some phases of an interior development have been telescoped and subconscious suspicions consolidated into conscious facts. Such a woman will hardly see things so clearly; she will probably postpone a clarification all the time. But the very question "What is wrong with our friendship?" can be asked only in a time when the personal situation means everything and the superior institution nothing.

It is true, tragic cases exist, caused for example by a wrong choice of marriage partners, psychological immaturity, ignorance about the nature of marriage or a belated awakening. But surely these defects can never prove that the other woman is the right one. They seem rather to indicate that there is yet another possibility of error. 'The great passion' does exist, and certainly also outside marriage. Dante was not married to Beatrice, nor Hœlderlin to Diotima.[1] The very great love in marriage is rare, though marriage may contribute much to the ripening of love; but it is equally rare outside marriage. What happens normally is that one had not sufficient strength to resist the attraction from the beginning, though one knew quite well one ought to have done so. This weakness has led to a friendship that is rotten within. But if a really great love breaks all the barriers, one ought to face the consequences. One has placed oneself outside the law, but should not make one's unbounded thirst for freedom into a virtue. Even so, such an attitude will be possible only to strong characters. If they prefer sin to renunciation, this is a matter for their own conscience; we cannot know the ways in which certain natures have to be purified. But one should not dramatize one's own weakness, indolence and self-indulgence into a tale of heroism. People of extraordinary spiritual stature are also capable of extraordinary friendships. Thus it may happen that the woman who is the spiritual friend of a married man may not only not disturb but even help his marriage. Such men and women will be devoted to their work, and take their responsibility to the community very seriously. They will master even an unusual destiny; but to master it means to make decisions according to one's conscience, and act accordingly, not to leave things to chance and perpetuate one's weaknesses.

A woman can hardly learn theoretically whether it is better for her to specialize in friendships with women or with men. But the single woman, too, must take account of the fact that human beings depend on each other. Just those in most urgent need of an understanding heart, whether of another woman, a man or a member of their own family, often find it most difficult to free

---

[1] Hœlderlin (1770–1843), German lyrical poet, whose love for the wife of his employer, Susette Gontard ('Diotima'), inspired much of his finest poetry.

themselves from the obsession with their own self. The way to the
other will be found only through the right form of self-love, not
through self-hatred. If a woman is permanently dissatisfied with
herself and does not like herself at all (in this case because she
refuses to accept her unmarried state), she will never attain to that
understanding of herself that will replace vainly desired self-forgetfulness by unselfishness. Now, we can become unselfish only if
we have found ourselves. For how can we leave self behind if we
still passionately seek it? And how could we not seek it if we have
never happily accepted and appreciated ourselves? If we have
not made a place for ourselves in our own heart? We need only a
narrow space within ourselves, where much will find room. But
this is where we belong. It is certainly curious that those who have
exterminated themselves from their own heart can never fill just
this heart. The right form of self-love seems to fill a leak which
would cause to flow away all other values we would like to appropriate.

We have argued throughout that in order to cope with life we
must first admit and accept the vocation given to us. However important our own attitude to our state in life, it must be conceded
that it is difficult to free oneself altogether from the influence of
general opinion. Today much of the prejudice against the professional single woman has been overcome. It is a sign of the positive development that these women are almost recognized pub-
licly as a separate state. Now, if self-esteem is to be strengthened,
a definite setting will be needed. Noble friendship demands a corresponding social life, which in its turn requires appropriate lodgings. Here things are on the move, as has been indicated elsewhere. It is not within the scope of this work to discuss the external conditions more fully.

In these chapters we are concerned to point out to unmarried
women their manifold human possibilities and to urge them to use
this capital. It is consonant with women's nature to penetrate to
objective values and to realize spiritual ideals by way of personal
relationships. Therefore social or individual contacts will always
have a special importance for them.

FRIENDSHIP WITH PRIESTS

A special form of friendship, which may come to every Catholic Christian, is friendship with a priest who has renounced attachment to a single person for the sake of the Kingdom of Heaven.

Surely the high-minded single woman need not anxiously avoid all intellectual and spiritual exchange with a priest. For it is precisely in him that she will meet a noble personality capable of introducing her to a higher view of existence, since he proves himself how celibacy can lead to a perfectly integrated life.

As a matter of principle, it must be conceded that such a friendship is possible; above all, because only man and woman together can represent the life of the spirit in its totality. The priest of our time must descend into all the depths of human life, and may not remain entrenched in the sphere of the 'sacred'. Hence he needs messengers to put him in touch with everyday life and indicate the direction his missionary activities are to take. This important 'material' will be brought to him chiefly by women, since they have access to the intimate spheres of life more readily than men. Hence it is only desirable that the religiously minded professional woman should be able both by her personal and by her objective qualifications to prepare the priest for the situation in the pagan desert, and to acquaint him with the way of life of those estranged from God. In the interests of apostolic co-operation there should be easy contacts between priests and lay women, based on mutual trust and reverence, without barricades on the one side and misplaced shyness on the other. Objective conversations on matters of interest without too much social formality would relieve the situation on both sides. Thus the priest would find an easier entrance into the profane life, and the lay woman into the sacramental sphere of the Church.

However, such a relationship will have a different aspect if it is not devoted to general apostolic tasks, but if a sacramental relationship with a confessor develops into a wider spiritual direction, so that all spheres of a woman's life will become part of her regular conversations with the priest. Such an intense spiritual relationship is possible only if the priest is attuned to her also in the human sphere. This may well be called a form of friendship, even though the exchange does not take place on the same level. Certainly every religiously inclined woman is fortunate to find a priest who will enrich her interiorly, discover to her the depths of union with God, and direct her attention to the needs of her fellow-men. The advantages of good religious direction are so great that a devout Christian should prudently accept also its drawbacks. For a woman these do, indeed, exist; we should deny the many-layered variety of human nature if we attempted to deny them.

If we have at last found someone who understands us and encourages our religious and moral aspirations, we shall hardly want to forgo this beneficial influence. On the contrary, we shall rightly try to make as much use of it as possible. It is a fact of experience that sympathy and understanding on the one side, and gratitude on the other, may lead to all but indissoluble unions far deeper than any social relationships. The party most enriched by them will certainly see in them a gift of providence.

It is in woman's nature that her mind, heart and imagination will also turn to the person to whom she opens her soul. Neither the most cautious guidance nor the greatest restraint on the part of the priest can prevent that this relationship will result in affecting the whole human being of the woman, and that the development of her personality will be somehow marked with his individuality. Yet she is allowed to share his life only in that narrow sphere formed in her by his spiritual direction. If such a friendship is kept within these limits, however deeply a woman may be affected by it, she ought not to be advised against it, and there will be no reason for anticipating unfavourable developments. Nevertheless, from time to time she will feel the pain of the resignation just mentioned.

Certainly innumerable women will be under the direction of the same confessor for years without the slightest difficulty. This will be possible for two reasons. Either it is simply a case of following a rule of life, without the whole personality being engaged in this direction, or the penitent herself may be one of those immature, pliable, unmarried women whose desire for partnership has remained dormant, because their womanhood has never been fully developed.

A man who appeals to a woman spiritually and intellectually cannot remain totally unimportant to her in the natural sphere, especially if she is of a feminine type and has not completely resigned herself to her unmarried state. For a woman needs no physical desire to fan her ardour; she is capable of being consumed by the fires of the soul. It would be foolish to avoid spiritual direction because of this danger. But it would be also unworthy of the serious desire for Christian perfection to pretend to attain the supernatural end without the aid of natural means, and to attribute disturbances caused by devotion to the person of the priest to mystical trials. Here a clear insight is needed for the sake of spiritual progress, which would be hindered by a lack of interior honesty. But if a woman is sufficiently disciplined to refrain from dragging the priest to whom she gives her confidence into the affairs of her secular life, she will reap abundant blessings from the direction she receives. She will grow to maturity through painful, perhaps unacknowledged, desires that cannot be fulfilled. But apart from this, her conscious resignation will bring forth inner joy and security, which will cast their radiance over her whole life. For it is part of a true culture to know the importance of frontiers and limitations. Yet within these there should flow a rich spiritual life, with room for genuine exchange and discussions of more than personal importance. Intensive spiritual direction of a professional woman in the world is impossible without the discussion of urgent contemporary tendencies and needs, which would also be profitable to the priest.

We should not fight shy of calling such relations with a trusted priestly adviser of long standing by the name of friendship. It can be lasting only if it be based on mutual confidence. These considerations are irrelevant, however, if the priest functions only in the confessional, in connexion with the Sacrament of Penance. In this case his human personality will play no part at all. But in the wider context of direction given in conversation, mutual understanding in the spiritual sphere is absolutely essential, else it will remain ineffectual. Now, in the case of a woman such a relationship will bring about interior attachments which must be properly recognized and controlled, else they will become a mysterious burden in the depth of her soul that will give her no peace. It is impossible completely to remove the priestly intermediary, who may be the first to open up to a woman the immense world of the spiritual life. Religion itself is full of mysteries, and so is its priestly interpreter, who, as a man, represents for her the other half of the world.

This subject may be rounded off by the passage from St. John's Gospel (20 : 17), in which the risen Lord says to St. Mary Magdalene who is weeping at the tomb : "Do not touch me, for I am not yet ascended to my Father. But go to my brethren and say to them . . ." Here the priest is placed between heaven and earth, or, rather, it is implied that he has no definite place. He mediates between heaven and earth, hence we cannot count on him as being always at our disposal. It is true, he gives us the fruits of his vocation, but we may not become attached to his person. Friendship with him is not situated within the closed circle of ordinary human relationships, but in the freedom of the children of God, which opens into the world above. Certainly, there is an authentic meeting between priest and woman in the pastoral sphere, in which they come to know each other, becoming conscious of the radiance of their personalities. But this communion is in spirit and in truth. They are not meant to become absorbed in each other, but to seek the eternal goal. No doubt a woman will sometimes deliberately have to recall this end of the friendship, which is expressed by the Cross. If she is not strong enough for that, she had better avoid closer contact with priests.

FRIENDSHIP WITH GOD

We must not conclude this chapter on the friendships of unmarried women without at least hinting at the security they would find in friendship with God. If a woman can say, according to Rilke, "You are the guest she receives in gentle evenings. You are the second in her solitude, the peaceful centre of her monologues . . ." then she has arrived at the stage where the question 'Why?' is changed into 'For what purpose?' If a man 'has' God, nothing can happen to him. This is a truism for the faithful, but unintelligible for those without the religious superstructure of life. Now, we would not like to be understood to mean by this that we consider religious faith an ornament fit only for adorning sensitive souls, but unsuitable for more robust, earthly natures. In order to avoid this misunderstanding we should perhaps rather have spoken of the religious roofing of life, so as to indicate that it is essential for a complete human nature to turn towards the Eternal One. There may be many people nowadays who have never discovered their own roof or summit, who are completely wrapped up in what is visible and tangible, and never look farther than the present, though they have made material provision till the end of their life. And there may be others who vaguely believe in man's 'religious destiny' but not really in God. Such people are not altogether averse to external worship, and swell the ranks of those who figure in statistics as members of some denomination. They are satisfied if life is set within a framework of religious ceremonies; even more, they are convinced on these occasions that they are themselves formed by religion. But they are related only to a mysterious 'It', to an intangible *thing*, both in the literal and in the metaphorical sense. Nothing can 'happen' between this thing and man. Certainly, the 'thing' provides rules and somehow arranges life. But one is no more intimately related to it than to the travelling agency responsible for the smooth working of our holiday arrangements. One darkly knows that, if one pays one's tribute properly—that is to say, if one neither commits murder nor steals; in short, if one is not grossly immoral—nothing can and ought to happen to one.

Few are really aware of the fact that faith is friendship with God or, better, friendship of God with man. He has begun it; He has called man by his name and will never forget him. He is always ready, a friend who constantly waits before our door; only most baptized people do not know this. What a help this Friend could be to the unmarried woman. She suffers so much because no one is completely at her disposal, because she must always ask if somebody has time for her. One's fellow-men are so unreliable! When do her friends write to her from pure affection, only to make the lonely creature happy? They write, because they want to get something off their chest, because they are just in the mood for saying something or other. People think of the recipient only if they are actually in love, or when they are already completely purified.

Yet God has written to His friends in such a way that each one of them is considered and addressed in his individuality. God cares for the religious-minded woman not just superficially and in general, but personally, in the living word of Holy Scripture. If anyone now disappointedly shakes her head and turns away, she has not yet let herself be really called; believing means to trust the friend, the fatherly, the motherly, the brotherly friend, according to the individual's needs. God, who is inexhaustible, who is greater than all, whose resources never fail, will adapt Himself. He knows what this, or that, or another woman needs.

Most people fight shy of trusting implicitly, of simply listening. "Yes, but I am not firm in the faith." "But do I have the right faith?" "And then, anyhow—no, it is impossible." It is strange, indeed; there is the constant misery, the struggle against the feeling of loneliness, the unrest, the unsatisfied desires. One knows one is 'a failure', one realizes the unrelieved childhood troubles, the great faults and the little bad habits. Every day one reads prescriptions for a good life in the papers. One starts, one stops again, one feels better for a little while—then one is again submerged in one's misery.

Why will the person who is trying to be religious not go to the Bible? Are the events described there really so boring, are the parables flat, the teachings sour morality? If a believing Christian asserts this, he can never have read in it. The single professional woman has a bookshelf full of reading matter; but she knows it all, it does not attract her. She would not dream of standing before the multicoloured backs, dipping into the individual authors to enjoy their cultivated and wonderfully silent company.

One thinks even less of making it a habit—and it would really be an excellent one—to take down the New Testament after the day's work. One need do nothing else but open it in the spirit of faith. God will do the rest. When all is so quiet that we are startled when the floor creaks, when the air seems to be humming with silence, when we are longing for the presence of another, haunted by gruesome imaginings, or when we are burdened by our own self—then we ought to open the Bible, sure of finding a friend. This kind of advice, of course, cannot be followed like a cooking recipe; though even a dish of food will not turn out well if one only mixes the ingredients with one's hands while one's mind is far from the work. This is even truer for 'recipes' of living. Certainly not everything depends on the training of the will, at least not on the active will that wants to be up and doing. It is far more a question of the interior will to self-abandonment, of an unquestioning readiness for existence. This is not the will in jackboots, the achievements of which can often be enjoyed by the senses; it is the willingness to be a creature. Because we are creatures, we sense tendencies in ourselves that cannot be completely cleared up only by inquiring reason; we carry remembrances that go beyond the temporal faculty of memory, we feel a profound desire for more than merely human fulfilment.

Such will be the preparations for a conversation with the divine Friend. There are people of exemplary hospitality, who will almost kill themselves when they have guests. The table bends under the load of dishes, no plate is left empty, the host is perpetually on the move. Always something or other is still missing. It is impossible to talk quietly as long as the meal lasts. Eventually the table is cleared; now would be the time. But by then the host is so exhausted by the preparations and the guest by his efforts to cope with the meal, that the really important things are left undiscussed.

Certain people behave in a similar way when they want to make contact with God. First they will make endless arrangements and preparations; they will read lots of books which they think ought to lead them there, and yet they will fail in their purpose. They think they ought to come to it with plenty of well-meant plans, but as this is impossible in busy everyday life, and quite hopeless after a full working day, they will achieve nothing. They think that one cannot just start reading the New Testament a few minutes before going to bed; so to speak *en passant*—that would be irreverent. So they decide against it, and do it neither today nor tomorrow—perhaps never.

The fact is that religious faith does not remain ineffective because reason cannot grasp it. The natural knowledge of God is accessible to every human reason prompted by a good will; for the supernatural knowledge, however, reason must be willing to follow the authority that guarantees the truth; it must incline the will to obey the will of God, and the precepts of His representatives. If a person entrusts himself to the teaching authority of the Church, he will also accept her priestly and pastoral ministrations. Thus he will know the range of his duties, the Sacraments, prayer and the twofold precept of love. This programme will provide so many personal suggestions and, what is even more decisive, will clear up so much the meaning and conduct of one's own life that such a person will be well able to live alone without the companionship of marriage.

Without an inner meaning, life dissolves into its diverse components. It contains nothing of importance beyond the present moment; above all, misery, need and adversities remain 'indigestible', like immovable pieces of rock against which the memory continues to hurt itself. The mirror of religious faith establishes order in the happenings of life, like the optical square in the coloured pieces of the kaleidoscope. Seen with the eyes of faith, life has an orderly pattern, in which everything serves to free the spark of eternal life from the suffocating weeds, and to reveal increasingly even now the eternal destiny of man. The infallible sign of this is growth in neighbourly love.

APOSTOLIC WORK AS A SIGN OF FRIENDSHIP WITH GOD

(Catholic Action, Legion of Mary, Secular Institutes)

There is no living love of God that does not react on men. This reaction produces the desire to work for men in the service of God's Kingdom. Everyday life offers innumerable opportunities for this in the manner of the 'Little Way' of St. Teresa of Lisieux. Nevertheless, it will prove difficult if one has to rely on one's own devices without any particular incentives. Energy will slacken, and with it interest in tasks of essentially 'ideal' value without much visible success. Besides, a serious Christian life in the world of today will seem folly to the outsider. People seeking to live from within, who refuse to compromise with the ordinary mass suggestions in questions of taste and conscience, have no home in the centres of life in the mass.

But man must have a home somewhere, where he knows himself understood and appreciated. Here the Third Orders, the Marian Congregations for people in the world, or the adult branches of the old religious Youth Movement, will offer a suitable background for the life of professional women. There are as many possibilities as there are human types. Within the Church everyone can find a group to suit her, to give her companionship and security.

In our time personal religious life is usually combined with the apostolate, by which we understand tasks undertaken for the Kingdom of Heaven.

There is first of all the comprehensive Catholic Action, which would offer the unmarried woman opportunities for deepening her religious culture. From there she could be led towards apostolic work.

The Legion of Mary is well known. It is an association of Catholic men and women of every age and condition of life, approved by the Church, which, under the guidance of Mary, the mediatrix of God's love and justice, actively helps priests in their apostolate. It is called the Legion of Mary because it is an army of lay apostles organized on military lines; its aim is to win back the masses to Christ. But as it is impossible to spiritualize men in the mass, its members strive to make personal contacts. Two by two the legionaries visit families in their homes, for their immediate aim is not the social apostolate but the religious renewal of hearts.

When this will have been achieved, the way will be free for a new social order in the spirit of Christ. In principle the Legion does not confine itself to a special definite form of activity. It places its members at the disposal of bishops and parish priests for any kind of apostolic work. The legionaries go from street to street, from house to house, from one family to another. They visit hospitals, sleeping quarters, poor-houses and prisons. They work in offices and factories, in schools and universities, for the Legion is a very active organization. Nevertheless, prayer is the source of its activity. For it knows that the apostolate is essentially the work of divine grace. The Legion is thoroughly organized, and takes possession of the whole human being; its members would find it difficult, indeed, to feel isolated or superfluous. The Legion's action will carry them, provided they are in it with heart and soul.

The problem, in fact, is not really that there are no ways to overcome loneliness. This could only be the case if one were living on an isolated island. The difficulty is only that many find it hard to walk in these ways. Faith is not strong enough to become a source of energy feeding the whole life. Thought and imagination are not occupied by faith, which in concrete fact means the Kingdom of God on earth, but for the greater part by longings to have their own natural desires fulfilled. Otherwise it would be easier to integrate religious ends into daily life. The difficulty of an immediate religious programme lies in the fact that it must be realized through discipline, self-denial and sacrifice, and can ultimately be attained only after death. Certainly faith will offer even on earth unimaginable bliss and joy, the first-fruits of a future happiness that can never be lost. But we must add, for the sake of truth, that the higher delights of religion are only for those who have really abandoned themselves to God for better or for worse. Here not everything depends on good will alone.

Nevertheless, it remains true that a life consciously based on faith will so enrich and support people that everyone who feels even a faint call to it should faithfully pursue this way. Today it is even possible for unmarried professional women to be completely at the disposal of God and His Church within the sphere of their actual work. By recognizing the so-called Secular Institutes, the Apostolic Constitution, *Provida Mater Ecclesia*, of February 2nd, 1947, has created an entirely new form of ecclesiastically established women's communities for the propagation of God's Kingdom in the world.

These communities, which are adapted to the needs of our present time, form a separate estate in the Church, in the same way as the religious Orders. They cater for women (in principle also for men) who remain in the world, living with their families or alone, yet according to the three evangelical counsels of poverty, chastity and obedience. After a period of formation and trial, they bind themselves by private vows or promises to obey the evangelical counsels and the Constitutions of their Institute. We will here describe in detail one of these Institutes, in order to give the uninitiated an idea of their spirit and activities, taking as our example the Institute of 'Our Lady of the Way' whose mother-house is in Vienna.

This Secular Institute was organized by professional women in 1936, and canonically erected on March 7th, 1948. By methodically striving for perfection it aims at giving its members a sufficiently thorough religious training and formation to fit them for furthering God's Kingdom in the world. The means employed are devotion to the interior life and observance of the Evangelical Counsels, to which members are obliged by vow.

The community of 'Our Lady of the Way' is especially anxious to preserve the character of a Secular Institute, hence it deliberately rejects community life. Its members live with their families, for whose support they are responsible if necessary. They dress according to their social position, and are in no way distinguishable from their surroundings by their customs or in any other way.

They combine the apostolate with their own sanctification. The former is to be exercised particularly within their profession. Hence much importance is attached to a sound professional training, and later to continued attention to progress and efficiency in one's work. The apostolate in the world is invisible; the Institute itself does not provide jobs, nor does it urge a certain 'line' on its members, nor interest itself in a particular department within the Church in order to gain a definite sphere of work and thus a platform for its activities. It accepts all professions, from the industrial to the intellectual worker. Its professional consciousness is solely religous, it penetrates external features from within, not the other way round. This was also the intention of the Holy Father when he asked the Secular Institutes to be the salt of the earth, the light of the world and the leaven in the lump. Members prepare for the apostolate in the world in common, but place and manner of these activities will differ. For in the opinion of this community,

if the external professional aims become too standardized, there
will be the danger of changing it into a mere utilitarian association. Its great ideal is to achieve genuine spiritual education and
sanctification, capable of changing the world by their very existence.

This is to be done by faithfully fulfilling the Constitutions.
These are animated by the spirit of the Ignatian Exercises, hence
are nourished on feeling and living with the Church. The guiding
principles of the community are, in a nutshell : God is the Lord,
Christ is the Way, Love is the Goal.

The core of it all is obedience to the superiors. It is a great
achievement to practise this in such a way that it will be truly
spiritually fruitful. The changing conditions of life will prevent
stagnation and empty formalism. For obedience has really to be
fashioned anew every day. This shows itself in practice in the
monthly accounts to the Provincial Director or other senior Sisters.
In these accounts the external work and conditions will be discussed, but the advising Sister interferes in no way with questions
of conscience. It is a truism that spiritual progress is impossible
without order ; in the same way, order is impossible without adequate book-keeping.

The spirit of poverty finds its place in the monthly balance-sheet
of income and expenses ; for larger or regular expenses permission
must be asked from the superiors.

We cannot here give an account of the daily spiritual horary,
which is adapted to work in the world. The spirit of the community is most clearly visible in the annual Retreats, in which the
Sisters of the different regions are gathered together. Otherwise
members of the various districts meet for religious celebrations,
Quiet Days, but also for lectures on a large variety of subjects.

The life of the Institute in general is adapted to the requirements as they arise. The Constitutions are sufficiently elastic to
allow for the many ramifications of life in the world. The main
difference between Secular Institutes and conventual communities
is clearly that every member lives by himself, or herself, 'outside'.
But perhaps it is not so evident in what way these Institutes differ
from the older religious organizations of Christians in the world.
Their distinctive feature is that they penetrate a person's whole
life, being a vocation in the same way as the religious Orders.
They involve strict obligations, and the evangelical counsels, confirmed by vow, are expected to be lived as perfectly as possible.

This form of life, however, could not be described as 'taking the veil' in the world. This metaphor would misrepresent the reality, for members of these Institutes live, unprotected by walls, unreservedly in the midst of this 'evil world'. For the world that is far from God is to be included in their total surrender to Him, expressed in neighbourly love. Now, since it is extremely difficult for the individual to persevere in this, it is done in community, and in obedience to rules and constitutions that are safe, because they represent the wisdom of the Church.

Naturally there will always be people who will shake their heads and ask what more is done by these organizations than by zealous Christians outside them. Perhaps there may not be 'more done'. It is not a question of collecting good works or achieving success that will show in statistics. But things are done in a different way, because they are done within the particular vocation to this religious state; it is God's will, a divine call. If people mistrust such a life, we can only say : "He that can take it, let him take it." The nature of a religious vocation will be discussed later. First we should like to mention some other modern apostolic institutes.

The 'Handmaids of Christ the King' in Vienna are a community similar to that which has just been described. It is especially designed for women engaged in church work, for whom it was originally founded. This, too, demands a life based on the evangelical counsels, and vows are encouraged. The Constitutions are not inspired by any religious Order, but are adapted to the needs of Catholic Action. The 'Handmaids of Christ the King' should be penetrated, above all, by the spirit of the Gospel, and burn with love and zeal for the honour of the divine King. Despite their wide scope, the Constitutions are so arranged that, if faithfully observed, they will always promote the greater glory of God. To give more details about this community would involve tiresome repetition. In 1952 it had more than a hundred Sisters, most of them living in Austria, and a few also in Germany.

The 'Sisters of St. Boniface' are a Secular Institute in Northern Germany. They do not take perpetual vows, but after a one-year novitiate join the community for three years, and later for life. The Sisters have a special name in the Community, but do not wear a habit. They receive their professional training for future work at colleges recognized by the Church or state; according to their earlier education and inclination they become kindergarten mistresses, nurses, social workers, teachers, doctors and so on. Of course, fully trained women are always very welcome too. The Mother House is in the Teutoburger Wald. Here the character of an Order is more pronounced than in the Institutes mentioned above.

The 'Women of Bethany' were founded by the Jesuit Father van Ginneken in 1919. They aim at converting the modern pagans in the old Christian countries. Their influence on Catholic life is very prominent, especially in Holland.

In Rome they have founded an Apostolic Institute for the training of young Catholics in their relations with non-Catholics, which is connected with the 'Foyer Unitas' in the Palazzo Salviati in the Piazza della Rovere on the banks of the Tiber. Since 1952 the Dutch religious have there been working among the non-Catholic visitors to the Eternal City, counting among their guests especially many English and Scandinavian tourists. They also do valuable work in other European cities outside their own country.

We reproduce a passage from the prospectus of the Grail, an Apostolic Congregation of young women (taken from *In heiliger Sendung*, Vienna, 1953) : "A movement of young women devoted to the lay apostolate of the universal Church. Founded in Holland in 1928, since then spread to many other European countries, North and South America, Australia, Africa and Asia. Its characteristic structure : it is built round an international centre of young women, who devote their lives completely to God and so provide the basis of unity and the source of spiritual power for the whole movement. Their programme is quite concrete : they want to make clear to the young women of all races and conditions, of every religion and *Weltanschauung*, their God-given vocation, and to help them to realize it in modern times. Their method is simple : they form centres of Catholic life, influence and attraction wherever young women can be found ready to give them a hearing. Their methods are adapted to the needs and possibilities of every country; their spirit is that of primitive Christianity; the saving Cross is its central mystery, and the love of the Cross the deepest inspiration of every young woman. Their vision is universal, expressing a tendency of the young women of the whole world to want to bring the world to Christ by a powerful concentration of all their virtues, talents and zeal." The international centre of this movement is the 'Tiltenberg' in Holland, where many events of the most diverse types are arranged open to young girls and women between eighteen and thirty years of age.

It will be clear from this that there are sufficient opportunities for religious activity that do not entail spiritual exercises far removed from the world. They will provide not simply occupation and 'amusement' for one's spare time; on the contrary, they are based on a religious attitude to life which will gather in all its bits and pieces. Perhaps our contemporaries will shudder slightly when faced with the demand to undertake religious obligations involving partial or complete limitation of their freedom in the world. The Secular Institutes just described do, indeed, require such obligations, even though they do not prescribe a community life in the accepted sense.

VIRGINAL LIFE

The right attitude to these questions has not yet been reached if they are seen mainly as a supposed narrowing of life. This is as foolish as if somebody were to consider his fenced-in garden more perfect than the beauty of uncultivated nature, simply because he can well overlook and tend this small plot of ground, with its few beds which he has planted himself; and if, on the other hand, he would deny that mountains, lakes and forests are authentic nature only because they came into being without his help. A man must leave his own narrow sphere behind, if he would gain the right view of the world and things. From the summit of a mountain he would see a surprising panorama which would change his impression of the whole landscape. Thus it is also with human life, if one considers its origin and its goal. It will not be seen for what it is if it be followed only to its germ in the womb, from which it is passed on to future generations. Certainly this is needed, but the physical structure of man contains only the conditions of his life; it cannot solve the mystery of its origin and destiny in so far as it is specifically human. Even if a man is not explicitly religious, he will yet suspect that there is a power above the insignificant individual existence which governs and calls men. The Christian knows his God, who has even made Himself like him in Jesus Christ.

He knows Him not only in the way one can acquaint oneself with scholarship and art; he has not only learned things about Him; no, he has even 'put Him on' in baptism and lives, as has been said before, in communion and exchange with Him. Now it is not only conceivable, but it has been proved by hundreds of years of Church history, that there have always been men and women, and still are, for whom union with God is of the utmost importance. They are always standing on the summit, so to speak, from which more than their own little self can be seen. At one time or another they have realized that, by renouncing their desires for their own personal well-being, the centre of their life has been shifted away from their own self, thereby greatly enlarging their personal horizon. If we follow the three evangelical counsels, we shall indeed make the threefold sacrifice of property, family and private life; but we shall gain a totally new conception of life on the infinite plane of the freedom that has been given to God.

Naturally, there is a great difference between the single life imposed by circumstances and celibacy deliberately chosen as a supernatural vocation, in preference to serving the natural propagation of the human race. The vow of virginity has an immense significance in a world that unhesitatingly prefers the achievement of a material end to the realization of spiritual values. As has been said, the point is not that something should be left undone, especially if one thinks that natural impulses ought to be repressed; the value of chastity is determined by the end for which it is desired and by the wholehearted sincerity of the effort. God's Kingdom needs people who will serve it with individual loyalty. It is highly desirable that there should be enough generous women with sufficient courage for the virginal life in its full religious meaning. They will have their special share in renewing the face of the earth. It is, indeed, possible to make promises or even vows of this undivided loyalty as an unattached individual in the midst of the world. But it will be extremely difficult to carry them out, and, moreover, require constant spiritual direction. Surely it would be far more suitable to do this in common with others who share our ideals? Christian life is meant essentially to be lived in community; moreover, our time needs groups that are examples of worthy forms of human association. The Secular Institutes are wholly adapted to bringing the Gospel message to individuals, and offering spiritual support to those attracted to this form of life. They are authentic efforts to cope with the situation of our time.

THE RELIGIOUS STATE

The readiness of women to devote themselves to works of Christian love is as old as the Church herself, and religious houses for women have existed from the first centuries. Vowed to vir-

ginity, they live together, protected by strict enclosure, under a
rule providing for constant prayer and charitable activities. From
the seventeenth century there have also been the so-called Congregations—that is, religious associations which have given up
enclosure for the sake of practical apostolic works, especially
nursing and education—whose members take simple instead of
solemn vows. Thus old ideals are preserved while being adapted
to the needs of later situations. Since there never is a straight his-
torical development and all human desires are fed from innumerable sources, forms do not change in such a way as to destroy each
other. New things will be added, while the old ones will yet continue their fruitful growth, and old stems will bring forth new
branches.

The 'Dominicans of the Incarnate Word' may serve as an
example of this development. They work in France and were
affiliated to the Dominican Order by its Master-General in 1952.
They are professional women who have received the Habit of the
Order, which they wear on the great feasts, but normally they
wear secular dress, in accordance with the requirements of their
professions. In choir they put on a long dark cloak. As their name
suggests, their example is the Incarnate Son of God who has
'dwelt among us' for our salvation.

This is the ideal these Dominicans in secular dress have before
them. They, too, follow men into all departments of their life,
which they are able to do through their professions. They take on
all kinds of different jobs as teachers, doctors and nurses, social
workers, manual workers and parish helpers. They want to exercise their influence, not only by setting an example, but also by
actively contributing to the Christianization of our world. Their
particular aim is to help in the work of salvation by putting the
Catholic social teaching into practice. This, of course, is not to
prejudice their task of working out their own salvation by aiming
at personal perfection. Their training is determined by this double
aim of furthering their own religious development and serving
their neighbour in a special way. After a period of postulancy and
a year's novitiate as elsewhere in the Order, they take a three-
years' course in philosophy and theology. The special professional
training begins only after this, unless it has been completed before
entering the Order.

Though they practise their professions outside, these Dominicans in secular dress strongly emphasize community life. They

regard it not only as their home but especially as an opportunity for making use of efficacious means of the apostolate, such as the liturgical life, time for meditation and study and the exchange of experiences.

This form of the Dominican life approved by the Church has been described in such detail because it represents a new stage in the development of the religious Orders. There are many other attempts on these lines. In the case just mentioned old and new elements have been combined; such established features as vows, conventual community, devotion to the liturgy and the contemplative life have been fused with new factors such as contemporary forms of life, philosophical and theological courses for all, special training for various professions, in which women nowadays work side by side with men.

Beside this quite recent development, the old ideal of the contemplative Orders is still flourishing. The best known is probably the Order of Mount Carmel, which the two St. Teresas of Avila and of Lisieux have made known to all who are at all interested in such things. Contemplation means union of the loving soul with God in prayer. The Carmelite way of life is austere, for Carmelites devote their whole life to reparation; prayer and penance are their great weapons, which St. Teresa of Avila calls "divine fortresses behind the lines". Happy are those who have realized the profound meaning of such a vocation and find their own contentment in it. Recently thirteen Carmelites, all under thirty years of age, have built their new convent near Turin with their own hands, hoping never to leave it throughout their life. Elsewhere, too, the contemplative spirit of Carmel is alive and at work, and its efficacy ought not to be under-estimated.

The practical apostolate of the women's Orders has always been alive in the Church. For centuries nursing and feminine education as well as the exhausting labours in the mission-field have been carried on by nuns. Long before the so-called emancipation of women was dreamt of, these Orders were demonstrating that women are capable of culture and civilization, and have shown what are their particular spheres. Apart from the most varied domestic and agricultural activities, women are especially fitted for nursing, and for the education of the young in all its aspects. In the case of a religious Order the superior and all-embracing leading idea will naturally be the service of God through the surrender of one's whole life. But this ideal elevation of the work shows even more clearly the spiritual powers latent in women.

The complete picture of women's Orders shows plainly how fruitfully women's activities can complement the work of men. The *raison d'être* of the feminine Orders and Congregations is certainly not to serve their masculine counterparts. Both branches are dedicated to the service of God, not to the service of each other. Nevertheless, the fact cannot be overlooked that as far as the earthly realization of the idea is concerned, the Fathers of an Order derive much advantage from their sister organizations and vice versa. In fact, the founders of such double Orders established women's convents with the express purpose of gaining from them support for the prayer and work of their men.

In the course of time the Sisters' own apostolic activities extended their scope. Nevertheless, they are the more stable element in the families of the religious Orders. For they are tied more closely to their convents, and being more inclined to the personal, to the episode and to emotional attachment to a person or a cause, they serve the same purpose as other women do in the natural family : they keep alive the tradition. Masculine and feminine enthusiasm have different effects. Many little traits from the history of an Order will be faithfully preserved and handed down by its nuns. They will also pay a tender respect to their religious brethren, with whom they are in contact, such as men would never bestow on each other, and which they need nevertheless. For unless women mediate to them the irrational forces of creation men will atrophy. That is to say, they will become one-sided, wooden and apt to over-simplify vital questions, a common weakness of the masculine *ratio* if left to itself. Women have analogous difficulties if left to themselves, and so it is important also for the nuns to be in spiritual and intellectual contact with the male members of their Orders. Moreover, they will thus be acquainted with contemporary problems, which should certainly be familiar to all whose apostolate brings them into touch with lay people.

In any case, a spiritually minded girl should give serious consideration to the religious vocation, when she thinks about what form her life is to take. Femininity will not suffer thereby, provided it be rightly understood. For if physical motherhood is renounced for the sake of a high ideal, its sacrificial aspect will yet be fully used. It is far less important that one's physical possibilities should be left unused than that one's whole existence should take a form directly opposed to one's nature. Today women fight shy of a religious vocation, not so much because they are afraid of not being able to live up to its ideal of purity, but because they fear to give up their freedom and, so they think, their personality. But, above all, they are terrified of the great physical demands made by such a vocation, which, in the teaching and nursing Orders, are, indeed, considerable. In addition, nervously unbalanced people are afraid of the monotony of regular convent life. They sense in themselves a lack of stability and perseverance, as well as such an intense desire for experience that even religiously inclined natures will vigorously reject the thought of a vocation.

Another expression of the instability of our contemporaries is the absence of family feeling. They find it hard to bear their solitude; yet they rarely realize that this can be traced back to their lacking sense of natural communities. A convent would offer so much security. By this we do not, of course, mean the external cares about board, lodging and clothes, from which the religious are exempt; we mean the integration into the great family conscious of its traditions. By entering an Order the person called to it leaves the no man's land, and is welcomed into a carefully constituted society of which, if suitable, she will become an organic member. Few people realize that the lack of freedom is considerably greater in modern collective society than in a community that has been organized with a view to man's eternal destiny. Despite all the difficulties of convent life, we tend to overlook that in such a life a human being is 'employed' according to his real talents. Discipline and lack of amenities are, indeed, conditions, but, looked at from the natural point of view, human dignity is not only preserved, it is the point of departure of very effort.

Anthropology is as capable of development as every other science. The new discoveries will naturally be useful also to those communities that work for supernatural ends. Even though men carry the seeds of eternal life in themselves, the methods of guiding them are changeable. Some religiously inclined women of a modern bent of mind are afraid they might miss the Resurrection if they went into a convent, because there they would be submerged in the past. In their view, entering religion would be suicidal to modern people. But their faith would seem to be lacking in drive and imagination. If we are really only anxious to serve the Kingdom of Heaven, surely our faith ought to be strong enough to move mountains, first of all the mountain of our own pusillanimity; but then it ought also to give us confidence that it will be possible to move the mountains of old-fashioned methods. The many new forms of religious life that have been mentioned above are an eloquent proof that this is possible.

Anyway, a person who decides to enter a convent must have a broad mental outlook and know in her inmost heart that a human being can be happy only if he transcends himself. If we have once, in a quiet hour, understood the meaning of human freedom, we shall be able to realize the wonderful destiny of those who, together with like-minded companions, surrender themselves completely to God. For our vital energy will increase if we overcome our egoism and penetrate beyond the limits of the merely material sphere; but to be aware of this needs standards not everyone can appreciate, though this does not diminish their value.

There is no greater human act than to offer oneself completely to God, who "dwells in inaccessible light" and "whom eye has not seen". Misfits will be possible, of course; yet in the nearly two-thousand-year-old history of religious Orders there are abundant documents that speak of the happiness of this vocation, which cannot be attributed to highly strung imagination. Quite different people arrive at the same experience, which culminates in affirming "the glorious liberty of the children of God" attained by giving up a worldly career.

The religious life is frequently called 'unnatural'. But in our age of technical civilization this is less true than ever. It can hardly be called very natural to live in a perpetual rush without natural pauses, turning the night into day and the day into a whirlpool. Surely it is far less natural than to follow conventual customs, rising with the sun and going to rest not long after it, spending one's evenly divided days in peaceful regularity. Work and prayer, meals and recreation, follow each other far more naturally than the quickly changing scenes of the film of our daily secular life.

As has been said, even Orders will have to submit to genuine changes in their mode of living; whereas, on the other hand, it is a good thing that there should be quiet oases that are not affected by new fashions. If we looked at history without seeing the Orders, those pillars of the eternal order, we should be seized by vertigo; for all the institutions that relied only on the strength of men divorced from God have proved unstable and transitory.

Many generous women have gone astray because they fell into the hands of tricksters and frivolous exploiters. Surely quite a few of them might have developed into motherly, contented nuns, if only at the decisive moment they had known the unpretentious but lofty ideal of the religious life, instead of giving way to fanciful daydreams.

DIFFERENT FORMS OF LIFE AND DIFFERENT SPHERES OF ACTION

When discussing possibilities of shaping our life, we had to include the religious vocation. No matter whether an unmarried woman chooses this way or another, her feminine endowments are there to be developed; for they are needed particularly in our own highly technical world.

The life that is fully consecrated to God needs a special vocation. But apart from this, every human being is destined to work out his salvation, and from this point of view all Christians are equal. No 'unorganized' Christian woman living in the world can regard herself as excluded from salvation. In other words, every life has its meaning, which ultimately visualizes the eternal goal, though this may be hidden in the humdrum daily round. It must be admitted that the knowledge of this end need not communicate an immediate joy of life; yet at decisive moments, when we have to endure and suffer, the hope of salvation will give felt support.

Now, today there are many people to whom religion means nothing and who yet look for a meaning in life. They do not wish for anything transitory, but want to have it infallibly attested that their life is of value. But to whom? It is a healthy human feature to try to probe in various directions; for it is natural to the spirit to seek for more than physical nature is able to grasp. Though the senses may be satisfied, possessions increase, and events move according to plan, yet an ill-defined longing for 'the whole' is left unfulfilled. Though we may have achieved or 'got over' this, that or the other, we have a vague feeling that this was nevertheless not all. This 'all' is a happiness that will fill our heart and mind completely and cannot be taken away by any adversity. Now, no man can give this himself, because he is a creature with limited possibilities. Nevertheless, his spirit is akin to the eternal Spirit; and if he be alert and sensitive to it, he will be given no rest and be reminded from time to time by an indefinite urge that man's true home is in the eternal regions. The call from there causes the soul to expand and to desire what transcends itself; it wants to go somewhere where its own limitations will be abolished, at the same time desiring something that will not deteriorate or lose its value. It rightly feels that there must be something like that else it could not desire it. This 'something' is the meaning of life, and there is only one. Anything else that looks like a meaning proves, if attained, to be only a secondary aim; having scarcely realized it, one will press on to other aims. The end of life is to fulfil oneself as a human being, to accept oneself and one's surroundings, and to establish a contact with them, the fruitfulness of which depends on one's own capacity for love.

A professional woman will be completely human, hence content with her fate only when she can spend herself for others. The key to life is the conviction that we are meant to serve our neighbour. If the motherly qualities of a woman remain completely unused in her professional work, and if there are no family obligations either, she ought to find some other outlet for them. Human needs are varied, and there are as many different ways of approaching people as there are interests. There are no hard-and-fast rules for helping them. Personal attitudes cannot be learned—for it is not enough to understand the situation. It is the same here as with so many other difficulties one likes to attribute to unfortunate circumstances or bad times: the chief thing is to resolve to open one's conscience and one's heart, to sacrifice a little personal comfort, regular habits and self-indulgence. We ought not to complain of interior emptiness if we do nothing to fill it. Those people are ordinarily happiest who are capable of following a certain rule of life, which means they are able to overcome themselves and will not give way to every slight impulse urging them to indulge their moods and get whatever they like. We simply cannot make a success of our life unless we are ready for restraint and discipline.

It is hard to understand why so many unattached women who suffer from their loneliness will not club together. None of them wants to leave her ivory tower, disregard her own fate and listen to others. They will pretend that people are 'so wicked', ungrateful and hostile. They ask first: What can I get out of it? instead of leaving themselves completely out of account and being open to others without constant comparisons, which end in finding their own lot much more lamentable than anyone else's. Yet there would be a vast field for unmarried women, if we think of the many young girls without a proper family background or even a grown-up person in whom they could have real confidence. It would be a truly noble effort and very rewarding, too, if they devoted themselves to such a protégée, even if only once a month. It would not be necessary that a woman with an exacting job should be constantly at the disposal of such a girl. One ought not to overdo things and not take on obligations until one has tried one's strength and capacities. If such a girl is kept at the right distance and not allowed to make too frequent use of this opportunity, it will probably be esteemed much more, and the influence of the older woman will be much more efficacious. Young people like to entrust themselves to a balanced grown-up person if they feel genuine love. If a woman has herself perhaps suffered from a feeling of insecurity in difficult years, she will now have the opportunity of giving security to someone else. Thus, many a torturing 'complex' of her own may lose its terror and finally disappear altogether if she realizes that she may be of some use to another, after all.

In such company we might also fill up some of the gaps in our own education. Theatres, concerts or exhibitions will assume a fresh importance if we visit them with a lively, enthusiastic young woman. Nobody need feel forsaken and lonely in a city which will provide so many opportunities to occupy one's time, ruling out, of course, the pursuit of enervating amusements. Nevertheless, people will keep complaining : If I only were not alone for all this !

Because our contemporaries over-emphasize the personal side, are wrapped up too much in their own history and are peculiarly sensitive to stimuli from the depths, they find it more difficult to recognize an objective order of values and keep its rules. This lack of objectivity prevents them also from taking the right view of a situation. In the case of women this one-sided way of looking only at their personal discontent might lead to the idea that all would be well if the social differences between the sexes were abolished. If only women were recognized as sexually neutral economic factors, so the argument runs, they would have reached the summit of their social significance. Yet this recognition alone will never satisfy a real woman, nor can a civilization bear fruit, if it abolishes the feminine element. The social structure will probably develop in a way that women will be progressively integrated into the professional and public life outside the home. This will always involve the danger of losing their specific feminine qualities. In so far as they succumb to this, they will have missed both their cultural and their natural vocation. This would entail in its turn the lowering of the general cultural level. These undesirable consequences can be avoided only by facing the issues, an attitude that will react favourably both on women's relation to themselves and to society. This will give them an inner sense of security, which again will banish the feeling of being forsaken.

It has already been pointed out that this feeling will also be allayed by caring for others. Not only youth needs our attention. An ageing population requires that lonely old people should also be cared for. Those women who have an exacting job will hardly be able to look after them to any extent requiring much time and effort, but they might do something for their entertainment. Healthy single women who keep complaining that their life is meaningless should make this a point of their programme. Serving one's neighbour has enough meaning in itself—but it certainly requires effort.

Another, though less striking, way of acquiring a true self-appreciation is open to us if we penetrate into the world of the spirit. This world contains inexhaustible marvels, but it will only reveal its treasures if we approach it whole-heartedly. In order to enjoy and be enriched by our reading we must be able to let go of ourselves, else we shall always stumble over our own ego, and hardly come to learn that interesting questions of world-wide importance need not necessarily revolve around our own fate. Yet many discontented people read only to find it confirmed that the world is evil, and that for this reason they themselves cannot be happy and good, either. The motto of our time seems to be 'Man in his forsakenness'. This will paralyse our joy of life, and especially the sense of objective values.

SUMMARY

Since it is so important to know the foundations of one's own life, we would summarize the section on the independent woman in the formula that she must remain conscious of her own basic human structure. By virtue of this she is a spirtual being capable of judgement and decision. From this point of view there is no difference between the sexes. In the same way, every single individual, whether man or woman, consists of flesh and blood, while the intellectual and spiritual being is assigned to a particular body. The interplay of these two may be harmonious or disturbed. If this constitution of man be admitted, it follows at once that the spirit, being capable of knowledge and directed to ends, is not necessarily subjected to the dictatorship of dumb instincts, but able to shape its own life. It is true, the formation of one's existence depends also on unalterable circumstances, yet the spirit is free to consent to alternatives. Much may be clarified by recognizing a situation; even more by bravely facing it.

Apart from this, the specifically feminine nature must also be known and accepted. The unmarried woman will probably achieve her full development and ultimate inner security only by consciously integrating into her life her renunciation of motherhood. An ostrich policy might here produce undesirable repressions, as in the case of the shy, clinging woman who will not, and often even cannot, leave the stage of childhood. Or some kink may develop; for example, the woman may turn into the type of the noisy bachelor girl imprisoned in her own ego. An even stronger deviation is the cold, inhibited masculine woman. Such failures might have been avoided if the lawful desires of womanly fulfilment had been allowed to come to light and had been patiently transformed in the intellectual and spiritual spheres.

We would therefore repeat : the single woman is not a defective type but fully woman in the unmarried state. She is meant to be intellectually and spiritually fruitful, and is on no account to allow her heart to dry up, since it is both entrance and origin of values.

Her receptivity may be moved by religious, æsthetic and moral motives, but will be most easily affected by personal influence. For she turns naturally to the living 'thou' and is attracted by personalities; hence her heart is quickly stirred to action. This will call forth the unifying and peace-making powers of the feminine soul, and certain fruits of genuine motherliness. All these will complement the technical world constructed by men ; they are the result of the intuitive feminine spirituality that flows from her heart.

The reader will probably take up one of three possible attitudes to our treatment of the problems of life. She will either be surprised that one should make such a fuss about the most natural thing in the world, namely life, giving the simplest things highfalutin' names. This reader will face existence without any problems, and may not even wish to be conscious of meaningful relationships, which she lives in naïve security. Others will never have enough problems, despite all their questionings and complications they will never arrive at a peaceful life ; they will read from a text only what applies to their own difficulties, without taking any notice of other attempts at solving them.

Finally, readers of the third type will be sufficiently mature first of all to let themselves be impressed by the subject as a whole. Though having their own point of view, they will yet be ready to admit and try others, and to ask how the conclusions might affect their own life. Happy the woman who has always known how to act, and whose womanhood has never given rise to vital questions she was unable to answer. Even so, she might afterwards find that she could, or ought to, have answered differently, if she had known more of the laws of life. In any case, owing to his psychosomatic nature and his sex, man is so constituted that his important decisions will be directed now more by the one, now by the other point of view. His outlook is affected by his nature as well as by his education and his surroundings. Thus it is possible to hold a view that is technical and material, another that is more physically natural, and a third which believes that the centre of being is the decisive factor in things both great and small.

5

THE AGEING WOMAN

Attitudes and views change also with growing years. Youth and old age have different problems. From whatever angle a woman may approach events, spring-time, maturity and decay will leave their marks on her. Though she may foresee the moment that will definitely remove her from the ranks of the young and be mentally well equipped to approach it, its arrival will always be important. There are three stages in the process of ageing. The first will bring signs of autumn noticeable only to herself; something is not as it has been, but her surroundings will know nothing about it. The second is marked by a change perceived by others as a decline. The third stage escapes one's own observation; yet the decay continues, and is mercilessly registered by one's surroundings.

CHANGE OF LIFE

This first and by far most painful phase begins gently about forty and ends with the notorious change of life. Through some incident or other a woman becomes aware that her bloom is fading. Her presence no longer has the same attraction. People value her abilities, her professional success and her good reputation. This last is always something like a retirement pension. Her suspicion will be aroused if people talk about her 'ability', and if her husband treats her as a 'pal' and talks about the beauty of other women. These are signals announcing the approaching dusk. It is true, all lights are still shining, but they appear slightly dimmed. These shadows will either give acute pain or be only registered as a nuisance, according to the degree of a woman's attachment to the world and her desire for admiration. About this time there may also arrive certain physical troubles, such as asthma, emphysema or heart disease. In general, however, the experience of getting older takes the form of other symptoms, such as slight disturbances of one's powers of concentration, curtailed and lighter sleep and similar signs. They are as yet only warnings, but just for this reason all the more uncanny, and the words 'never more' will often appear before the inner eye. At twenty a young girl thinks she is alone in the world; at thirty she will discover other women beside her, and the woman of forty will notice young girls who look up to her. The girls are charming, but she herself is only to be respected. She may pretend that she gladly enjoys this deepened maturity, but this is not true. If she tries to disguise her weakness, she will suffer from it only the more.

She will then gradually approach the change of life or climacteric. This lasts roughly from the forty-eighth to the fifty-fifth year, during which period her organism undergoes important changes. Enough is known about the hormones, the mysterious interaction of the fluids, the delicate ramifications of the nervous system and the chemical changes in the body, to make people understand how important it must be for the entire economy of the body if a substance such as is contained in the germ glands is gradually removed. This does not remain in its place of origin, but will be distributed throughout the body, causing increased activity in other organs of specially delicate build. Hence there will be many disturbances, when this extremely important substance of the germ glands ceases its normal functions.

We have further to consider that, owing to the close relations between the activity of the endocrine glands and the vegetative nervous system, this latter will also be affected. Many pathological symptoms are probably due to disturbances of its regular activities. Though it has long been generally recognized that the constitution is of decisive importance for the extent of the complaints, we have little definite knowledge about it. Nevertheless, it all explains why the change of life can take such different forms. Some women will hardly notice it, whereas others will suffer from many disagreeable symptoms.

The most important of these are unpleasant disturbances of the circulation. Flushing or sudden giddiness, stinging headaches, occasional pallor and fainting fits are well known. Even worse are humming and ringing noises in the ears and a numb feeling in hands and feet. In the morning it will sometimes take very long to start and get rid of stinging, coldness and stiffness in one's fingers. The most recent investigations have shown, however, that just these disturbances of the circulation respond to treatment with vitamin E.

Other women will suffer from rheumatic pains in various places. Today they may find it impossible to turn back their head;

tomorrow they cannot do their hair because they are unable to lift their arms properly. Backaches will often be a veritable theme with variations, continuing throughout this whole phase of life.

Broken sleep is particularly unpleasant, especially if the disturbance lasts for hours and is accompanied by black thoughts. Others are frightened by sudden fits of perspiration. Sometimes a medical examination will reveal high blood pressure, which can be the cause of many other complaints. However, this must remain within certain limits, if it is to be attributed only to the change of life and not to a defect in the circulation.

The skin, too, may show pathological changes during these years; the face as well as hips and abdomen may get abnormally fat. Other women will be subject to trying skin irritation which is difficult to cure.

Differently constituted natures may be liable to fits that look like bronchial asthma; occasionally there may also be states of cramp in the digestive and urinary tracts.

In the case of some women the thyroid gland will function irregularly in these years. Other known symptoms are temporary metabolic disturbances, inflammation of the joints and pains in the bones.

This, then, is a list—which might even be lengthened—of unpleasant physical symptoms which may all be met with in the period of the 'dangerous age'. Nevertheless, it would be a mistake to think that these years are called dangerous because the organism is seriously threatened by so many complaints. Fortunately contemporary medical science is sufficiently advanced to be able to help in many ways; for example, by prescriptions made up of hormones, vitamins and calcium, which latter is good for certain special states. Here a woman must trust her doctor to give her the right kind of treatment. Nevertheless, these manifold, often ill-defined complaints and symptoms will in no way endanger the life of the patient. This age is dangerous rather because, apart from physical discomfort, it is subject to moodiness, irritability and lack of self-control. It is true, all these states will disappear once the sexual equilibrium has been completely restored. Some women, however, cannot rid themselves of the fear that they are not only not well but even seriously ill; or, apart from such depressions, they misinterpret the physical symptoms, regarding them as the first indications of a grave illness; thus they will actually make themselves ill with the idea that their body is disintegrating altogether.

The doctor will try to calm his patient; but this will be of no use. She will distrust his advice and imagine that his diagnosis is wrong. Seeking medical help, she will not feel she has found it if the doctor explains that despite all her ailments the state of her organism is normal. The danger of this transition period lies in the disproportion between objective illness and subjective discomfort. If a woman cannot bring herself to trust her medical adviser and is unable to cope with such pranks of fate, she will really become ill. If she takes too much notice of her condition, the unpleasant symptoms will grow immeasurably and result in a psychological catastrophe.

This period of transition, during which the full physical powers of a woman are transformed into the ultimate maturity of her personality, might be called the illness of the healthy; it is part of woman's general destiny.

Before discussing the psychological difficulties of this time and the ways to overcome them, we would say a word about physical and beauty culture. Walking and other sports and exercises should not be given up unless serious complaints diagnosed by a doctor make them inadvisable. In these years some types lose their youthful figure. If questioned more closely, these women will generally admit that they prefer rich food. Here excellent results will be obtained by reducing fats and sweets; one milk day (one and a half pints) or one fruit day (two pounds) a week would also be useful. For the slowing down of the metabolism inclines to stoutness. If the glandular system is healthy, moderation will here be the simplest and most effective remedy. Slight massage and Turkish baths will also promote a better circulation of the fluids and remove dross. In fact, a woman who has reached the peak of life should begin to devote one day a month to the care of her body, if she has not yet done so. Good artificial teeth, skilful make-up and well-dyed hair are not artifices of the devil. If a woman is desperately unhappy and unable to cope with life when symptoms of middle age become noticeable, she had better do something about it and use, with reason and moderation, the technical devices that will produce a youthful appearance. For nervous irritability we would advise hydropathic treatment, from hot and cold footbaths to cool rubdowns and various forms of showers. Sage-tea, if taken regularly, will diminish perspiration. A hormone treatment should be undertaken only under medical supervision.

It goes without saying that the abnormally excitable nervous system should not be further stimulated by taking large quantities of coffee, strong spices and much salt.

If bleedings occur after having ceased for an appreciable period of time, a specialist should be consulted. An annual gynæcological examination is advisable, in any case. If everything is in order, this certainty will be a comfort; if not, incipient diseases will be treated in time and will mostly be completely cured.

Apart from these more or less external symptoms there are interior upheavals, which a woman will find much more difficult to bear, and which will make her sometimes a stranger even to herself. Under the influence of organic changes she will once more be seized by an increased longing for love. Desires that have long seemed buried and done with will awake once more and be felt strongly enough to suggest possibilities of fulfilment that do not actually exist, for her powers of adaptation are not equal to the momentary emotional storms. The fully formed personality will give way before their immediate urgency, and the fact that the unmarried woman had not only resigned herself to her situation but even really mastered it will temporarily be relegated to oblivion. She has made her way alone, and will continue to do so unless her present difficulties cause her to fall into the error that her past life has been completely wrong and that she must find a partner by hook or by crook. Sometimes the instinctive urges may even be so overwhelming that she will not desire a permanent union, but only a quick delivery. In this way women may sometimes panic into an unworthy liaison which will give them a short relief and a long sorrow. In such cases understanding, discussion and temporary careful guidance would bring comfort. Thus a short, painful period could be endured more easily and would usher in a fruitful time of peace.

Good marriages of twenty years' standing will sometimes come to a tragic end, because the ageing husband is seized by an irresistible passion for a young woman. He will become indifferent to his wife and children and fall in love with a girl who might well be his daughter. No reasoned remonstrations, no domestic scenes can prevent him from becoming unfaithful. Such a man has heard the worm ticking; the feeling of being on the decline has begun to hamper him professionally; his unrest and irritability have caused setbacks in his business, and the love of his wife has not succeeded in calming him and putting him on his feet again. Suddenly a bright young thing crosses his path. The 'man with the grey temples' not only excites her admiration, but she obviously falls in love with him and gladly accepts his courtship. From that moment he is completely changed; he becomes youthful, elastic, full of masculine vigour. And lo and behold, the business reversal is overcome, too—all things seem to have been made new.

The wife who belongs to this husband will probably be in her late forties. Her justified sorrow, which may understandably even turn into despair, will add years to her age in a moment, and cause her to lose all her charm. There will hardly be an opportunity to talk things over quietly. She will be excitable and irritable, anyway, during these years, and he will listen impatiently with one ear, anxious to be gone as quickly as possible. His reason will tell him that he is at fault, but his heart will defend his newly found love all the more eagerly.

If a woman values her marriage and sees in it a higher meaning, she should force herself time and again to be patient, and strive gradually to win back her husband by equanimity and understanding. This is more easily said than done. Nevertheless, it is the only way to ward off disaster. A woman should not give up her marriage only because her husband is momentarily not in full possession of his reason and imagines that he 'cannot help it'.

In a quiet hour the wife, too, should ask herself what he may not like in her; perhaps she has indulged bad habits, easily lets herself go, bothers him too much with domestic affairs and takes too little interest in his profession and hobbies. Her motto should be not to give in and to keep on trying anything likely to change the situation.

It has to be remembered that in the sexual sphere the process of ageing differs for husband and wife. In her Indian summer the wife will gladly do without married intimacy, whereas the husband will not. Estrangement in this has sometimes caused a man to seek another woman. Yet it must be added that a wife whose sexual desires cease prematurely will often have been guided wrongly by her husband in the long years of their married life. He can hardly have known how to make her inclined to his wishes, and his understanding of the feminine mentality must have left much to be desired. So both have been left unsatisfied—she in the human sphere, and he as a man. The young woman who has crossed his path certainly attracts him sexually, and the bond will become so strong only because often a desire pent up for years finds at last its fulfilment. The mutual attraction of the sexes is fundamentally a mystery that may sometimes reach into demonic depths. Man being an imperfect being, he simply cannot be so sure of himself as he sometimes imagines. Unless he firmly believes in a spiritual meaning of life, he will always easily give in to sensual passions, without even suspecting that he could equally passionately give himself to an ethics or a religion. In fact, he will only reach the summit of his being when the opposition between the lower and the higher passions will be resolved in the painful sacrifice of a subjective satisfaction that will lead him to a higher form of life. Only if a person has achieved this will he realize how fruitful all his sacrifices have been.

It would certainly be better if things were not allowed to develop until a man be firmly attached to another woman. During the critical period husband and wife ought once more to turn to each other and examine the faults that may have developed in the long years of their life together. Some men are too dry and unsympathetic at home, without delicacy of feeling and chivalry. Women worried by the change of life will be inclined to scenes, tears and moodiness. So both parties will find it difficult to come together. But they should really for a time forget themselves and think of the other. They ought to give some consideration to the sufferings and difficulties of their partner and not pour oil on to the flames, but at the right moment try to help the other.

Just as a human being will not achieve perfection only through physical labour, so the fullness of womanhood does not coincide with the flower of youth. Though from now on a woman may be denied the fruit of the womb, she may only then be able to bring forth the ripest fruit of her human capacities. If she is able to interpret the storms of the sexual decline as the spring gales of a new, enriched humanity, she will patiently bear and overcome the manifold discomforts of this time, such as moods, the various pains and other complaints.

Some easily applied remedies have already been mentioned, such as change in diet and hormone therapy. But this does not absolve the patient from having to cope with the situation herself. It is easier to bear an ineluctable fate if it be accepted than if one continues to revolt against it. If during these difficult years women are sorely tried by a lack of balance and various pains, they should not forget that ageing is maturing. A poet has written : "Do not say to the stone, you decay, when it matures into crystal." This should be our guiding principle. The discomforts of the change of life may be seen to be the after-pains of the storms of the blood that have embittered the years, darkened the view and deflected the course of many a woman.

The evening light has a special brightness that sheds a mild radiance over the world. The change of life bravely endured will result in a wisdom of the heart that can never be lost. Such women will be familiar with life, no strangers to suffering, and their greatest joy will be to give to others. The world needs not only the energies that press forward, it is also well served by the powers that preserve. And who has more of these than the mature woman who—we may well admit it—is physically past her prime?

If, after the ups and downs of life, a person knows how to recollect and find herself, she will be able to shine by her own radiance. Her quiet goodness, her wise patience and smiling calm will be a consolation, a stimulant and a guide to others. Such are the fruits of a life in which the 'dangerous age' has not been feared, but consciously endured and conquered.

PSYCHOLOGICAL SIGNS OF AGEING

It is very difficult to distinguish scientifically between 'normal' and pathological signs of age. Despite exact scientific methods, senile decay is even now difficult to distinguish from specific diseases. There is also little certainty in how far the changes in the organism that are due to age prepare for certain illnesses. For example : Are the pathological tendencies of the circulation only a sign of age or themselves an illness? Is heightened blood pressure in advanced years normal or abnormal? The lowered capacity and the diminished power of reaction of an old organism are certainly a source of danger. Age is subject to illness and mostly ends through it. According to pathological anatomists, death is very rarely due merely to age. In any case, medicine nowadays investigates many diseases that appear in later years, such as heart troubles, arterio-sclerosis, diseases of the joints, enlargement of the lungs, degeneration of the kidneys and diabetes. Illnesses caused by infection often take a different course in the case of old people ; they show few general symptoms and fever, last for a long time, and rarely allow of complete recovery.

However, we are more interested in the psychological attitude of old people, though even here there are no rules that would apply to everybody. In what way and how quickly people age depends on their constitution, profession, surroundings, experiences and misfortunes, as well as on the illnesses and accidents they may have had. Character, too, has something to do with it. By their looks and mental attitude many people will give the impression of being quite old and spent even at the beginning of fifty, whereas others are still vigorous, lively and in full possession of their physical and mental powers at seventy or eighty. In other cases, again, there may be a disproportion between physical and mental conditions. Though physically much older, people may be mentally fresh and unwithered, and vice versa.

When a woman is past the change of life she will gain in interior calm and firmness; though tenderness will give way to masculine roughness. With progressing age both sexes will generally become more like each other. In a home for old people in Switzerland the interesting fact has been established that old women are better able to accept and bear hardships than old men, but that they have a more vivid memory of misfortunes even if these are long past. Old men were found to be more resigned or indifferent in this respect.

Generally speaking, we may say : In old age the psychological situation and the attitude to life are quite different from what they were in youth. Above all, individual traits become more firmly fixed. Youth may be compared to a touched-up portrait; in later years the embellishing touches will disappear ; attitudes and aims can no longer be changed. An easily frightened woman will become even more so; a mean one still meaner, a jealous one hardly more reasonable ; the type of the 'queen mother' will scarcely be more inclined to abdicate. If they had once expected the time of retirement to yield gains for their personal life or even increased activities, things will look very different once this age has been reached. They will inevitably stiffen and their reactions will be blunted. The world seems to glide away. When a person grows old, he will, in fact, become more silent and turned in on himself, his interest in the outside world will lessen. He will accept new things with difficulty and become less capable of enthusiasm.

All this is no doubt connected with physiological changes. It will be noticed with dismay that one's memory begins to deteriorate ; first one cannot remember names, later other gaps will appear, which unfortunately concern contemporary events

and impressions. This will slightly loosen contact with one's surroundings. On the other hand, events from the first years of one's
marriage and even from one's childhood will come back. This
awakens the interest in tradition and in one's family history. But as
the young people will hardly sympathize with this, old persons will
be subject to feelings of inferiority and be painfully conscious of
their inability to keep up with the times. They realize that they are
no longer swimming with the stream, but have been thrown on to
the bank.

All sorts of infirmities keep on increasing. The failing memory
becomes more noticeable, so does deafness. These and other dis-
abilities make life very difficult, and often young people will get
annoyed when they are inconvenienced by them.

Naturally it depends entirely on the old people's character and
former habits how they will finally react to this. Some are unable
to overcome their bitterness, becoming completely wrapped up in
themselves and thinking of nothing but their own needs and well-
being. Anxious hypochondria may become a heavy burden not
only to themselves but also to their surroundings. This, it is true,
is an extreme case, though it is well within the limits of possibility.
We do not think it necessary to discuss in this context actual old-
age diseases that accompany the disintegration of the personality.

III

PERFECTED WOMAN

THE FINAL ACHIEVEMENT

How to cope with old age is a vital question that also concerns women. Its solution will depend on their attitude to loneliness. Being free to move about, the young unmarried woman will be able to find many interests outside her ordinary sphere of life, but this will become more difficult when she is getting older. If an old person is disturbed in his normal ways, he will often pay for it with indisposition and subsequent bad temper. Thus the older woman is rather left to herself, and this knowledge is painful.

What will be her position if she lives together with her family? We are now thinking of the grandmother, after her husband has died. If there are grandchildren in the family, the scope of her activities is obvious and will depend on her strength, though the way in which she will accomplish them depends largely on her mental maturity. This will really exist if the older woman is satisfied, not only with her achievements, but also with what has been denied her; if she is not jealous of the younger ones who are in full possession of their powers, and lets them arrange their lives without always wanting to judge them by her own standards. The art of keeping silence is truly an art of old age. Outer forms will change; modern technical developments have brought about revolutions which the old people alive today are finding almost impossible to grasp. The present generation of men and women of advanced age experience not only the normal difference between young and old; they are faced with a real break between two eras that goes right through their life. The young, too, ought to take this into account.

If a woman loses her husband after thirty or forty years of happy married life, the wound will certainly never heal completely, the sorrow of the widow will never be quite overcome, even though it may diminish with the years. We mean here the sadness of having to say good-bye, and the feeling of forlornness. Man is made of flesh and blood and reacts in a natural and human way. This does not mean that there is no sense of being destined for eternity. It does not signify a lack of faith if sorrow is experienced precisely as sorrow. What matters is how it is accepted and integrated into one's life.

If we would seriously discuss the problems of older people we must frankly admit that this is the time to face the thought of death. So many agonies of conscience are in the last analysis agonies at the prospect of death. So much nervous unrest is due to the feeling of a shadow which a man is always trying to escape, and he will rather bear the loneliness of old age with sluggish resignation than face the deepest question of life, which is death. The earlier a person concerns himself with this, the more harmonious and fruitful will be the evening of his life. The more deeply he draws death into his life, the more serenely he reckons with its reality, the more securely he will live, the more contented will be his last years. We do not mean by this a dull, indifferent resignation. Man's soul is destined for immortality, and he deceives himself if he thinks he can face his end with equanimity. In every man there is a religious core which tends towards the eternal fulfilment of life, and even if he denies it this is no proof of the contrary. The question of the meaning of life is transformed by death into the question of supernatural perfection.

Because this is the great question of human destiny, we would say a little more about it. Ultimately death remains the great stranger. However much we may know about it from the physiological point of view, we cannot deceive ourselves on one thing : life does not glide smoothly, and as it were seamlessly, into death. While the dead body is still resting in its coffin, the spiritual part of man has left the earthly life and taken its first step into another reality.

Death is an end, the irrevocable termination of all the sweetness and bitterness of earth; it is and remains difficult and completely unintelligible if our life, our thinking, feeling and enjoyment is only circumscribed by this earth. For death does not follow from the inner necessity of human existence, it is the fruit of sin.

This affirmation may sound strange to someone who imagines that he is free from guilt, quietly resting in himself. There certainly is the biological and the 'biographical' death, in neurotic cases death may even be sought, and there are also circles that speak of 'shaping death'. Yet if the inmost feeling be consulted, it will answer that the ultimate fulfilment of man is not death but life ; a life, of course, that must be worthy of man and in harmony with his nature.

Now, human life is not natural in the sense that only instincts and appetites have rights in it; but, and this cannot be stressed often enough, mind and spirit, too, belong to man's nature. Hence it follows that the 'natural' course of human life is set in history; that is to say, this particular life moves between a beginning and an end. The beginning of a man cannot only be equated with the fact that an ovum, under a natural compulsion, unites with a sperm cell; for at this very moment he also receives the 'breath of God' as a spiritual soul. Moreover, his parents have come together, because they were longing to rise above themselves; for meeting and relationship are part of human existence. Man is born as the result of a meeting, as the result of a meeting he conceives and brings forth his allotted work. Now, meeting demands response and decision. Man will constantly give evidence of being capable of these high activities and will always prove his worth in their exercise. For the less easily satisfied he becomes with these encounters, the less he entangles himself in lower relationships but is driven on by those of his own standard, the more he will tend towards higher values, and ultimately to the highest, which is God. The never satisfied longing of a man is born of his desire to meet the absolutely valid divine reality. For God has created him and given him a soul. He had once been called into existence in order to tend without hindrance to the meeting with his Creator. The will and desire of the first man were such that he could without distraction make a bridge towards the fount and essence of Life. In the darkening that followed the first sin, the arch that had linked man with God was broken. Since then there has been no immediate transition to eternal life; instead, there has been death.

Man as a creature has always been destined to have a beginning and an end. Yet the wall of death would not have been erected had the faithful trust in God the Father not been destroyed in the first human couple. The biological laws of heredity will certainly not tell us this. For the work of grace is ultimately unintelligible; it obeys no natural laws, but only the giving love of God. Hence every individual human being will always have to prove whether he is at all receptive to the call of the all-preserving Creator, or if he vegetates without hope in a narrow circle of resignation until his heart ceases to beat in the bitter agony of death.

Though death is actually the ultimate consequence of sin, it is not the final destiny of man. It means change and judgement, and so it may truly be described as the 'great stranger', for the eternal truths always find an authentic expression. We may think, for example, of the famous *Dance of Death* of Luebeck, of the unforgettable expression that Bernt Notke (*c.* 1500) has given to death as the last companion of all men. If we silence all other voices and let the cry 'Everyman, Everyman' ring in our interior ear, we shall hardly be able to discount the credibility of this warning.

Death has something dark and threatening; to deny this would falsify human reality. Yet its strangeness is tinged with a charm that commands reverence; its darkness is not a thick blackness, it is filled with a gentle light. For death has become something new; its finality has been abolished through the Atonement; the sacrificial Death of Christ has given meaning to our death.

For He has died for us and thus redeemed us to eternal life. This fact cannot be changed, even though it may not be recognized. Nevertheless, it means much for the individual human life if it is allowed to have part in the fruits of Redemption through the free act of faith and the acceptance of the grace of God.

From the point of view of the truth of Redemption, death is not an end but a transition. The dancer Harald Kreutzberg has succeeded in representing the full meaning of death in an overwhelming mimic dance. In one of his creations he shows the terror of death, but at the same time he points with an arresting gesture to the shore beyond. In this dance death is seen in the way it has always been understood by Christians, as a beginning, a start, as the first, though terrifying, step to a higher stage of life. This new form of life is characterized by the Resurrection. The redemptive work was completed only in this third act, that followed crucifixion and death. Suffering and death by themselves are incomplete; they need to be made whole by the Resurrection.

If death is the beginning of a new life, judgement is the threshold the soul has to pass when it leaves its body. This judgement, which is nothing else but a comprehensive knowledge of self, may perhaps be pictured as the complete developing of the photographic plate of life, which has till then been stored away in the dark-room of the earthly destiny. Now, however, it will be visible, fully worked out in all its details. It will certainly reproduce the achievements as faithfully as the failures. The Name of God will protect those who have hallowed it. The final picture of life will be lit up by the light of faith; even a poor, repressed and miserable existence may be transfigured if God has entered into it.

Risen man will be fully elevated to the reality of the Triune

God. He will be filled with a knowledge such as cannot be fathomed on earth; God's design for the world will surround the elect like a magnificent frame. The thoughts painfully worked out by the toil of centuries will then be known not one after the other, but altogether in the eternal Now. The risen men will experience an ineffable peace, because they rest in an order which all must admit to be perfect. For God Himself is the content of eternal life, and everlasting adoration will be its beatitude. All disquiet and doubt, every shadow, slackening, disgust and weakness will have ceased. Perfection has been attained through death, for which all one's life should be a preparation, even though it may come only after many years.

In the presence of death all that has belonged to the body will fall away; the hands will let go what they have gripped, the noise of the world will fade; the things will release men from their protection, every single covering that hid the soul will fall off, everything transitory will pass. Only the centre of self, the soul, will resist, transcending its own grave. And lastly the perfection of the creatures will be fulfilled in the glory of God.

FORMED OLD AGE

YET how many people will gain these insights by the efforts of their thought? Surely not many; for only few will rise above the things that are within easy reach, near in time and tangible. The process of ageing certainly means not just decay, resignation of one's office on behalf of the next generation; on the contrary, it includes also the gathering in of the harvest, ascent to recollection and contemplation, and the taking over of another office from the eternal shores. This task is prepared by nature itself, when it refuses breathless hurry and causes the thirst for new experiences to fade. It is consonant with the process of ageing that community feeling should be weakened and one's own characteristic features assert themselves. Hence it is important for growing old peacefully to be able to indulge one's special inclinations and hobbies, and to have a home of one's own, however humble, where one can live according to one's own ideas.

We need hardly emphasize how difficult this is, if several generations have to live with each other in a very limited space. There simply is no recipe to tell us how grandmother, parents and children are to get on together in one room. Only athletes of self-denial could be sufficiently sensitive to the others' needs to make such a life possible; though this extreme case will not occur very often.

The evening of life should really become an evening; it should be organically connected with the past, and show that a man has achieved a whole, partly by his own efforts, partly by what had been given him. Even his errors and setbacks should be integrated into a final meaning. This will be revealed in the measure of love with which one has encouraged oneself and accepted the manifold incomprehensible reverses of fate. It is true, we can accept these— which means as much as answer them—only if we know our names have been called by a transcendent power; that is, by God. If a man is nearing the ultimate frontier, he will find it difficult to attune himself to it merely by his own unaided humanity. There have always been atheists who were so deeply rooted in goodness that they did not fear their approaching end, and faced it with composure. But the security of these men was precisely the fruit of the spirit they denied. They contradicted the hypothesis of man's independent creative spirit by their very personality and work.

An old person desires spontaneously a retired life and a quiet occupation with something he holds dear. A woman, especially, will have opportunities for so many charitable services within as well as outside her family that she need not feel at all useless, even if her infirmities should be more than average. The difficulties of old people are usually due, not so much to their situation as to their character. As has been said above, the characteristics become more pronounced, especially also the tendency to grumbling and complaining about all sorts of discomfort.

There will certainly also be situations when an old-age home will become absolutely necessary. This should not be left too long, when the old person is in a state of complete debility. She should also be properly prepared for it; sometimes a sudden change of surroundings will result in a complete breakdown which, after what has just been said, is quite understandable. It will be best to choose a time when she is still capable of moving about and taking an interest in her new home. Nowadays these homes are generally given a family character, where the inmates can live at least a little according to their personal liking, and need not abandon their favourite habits. As a perceptible consequence of the lower birth-rate, there are even now increasing numbers of old people who are not looked after by their family, and who have simply no other choice but to enter a home. It will hardly be possible to avoid all drawbacks; nevertheless, it is only just to point out that much has already been done to give old people a pleasant home.

In view of the increased duration of human life, the question of making a success of old age is very important. For the sake of preserving good health, everything ought to be done in time to prevent avoidable harm. A suitable way of life should be wholesome and natural, practising moderation in all things. Annoyance and bad temper, the incredible rapidity of the machine age and too many stimuli of the nervous system, act unfavourably on the expectation of life. For, as has already been said elsewhere, the vegetative life centres are very susceptible to external influences. Hence times of relaxation and complete rest should always be provided to balance the strain caused by our technical civilization, and no effort should be spared to obtain sufficient sound sleep. If one has been working hard all day long, one should allow the emotions an outlet in the evening; whereas if one's occupation is monotonous, one will need an intellectual stimulus, according to one's cultural standards. No woman should completely remove sports and beauty culture from her programme, though here right choice and moderation will be particularly important. On the other hand, intellectual and spiritual recollection and the development of, and conscious care for, human values will be just as necessary as physical recreation.

VITAL QUESTIONS OF WOMEN—FATEFUL QUESTIONS OF THE WORLD

TODAY it is certainly one of the most important tasks of feminine education and self-training to rouse and keep alive the consciousness of human values. Woman's nature tends towards the individual personality. Before looking at somebody's achievement, her watchful eyes will notice his personal state of mind and health. It is a good thing that this feminine quality should somewhat soften the standardizing tendency of our technical civilization. Much would already be gained if people recognized that the undeniably remarkable technical abilities of modern man are matched by the spirituality of woman that draws its strength from life. Women are there and co-operate with men—to deny this would mean flying in the face of facts. A new picture of woman begins slowly to take shape, of a woman who becomes conscious of herself without exaggerating her importance, who sees herself as the defender of human dignity, where the over-rationalization of the technical apparatus has led to defects. Therefore it is important not to try to limit women to only one function. Today motherhood is by no means her only task; many others are waiting for her in public, political, social and cultural life. Wherever there are human relationships—and they are everywhere—women are destined to create the right atmosphere.

This, it is true, needs mature humanity. It needs women stunted neither in their physical nor in their spiritual growth; knowledge and mastery of the body will be as necessary for this as a rich intellect and sensitivity. Natural grace belongs to their structure; but it does not imply intellectual inferiority. Whoever frequents educational and cultural institutions will admit the fact that they are greatly enlivened by the feminine element.

If we compare the women of even only a hundred years ago with our contemporaries, we shall recognize a great change. Today they are no longer tied only to the home; the sociological situation has called them into the front-line of life. It must be admitted that this development has produced a crisis of the family. But this statement will immediately call forth the question whether the middle-class home of the nineteenth century was really the ideal of a family in its full moral sense? In any case, there can be no putting back the clock of human development. Besides, the ideal of women confined to their physical functions and to the bringing up and education of the children has existed only in times when 'total man' was able to rule unrestrainedly. Otherwise they have always supported and complemented man's work. We need only remember the 'valiant woman' of the Old Testament, the prophetess of antiquity, the Teutonic valkyrie and seer, the princesses and abbesses of the early Middle Ages. The times of hetæras and courtesans have always been times of decline, just as when, in the Third Reich, women were encouraged to bear children without being accorded the dignity of motherhood.

It is perhaps a novel feature of the present situation that women themselves are responsible for this stocktaking; the new idea of woman does not come from man, who is weary after two wars, and feels uprooted and without a sense of direction. Man wants to have his peace—by which we mean not embittered resignation, but security and human warmth. He, too, is fed up with empty little women as well as with masculine perversions. Our fashions, with their stress on the feminine line and their hints of grand-mother's days, are significant. They indicate the desire for healthy, generous femininity which embraces reality as it is.

At the risk of being unpopular, we would repeat that man contributes little to shape modern woman; she fashions herself. His ideal becomes more and more that of the mature, self-reliant woman. It cannot be due to chance that for decades the public has been attracted by well-known, mature actresses, and not only by flappers and pin-up girls. The choice of subjects for films is equally significant.

How far women are already capable of governing themselves is proved by the innumerable professional and cultural women's organizations. Congresses in which women play a part, or which are specially concerned with their interests, indicate their present situation. They have not yet been officially 'recognized' by man; in many departments of life, where they have long been doing their share, they are certainly not yet regarded as colleagues with equal rights. Many men still consider admiring submission to masculine superiority as the only possible attitude for a woman. Yet her creative contributions have become indispensable in the unofficial scale of values.

Today no doubt women do have their possibilities. Of course

they must not worm their way into spheres that do not belong to them. But they have their economic and cultural tasks. The world is waiting for the right share of feminine influence also, or perhaps especially, in the sphere of international co-operation. For human dignity and human rights, the care of the family and cultural exchange, especially a deep love of peace based on religion will be a concern of women always and everywhere. Certainly it cannot be denied that new rights will also have their new dangers, an enlarged horizon may result in overstepping frontiers. If we are encouraging women to recognize their own possibilities and the manifold tasks for which nature has fitted them, this does not mean that we would like a world governed by women. Yet the cultural development of feminine abilities and crafts may even induce men to give a greater place to the imagination in their own way of life, and show them the happiness of a full human development. The soulless standardization of mass society cannot be redeemed except by woman, at rest in herself, when she brings man home in the deepest sense of the word. All this is not easy. It needs interior riches, but also renunciation and much self-discipline. If women are to be equal to this vocation, they will have to understand that slow growth is more effective than enforced accomplishment. Acquired rights are founded on personal sacrifices. If coming generations are to build up families and civilization in peace, this will be largely due to the greatness of the present generation of women, if they will strive to attain true culture, greatness of heart and a sure moral sense.

Women have not yet achieved everything, and not everything rests with their initiative. The problems are interlocked. Yet they are mentally sufficiently mature to do much for their own cultural advancement and development. If they fail to seize the propitious moment for this they will miss much, not only for themselves, but for 'the historic hour'. All this depends on their own interior elasticity, power of decision and quiet conviction of their own obligation to life. It is no excuse to complain about difficulties. No one can prevent a woman from achieving the full human development consonant with her nature, which is the unfolding of the truth that is in her. Truth unfolded is efficacious by itself, and calls forth its complementary truth. Thus man might light his fire from the spark of woman's interior growth, and through it learn how to wield his power over the technical unity of the world in peaceful security.